interrogating TEXTS

General Editors
PATRICIA WAUGH AND LYNNE PEARCE

CUNNING PASSAGES

New Historicism, Cultural Materialism and Marxism *in the* Contemporary Literary Debate

Jeremy Hawthorn
Professor of Modern British Literature,
University of Trondheim, Norway

History has many cunning passages ...
T. S. Eliot, 'Gerontion'

A member of the Hodder Headline Group
LONDON • NEW YORK • SYDNEY • AUCKLAND

First published in Great Britain in 1996 by
Arnold, a division of Hodder Headline PLC
338 Euston Road, London NW1 3BH
175 Fifth Avenue, New York, NY 10010, USA

Distributed exclusively in the USA by
St Martin's Press Inc.,
175 Fifth Avenue, New York, NY 10010, USA

British Library Cataloguing in Publication Data
A catalogue record for this book is available from the British Library

Library of Congress Cataloging-in-Publication Data
A catalog record for this book is available from the Library of Congress

ISBN 0 340 59853 0 (Pbk)
ISBN 0 340 66308 1 (Hbk)

Printed and bound in Great Britain by
J W Arrowsmith Ltd, Bristol

CONTENTS

GENERAL EDITORS' PREFACE

Interrogating Texts is a series which aims to take literary theory – its key proponents, debates, and textual practices – towards the next century.

As editors we believe that despite the much vaunted 'retreat from theory', there is so far little material evidence of this supposed backlash. Publishers' catalogues reveal 'theory' (be it literary, cultural, philosophical or psychoanalytic) to be an expanding rather than a contracting market, and courses in literary theory and textual practice have now been established in most institutions of Higher Education throughout Europe and North America.

Despite significant improvements to high school syllabuses in recent years, however, most students still arrive at University or College ill-prepared for the 'revolution' that has shaken English studies in the past twenty years. Amid the welter of increasingly sophisticated and specialized critical works that now fill our libraries and bookshops, there is a pressing need for volumes like those represented by this series: volumes that will summarize, contextualize and *interrogate* the key debates informing contemporary literary theory and, most importantly, assess and demonstrate the *effectiveness* of the different approaches in the reading of literary texts.

It is, indeed, in its 'conceptual' approach to theory, and its 'interrogation' of theory *through* textual practice, that the series claims to be most strikingly new and distinctive. Instead of presenting literary theory as a series of 'approaches' (eg., Structuralism, Marxism, Feminism) that can be mechanistically 'applied' to any text, each volume will begin by examining the epistemological and conceptual frameworks of the theoretical discourse in question and examine the way in which its philosophical and political premises compare and contrast with those of other contemporary discourses. (The volumes on *Postmodernism* and *Dialogics* both consider their epistemological relation to the other, for example.) Each volume, too, will provide an historical overview of the key proponents, texts, and debates represented by the theory, as well as an evaluative survey of the different ways in which the theory has been appropriated and deployed by literary critics. Alongside this informative and evaluative contextualization of the theory, each volume will perform readings of a selection of literary texts. The aim of these readings, as indicated earlier, is not simplistically to demonstrate the way in which the theory in question can be 'applied' to a text, but to question the suitability of certain aspects of the theory *vis-à-vis* certain texts, and ultimately to use the texts to *interrogate the theory itself*: to reveal its own inadequacies, limitations and blindspots.

Two of the most suggestive theoretical keywords of the 1980s were *dialogue* and *difference*. The *Interrogating Texts* series aims to (re)activate both terms in its attempt to map the great shifts and developments (the 'continental drift'?!) of literary theory over the past twenty years and into the twenty-first century: the differences both within and between the various theoretical discourses, and the dialogues that inhere and connect them.

Eschewing the mechanical association between theory and practice, it should also be pointed out that the individual volumes belonging to the series do not conform to any organizational template. Each author has been allowed to negotiate the relationship between theory and text as he or she thinks best, and in recognition of the fact that some of our theoretical categories will require a very different presentation to others.

Although both the substance and the critical evolution of the theoretical discourses represented by this series are often extremely complex, we hope that the perspectives and interrogations offered by our authors will make them readily accessible to a new generation of readers. The 'beginnings' of literary theory as a revolutionary threat and disruption to the Academy are fast receding into history, but their challenge – what they offer each of us in our relentless interrogation of literary texts – lives on.

Lynne Pearce
Patricia Waugh
1996

ACKNOWLEDGEMENTS

Most of this book was written during a year's leave spent in Austin, Texas from summer 1994 to summer 1995. I am grateful to my employer, the University of Trondheim, Norway, for granting me leave for this period and for covering the cost of a number of extra expenses. I am also grateful to the members of the Department of English at the University of Texas at Austin for inviting me to spend a year in Austin and for being very generous and hospitable hosts, and to the staff of the Perry-Castaneda Library and of the Harry Ransom Research Center for giving me much welcome assistance in tracing materials. Particular thanks are due to Alan Friedman and Elizabeth Butler Cullingford, who did so much to make my wife and myself feel at home in Austin. My wife Bjørg helped to keep me sane and (extremely) well fed, and shared my enthusiasm about trips to visit the Liberace museum at Las Vegas, Graceland in Memphis (where for the first time in my life I saw a gravestone with a © copyright sign under the inscription), and Buddy Holly's (non-copyrighted) grave at Lubbock. After such disquieting encounters with the encroachments of culture and property upon each other I returned a sadder if not a wiser man to the challenges of the literary text.

Various friends helped me trace – or made me aware of – relevant material, and read and commented on parts of the book; I am grateful to Gordon Williams, Domhnall Mitchell, Jakob Lothe, Jeffrey Wainwright and Iain Wright for their advice, information and criticisms. They are not responsible for errors or inadequacies in what I have written.

The author and publisher wish to thank the following for permission to reproduce copyright material. The author and Suhrkamp Verlag, for quotations taken from Hans Magnus Enzensberger, 'The Sinking of the Titanic', published in English translation by Carcanet Press (1981) and by Paladin Books (1989); translation copyright © 1980, 1981 Hans Magnus

Enzensberger; original German edition *Der Untergang der Titanic* (1978) copyright © 1978 Suhrkamp Verlag, Frankfurt am Main. Penguin Books Ltd and Oxford University Press Inc (New York) for the full text of Geoffrey Hill, 'Ode on the Loss of the "Titanic"' (8 lines), from 'Of Commerce and Society', from *Collected Poems* by Geoffrey Hill (page 50), (Penguin Books, 1985) copyright © Geoffrey Hill, 1959, 1985. Reproduced by permission of Penguin Books Ltd and Oxford University Press Inc. Peter Walton for three lines quoted from his poem 'Details' copyright © Peter Walton, 1993.

Part One

THEORY

*Textualism and
Historicism*

1

INTRODUCTION: TEXTS AND HISTORY

The Blind Eyes of Criticism

This is a book about the representation of history and about strategies of reading. Stated thus baldly the two topics may seem rather strange bedfellows, and part of the purpose of these introductory comments is to give some hint of the ways in which I will try to establish their interconnections. The particular reading strategies with which I am concerned are those which can loosely be termed 'historicist', those which are committed to the belief that literary works are most fruitfully read in the illuminating contexts of the historical forces which contributed to their birth and the historically conditioned, and changing, circumstances of their subsequent life. Such a project requires that one have some conception of the ways in which human beings relate to the past, the ways in which they trace the cunning passages of history and depict them in cunning passages of their own. But it is not just professional or academic historians who trace and compose such passages: literary works themselves are frequently concerned to investigate and depict the past. It is natural for us to inform our own processes of reading with the insights such works themselves offer into the reading and depiction of the past. Thus almost inevitably there is a reflexive element in any serious discussion of historicist approaches to literature, one which ensures that the critic or theorist must continually measure the adequacy of his or her interrogations against a standard set by many of the works he or she is studying.

In spite of its emphasis on historicism this book starts with a discussion of textualism, and, in particular, of those theories and theorists who have been unsympathetic to or unconcerned with historicist criticism. This is because such theories and theorists have played a major part in the formation of a new sort of historicism in the past decade or so. I should explain that in the pages which follow I have abided by certain terminological conventions. The term 'historicist' I have used, as in the paragraph above, as my most general umbrella term. The term 'New Historicism' is typically used in two rather different ways: either as another umbrella term to describe all of those historicist theories of both history and literature which are informed by textualist and post-structuralist ideas and which break with more traditional historicisms; or as a label for one particular group of (mainly American) writers who are thus distinguished from those (mainly British) cultural materialists whose own New Historicism owes much more to a tradition of Marxist analysis towards which their American colleagues are hostile or indifferent. There is no easy way round these terminological complications; the convention I follow in the book is to use 'New Historicism/New Historicist' as my blanket terms covering both American and British writers, and to refer to 'American New Historicism/New Historicists' when I want to narrow my focus.

Graham Holderness has attempted to differentiate between 'old historicists' and the American New Historicists as follows: 'Where the old historicism relied on a basically empiricist form of historical research, confident in its capacity to excavate and define the events of the past, New Historicism drew on post-structuralist theory, and accepted "history" only as a contemporary activity of narrating or representing the past' (1992, p32). Holderness's argument is supported by the editors of a recent collection of essays concerned with New Historicism:

> For the most part new historicism can be distinguished from 'old' historicism by its lack of faith in 'objectivity' and 'permanence' and its stress not upon the direct recreation of the past, but rather the processes by which the past is constructed or invented. Unsettling, transgressive, at times contradictory, new historicism tends to regard texts in materialist terms, as objects and events in the world, as a part of human life, society, the historical realities of power, authority, and resistance; yet at the same time, it rejects the idea of 'History' as a directly accessible, unitary past, and substitutes for it the conception of 'histories', an ongoing series of human constructions, each representing the past at particular present moments for particular present purposes. (Cox and Reynolds 1993, p1)

Thus there are those literary critics who believe that their task is (as Cox and Reynolds have it) 'the direct recreation of the past' – that is, the recapturing of the objective meaning of the literary work, a meaning that was forged into the work at its time of creation and which is there for the careful critic to recapture, fused into the work like the name in a stick of rock. Other critics believe that literary criticism is more 'an ongoing series of human constructions, each representing the [work] at particular present moments for particular present purposes'. This is how John Drakakis poses the alternatives:

> Can we regard all of these texts simply as antiquarian documents, remnants of a world we have lost, or do we, through the constitutive agencies of academic criticism, reformulate them as *universally* applicable texts? To put the issue another way, do these plays *mean* in some objective sense, or do we confer meaning on them through a complex process of cultural inscription? (1992, p1)

Central to the turn to history in literary studies has been a belief that such issues are not only a problem for historians. If the old historicists were 'confident in [their] capacity to excavate and define the events of the past', their counterparts in the field of literary criticism such as the New Critics were equally confident about the transhistorical life of the literary work, a work possessed of an objectivity and unchanging identity which it was the job of the critic to quarry and report on, unencumbered by as few footnotes as possible. But if, following a range of recent thinkers, the object of history is at least partially constructed by the historian, what of the object of literary criticism? If historical events are no longer to be taken as substantial and objective, what of plays, poems and novels? Are literary works the prostitutes of cultural life, dehumanized by the fantasies which successive readers and cultures project on to them – or are they possessed of some independent identity, some power to resist such readerly appropriation, something that makes a reader's desire to talk with their authors or characters more than the textual equivalent of harlotry?

In all this I remain convinced of the indispensability of the Marxist tradition to the project I outline. It is my belief that for all the errors and weaknesses to which this tradition has been prey, it alone provides us with a workable theory of historical determination, a means whereby determining factors can be ranked in terms of their importance, their power. It is for this reason that my sympathies are with cultural materialism in most of the debates that I trace. Cultural materialism, it seems to me, has succeeded in welding crucial insights of non-historicist theorists (such as, for example, the inescapably rhetorical element in all attempts to describe the past) on to the fundamental understanding of historical process which I believe to be contained in Marxism. Twenty-five years ago, Graham Hough wrote that any attempt to 'give some intelligible account of the relation of literature to the social order' had only one methodology to appeal to: 'To think on this subject at all requires some application of Marxism' (1970, p57). The collapse of communism – the political system which claimed to base itself on Marxism – and the replacement of monolithic Marxism by the flower of a thousand new Marxisms may make this claim seem quaint and outdated. For me, however, the explanatory power of Marxism did not collapse with the Berlin wall. Readers can judge the results of such waywardness by the literary readings for which it is responsible in the second part of this book.

Reviewing a series entitled *The Welsh Classics*, Byron Rogers has noted the peculiar effect caused by the fact that the Welsh language has changed so little over a thousand years that the modern Welsh-speaking reader experiences a sense of 'peculiar intimacy', a peculiar intimacy which can coexist with a shocked awareness of the utter strangeness of aspects of the life preserved in these so linguistically accessible texts: 'With old Welsh poetry, you close one eye and you are in the remote past; close the other and you are in the present' (1994, p8).

English-speaking readers reading the literature of the past written in English cannot lay claim to a language which has changed little in a thousand years. Nonetheless, that tantalizing feeling that we are dealing with people, situations and events which are both reassuringly (or uncannily) familiar and dismayingly foreign is one which comes to most – perhaps all – readers of the literature of past ages. Literature comes to us from the past, yet it puts us on terms of apparent intimacy with the long-dead, gives us access to the experiences, beliefs and thought-processes of those who lived in circumstances utterly unlike our own. The experience (or illusion) of such time-travel has only been an option for human beings comparatively recently, and has been open only to those men and women who belong to literate cultures. For those living in preliterate cultures the past as preserved in myth is quite different from that to which we have access; it is a past already made familiar, already *naturalized*, as current jargon has it. Whichever eye he or she closes – to pursue Rogers's figure of speech – the audience-member of an oral culture finds him- or herself looking at much the same thing.

Literary critics, like readers, can choose to close a metaphorical eye so as to render literary works less complex and contradictory. And recent literary criticism has often found it easier to work with one eye closed, concentrating either on the sense of intimacy and familiarity provided by a literary work while banishing the problems of the remote and the alien to the occasional explanatory footnote, or, alternatively, by seeing the world of the literary work as a foreign country through which travel is possible only if a comprehensive guidebook is provided for voyagers who must never be allowed to believe that they can talk to the natives without an interpreter.

Keeping both of one's eyes open is a good deal more difficult than restricting oneself to a monocular view of literature – or of anything else, come to that. But for me it is, more than anything else, what makes the literary criticism produced by cultural materialist critics so much more challenging and worthwhile than the many varieties of monocular criticism which have bloomed and faded with such rapidity in the last couple of decades. I believe that we misuse and undervalue literary works when we approach them with one eye closed – trying either to deny their pastness and assuming that they speak a universal language that knows no single time and place, or trying to deny that there is any continuity of human experience across time and cultural difference which allows a work of literature from the past to *live* in the present. Indeed, I think that we may have to confront the paradox that we can sometimes feel closest to the life of the past at just the point at which we sense its difference and alien nature most strongly – just as we experience intimacy with other individuals most strongly not, normally, when they seem most like us, but when their separateness, distinctness, difference – their independent identity – stand out in sharpest relief. (I might add that I find it ironic that those who would be most shocked and repelled were one to argue that peoples in different, contemporary cultures share no common humanity seem prepared confidently to assert that those living in cultures separated by time rather than place cannot be said to have any common possession to which the label 'human' can be attached.) My commitment to humanism is, like that to Marxism, unfashionable. But with the decline of Marxist anti-humanism an adherence to these two isms may seem less outrageous than it would have done twenty years ago.

What I hope will become clear in the second part of the book is that the reading of literary works involves struggle and effort. Meaning, significance, fulfilment are not to be found sitting obediently and expectantly in literary works, waiting for the pages to be opened so that they can troop out into the reader's head. What we get from our readings we get as a result of a mental struggle which is informed and directed by our theories and ideas – whether or not we are conscious of these. My long case-study of the literature of the *Titanic* disaster attempts to chart the mediations and transformations which occur when a striking historical event is depicted, displayed and discussed in works of literature, along with the changes which take place in such processes as the event in question recedes in history. I do not believe that any reading of the works I discuss has to retrace tortuously these mediations and transformations – the aim after all is not to get back to a starting point located prior to the writing of the works. But I do believe that the serious reader needs to have the existence of such transmutations and chains of influence in mind as he or she grapples with such works.

Some of the literary works I have chosen – W. H. Auden's 'Spain' and Joseph Conrad's *Nostromo*, for example – seemed almost to select themselves for this book. In others the potential fruitfulness of a historicist reading was either obscured (as in the case of John Keats's 'To Autumn'), or resisted and denied (as in the case of Henry James's *The Turn of the Screw*). Although I have entitled my second section 'Interrogations', it should be clear that some literary works collaborate more willingly with their historicist interrogators than do others. But, as in real life, it is often those least willing to collaborate who are possessed of the most relevant and valuable information.

Cultural materialists have argued most tenaciously in recent years that all reading is situated, and is conducted from concrete and specific social, cultural and political positions. While the American New Critics have often talked of our construction *of* the past and its texts, the cultural materialists have reminded us of our construction *by* the present and the culture in which we live, move and have our being. All reading is transactional. And because reading is an active and transactional process literary works investigate us while we investigate them. The chapters in the latter part of this book will, I hope, help the reader to isolate and appreciate potentialities in the works discussed. They will also, inevitably, tell the reader something about me. The reader should remember, however, that he or she is not immune from this process of interrogation. Literary works have their eyes on you.

2

THE CHALLENGE OF TEXTUALISM

Shades of the Prison-house

Many of the most fundamental theoretical battles of the 1930s and 1940s in the field of literary criticism involved an opposition between, on the one hand, a formalism that argued the irrelevance of 'context' and saw the life of the text through history to be guaranteed by a transhistorical 'human nature' which it both stemmed from and appealed to; and, on the other, various forms of historicism (dominated in the 1930s by a particular variant of Marxism) which denied the text any life apart from that released by and revealed through its incorporation within its genetic context.

I
Old Wine in New Bottles

Such battles of theoretical titans have, since the 1960s, given way to guerrilla wars and skirmishes between younger godheads – more complex and sophisticated views of the literary work's textuality and of its historicity. The titans are not yet dead, however, and their subterranean clashes still find forms of expression in perhaps more local theoretical disagreements. Many examples of the tenacious survival and perseverance of these theoretical polarities could be cited, but one will perhaps suffice.

The title of Ross Chambers's study, *Story and Situation: Narrative Seduction and the Power of Fiction* (1984), suggests straight away a contextualist approach: story cannot be studied apart from the (or a) situation which gives it meaning. Some of Chambers's opening remarks do much to confirm such an initial impression; indeed, the first sentence in the book would seem to place his study firmly in a contextualist camp:

> With the waning of structuralism, it has become clear that, in general terms, meaning is not inherent in discourse and its structures, but contextual, a function of the pragmatic situation in which discourse occurs. (1984, p3)

A meaning that is not inherent in discourse would, we might well expect, involve the situating of literary works in precisely those extra-discursive contexts that could be relied upon to help generate meaning, and this is Chambers's next proposal to his reader:

> So, it is my further suggestion that the study of narrative as transaction must open eventually onto ideological and cultural analysis of these enabling agreements, that is, onto what Clifford Geertz might call 'thick description.' 'Sarrasine' is as embedded in the male-female relationships of Paris in the 1830s as 'The Purloined Letter' is in a certain American mercantilism, while 'Sylvie' presupposes, with its bid for understanding, the desperate estrangement, in the bourgeois culture of the 1850's in France, of such marginal figures as the poet, the dreamer, the lover, *le fou*. Similarly, 'The Figure in the Carpet' and 'The Dead' propose in their different ways striking images of alienation, in the little world of literary criticism remote from the 'vulgar' and in the figure of Gabriel Conroy, ill at ease in the (vulgar) Dublin society to which he panders, without being able to become the messenger of a reality radically opposed to that society. (1984, p9)[1]

Some of the terms here might confuse a Marxist of the 1930s, and some of the detail might prompt the objection that the proposed 'enabling agreements' were not sufficiently fundamental and determining, but so far the general thrust of Chambers's argument would be familiar and welcome. Suddenly, however, our transposed 1930s Marxist would find him- or herself being presented with something that, to him or her, resembled not the one titan but the other, not a belief in the dependence of the text on particular contexts, but its self-sufficiency and independence of them:

---

[1] 'Thick description' is a term associated with the anthropologist Clifford Geertz, who takes it from the philosopher Gilbert Ryle. For Ryle, thick description goes beyond a mere description of – say – physical gestures and movements, and takes wider social and cultural implications and meanings into account. It can thus be seen to sit very firmly in a contextualist camp, denying the essentialist view that messages have an intrinsic meaning independent of social, cultural or historical context. Chambers's commitment to 'the study of narrative as transaction' also bespeaks an anti-essentialist commitment, implying as it does that meaning is the result of a transaction between teller and reader/listener rather than implicit in the interpreted text. See Clifford Geertz, 'Thick Description: Toward an Interpretive Theory of Culture', the first chapter of *The Interpretation of Cultures* (1973), and Gilbert Ryle: 'Thinking and Reflecting' and 'The Thinking of Thoughts', both of which are reprinted in the second volume of Ryle's *Collected Papers* (1971).

> Not the actual historicity of texts, but the markers, within them, of
> historical situation – these are what a renewed narratology, concerned with
> the phenomenon of point, might take as its object. (1984, p10)

Is this not the New Critical belief that the text carries with it all the context
its readers will ever need – writ new? Sure enough, a few pages later,
Chambers is using that term much favoured by the New Critics: 'autonomy':

> [The literary text's] characteristics as a literary text derive precisely from
> its autonomy (what in a previous chapter I called its alienation), the
> autonomy we give it as readers, an autonomy that cuts it off from 'original'
> or determining circumstances of narration, such as a controlling individual
> consciousness, a 'subject' solely responsible for meaning. These are, of
> course, the characteristics of interpretability, the availability to the activity
> of reading that enables the text to produce ever new meanings. Such a text
> can be treated as a stable or inert thing, predetermined by an intentionality
> (whether that of a fictional consciousness or that of an author), only at the
> risk of severely impoverishing it and depriving it of what gives it its value
> as literary discourse. (1984, p19)

How is it that we started with a meaning that is contextual, can only be
contextual, yet have apparently ended up with a meaning that is a property
of the autonomous text? Part of the answer to this question may just be
that Chambers is not wholly consistent in his argument, and indeed he
does admit that his analytical model is to a certain extent in philosophical
disagreement with the model produced by his analysis (1984, p22).

To answer the question in a more satisfactory way, however, and in a
way that takes in more than just one theorist, I believe that we have to turn
our attention to a range of extremely complex discussions of textuality and
of contextualism which have taken place during the past two decades or
so, discussions which have attempted to reconcile many of those claims of
formalists and historicists which seem at first sight to be irreconcilable. But
first it may be appropriate to ask some rather fundamental questions.

II
What is a Text?

The question seems odd, not least, perhaps, because it comes at the start of
a book concerned with literature and history. But it will seem less odd to
those who have witnessed the centrality of the notion of textuality to recent
debates about the life of literature in history. One of the paradoxes about
the turn to history in literary criticism is that, as Chambers points out, it is
only because texts are able to escape from confinement to one time and one
place that the problem arises at all.

Texts are fixed arrangements of signs designed to have a certain independence of time and space; they are typically *intended* to be accessible to human beings (or human-controlled entities) who (or which) are separated from the producers of the texts by space or time at least to some degree. However, this relative independence of time and space is a problematic matter. A text designed to have a relatively circumscribed independence of time and space may turn out to be capable of surviving much greater temporal and spatial removal. The letter I write to my wife today may be read, for all I know, by someone ten thousand years hence. Thus although the text may be designed to have a certain independence of time and space (what Chambers refers to as the literary text's autonomy or alienation), it is normally designed to be read within a particular context – that is, in accordance with a set of interpretative conventions associated with a given discourse or institution. This goes some way to explain the seeming paradox that a body of work such as Shakespeare's sonnets, which repetitively rehearse their own survival in future, unknown contexts, and their preservation of aspects of the lives of their creator and his subjects, should actually have spawned an immense activity on the part of scholars aimed at recapturing what is perceived to be a missing, meaning-conferring body of contextualizing information. While the sonnets themselves speak confidently of what they will preserve for future generations, so far many of these future generations seem to have been most preoccupied by what the poems do not preserve. It would appear that while the possibility of his sonnets being read in ages to come formed part of the *subject* of Shakespeare's muse, in an important sense the poems were not *intended to be read* by these coming generations. If we put the poems into the context for which they were intended, we must recognize that we are not part of that context: paradoxically, a successful genetic recontextualization of the sonnets might exclude ourselves.

Texts are not, then, ever completely independent of time and place. Jerome J. McGann has sought to alert his readers to the dangers of excessive decontextualization, to the need for the reader and critic to beware of precisely that quality of works of literature that gives the critic access to them in the first place:

> [T]he entire tradition of poetry comes into our hands in textualized forms. The problem then becomes: how are we to preserve and encourage a dialectical understanding and engagement with imaginative work that descends to us in those profoundly nondialectical forms we call texts? (1988, p22)

Another way of pin-pointing the issue is by having recourse to a distinction which has been given wide circulation by recent narrative theory – that between *énonciation* and *énoncé*, where *énonciation* is the *act* of making an utterance or statement, an act of meaning-creation in which the utterance or statement produces or enables meaning through its links to the specifics of the whole act-in-a-situation, and *énoncé* is the result of that act, the utterance or statement 'itself'.

III
Textualism and Contextualism

The distinction between *énoncé* and *énonciation* is one which can be made because linguistic utterances are capable of being fixed and reproduced in a way that – for example – gestures or caresses are not. As soon as writing exists to transfer the difference-system of language to fixed and stable signs, anything in language can be *textualized*: expressed in signs which are not subject to the vagaries of memory. One cannot divide a caress into *énoncé* and *énonciation*. On the other hand, we should remember that the distinction *is* a theoretical one: in practice there is no *énoncé* without *énonciation*, and vice versa. We can choose to concentrate more on the one than the other, and this is what monocular criticism – as I called it in my Introduction – tends to do. These two biases we can name *textualism* and *contextualism*. Whereas textualism (a term I take from Richard Rorty) admits of no reality that is extratextual, and sees our world as textually produced – a prison-house of texts – contextualism denies the specificity of texts and attempts to deflect textual meaning back into the text's (normally) genetic contexts. Textualism could be defined as an insistence on treating the literary work as *énoncé* rather than *énonciation*, and we can see the contextualist reaction against textualism as an attempt to reunite the *énoncé* with its original (or successive) *énonciations*. Contextualism can be seen as the product of a suspicion of textuality itself, a fear of language that is un-fettered by fixed meaning-determining contexts. Contextualism at its most extreme can seek to collapse *énoncé* back into *énonciation*, to transfer responsibility for the poem's meaning to its contexts of genesis and reception. It can seek to limit or qualify the relative independence of time and space enjoyed by the text, and at its most extreme can attempt to reject any literary meaning that is not overtly linked to originary or genetic contexts. John Frow, for example, argues that many of the contributors to Peter Widdowson's influential anthology *Re-reading English*

> reject a textually oriented criticism in favor of an analysis of the social conditions of literary production: meaning is displaced outside the text, but displaced most significantly to another disciplinary discourse: that of history. The assumption that textual meaning can be read off from the conditions of its production is made possible by the elevation of an apparently nontextual mode of knowledge over one which is explicitly textual. (1986, p123)

I want to agree with Frow that the way out of the errors of textualism is not by way of collapsing textual meaning and significance back into the conditions of the text's production (and I would add that the way out of genetic reductionism of the sort Frow claims to find in *Rereading English* is not by way of a dehistoricized textualism). Francis Mulhern has suggested, usefully, that if 'the idea of a perennially self-identical text is a humanist dogma, the antithetical idea of an ever-self-differing text is an academic-libertarian trifle' (1992, p22). He does not use the terms *textualism* and *contextualism* in this context, and indeed it seems that what he has in mind when he talks of 'an ever-self-differing text' is more the result of the deconstructionist's unfettered play of signifiers than a text subject to incessant (and total) redefinition through incorporation in a succession of different contexts. His comment has, nevertheless, the virtue of drawing attention to the weakness academics have for oversimplified solutions: either ignore the text's changing life through history, or collapse the text and its identity into this changing life or into the forces which produced the text.

The aim of a 'dialectical understanding and engagement', as McGann expresses it, has to be that of avoiding both sorts of simplification. I stress this point because there is a danger that we may be led to believe that anti- or ahistorical approaches to literary works are the invention of modern theorists. They are, rather, a development of a capacity inherent in texts, the capacity to move organized and stabilized systems of language out of their originating and explanatory contexts to quite different contexts. We should therefore remember that if there were no possibility of examining texts apart from their originating contexts, there would be no texts to examine. We need, in other words, continually to bear in mind that reading a text will always involve a sense of lack, that lack which is the necessary precondition of textuality. If we want always to have a meaning that is fully integrated with an expressive genesis we must remain with gestures and caresses, or with linguistic utterances expressed to their recipient in person-to-person contact. Alienation is a necessary condition of textuality: we can do what we can to lessen this alienation – and much of this book will discuss different ways of achieving this goal – but reading texts will always involve balancing the necessary alienation of the text with the fact that texts release their meanings only in determinate contexts. Those who embrace the text's alienation and ignore the fact that it lives only in a succession of meaning-generating contexts end up in formalism; those who deny this alienation *in toto* end up in reductionism, collapsing the text back into its genetic or receptive contexts.

It is, however, a paradox that for a text alienation is also, simultaneously, integration. Many have believed that as the text is alienated from the context of its production it becomes free-floating, complete unto itself, self-identical. But a literary work always exists in a complex of different contexts at any given time: even at the time of its first publication the contexts in which it is read will not be identical to those from within which it has been produced. Literature is, then, permanently in process of being recontextualized: those who congratulate themselves on looking 'only at the text' are actually incorporating it into a context so familiar that it is invisible to them – a process modern theorists call naturalization. John Frow has suggested that the text's naturalization within its genetic context has to be countered by means of a process of 'unframing' as a result of which it becomes 'subversive of its own legitimacy' (1986, p228).[2] Frow's Marxist perspective is one which is fundamentally opposed to the belief that meaning inheres in a text like the DNA in a piece of preserved tissue. But as I have pointed out, there are opposing traditions which believe that texts carry their own meanings. The New Critics constituted one such tradition, and Jerome J. McGann has argued that a comparable essentialism is also a part of the interpretive positions of Paul Ricoeur and Jacques Derrida. According to McGann, both Ricoeur and Derrida agree

> that a distinction must be made between text and event, and that 'meaning' – whether ontic or illusory – is a textual and not an eventual function. Their manner of distinguishing text from event produces a shared inclination to 'textualize' experience, and to see the reasoned disposal of experience – its manipulation and its interpretation alike – as an exegetical operation. (1988, p18)

For McGann, in contrast, textuality is not an escape from or an alternative to what he calls eventual meaning, but a necessary precondition of such meaning. Texts allow us to separate meaning from event, it is true, but only by reincorporating meaning into new contexts – new events.

Texts belong to the very latest stage of the development of the human race. Historically, there is something qualitatively new about a highly literate society, a society in which not only do all have access to texts, but all have access to certain key aspects of their society and culture – and to themselves – *only* through the medium of texts. Even if we can trace back written texts a few thousand years, a modern Western society is permeated by textuality in quite a different way from the way in which, say, medieval English society was. Even an illiterate living in a modern Western society will live a life dominated by texts, although many of them will not be written ones. Although the use of signs – linguistic and non-linguistic – is a central part of being human, our learning to deal with texts is not part of our biological inheritance but has to be imparted exclusively through the medium of culture; indeed, for us culture *is* to a considerable extent a learning to deal with texts. And it is a complicated process.

Because they can move about in space and time, texts are powerful things. They are the latest product of that process of development which has progressively freed human beings from a real prison-house, that of concrete immediacy. Texts help to release human beings from the confines of the here-and-now, the first and greatest stage of which process was the development of language. Just as language allowed human beings to contemplate themselves and their world at a distance, and thus provided the human race with a vastly increased power over nature (a nature which

---

[2] Frow writes as a Marxist, and his case for 'unframing' has a clear political underpinning. But a similar case is made from an apparently more politically neutral point of view by Ross Chambers, who argues that 'the reader, who is in a position to perceive the ideological and cultural constraints that have limited the text's self-conception, has a responsibility to free the text from its own limitations' (1984, p27).

includes ourselves), so texts provide us with immeasurably more complex and detailed pictures of our world, and allow us to deal with a reality which is more negotiable because aspects of it are presented to us in a stable and reproducible state. If, for example, we had only performances and no written texts of the corpus of – say – English drama, our ability to *use* this material would be a fraction of what it actually is. In the pages that follow I will be concerning myself with the dangers and problems which flow from the transportability of the text, and I will be exploring various suggestions which have been made as to how the text can be recontextualized in different ways, suggestions which I generally support. But at this stage of my argument I want to insist that the transportability of the text, its relative independence of time and space, must not be seen as merely negative. Texts would not have become so important in modern cultures did they not perform important rôles, rôles which they could not perform if they did not have temporal and spatial mobility.

As I have argued, however, we should not allow this perception of the text's transportability to lull us into believing that because texts can move from place to place, and period to period, they have no connection with the realities of any time and place. It is not just our modern textualists who are guilty of such misconceptions: those who deal only with documents have always been susceptible to the belief that there *are* only documents, or – a weaker variant – that documents are more important than the realities which they mirror, intervene in, or initiate. Here is the unnamed naval captain in Joseph Conrad's novella *The Shadow-Line*, thinking about a shore-official with whom he has just been in contact:

> He had known me only by sight, and he was well aware he would never see me again; I was, in common with the other seamen of the port, merely a subject for official writing, filling up of forms with all the artificial superiority of a man of pen and ink to the men who grapple with realities outside the consecrated walls of official buildings. What ghosts we must have been to him! Mere symbols to juggle with in books and heavy registers, without brains and muscles and perplexities; something hardly useful and decidedly inferior. (1985, p34)

It will be noted that Derrida is not the first to believe that there is nothing outside the text. If those who live by the sword perish by the sword, it would seem that many of those who live by the pen – shore-officials, French philosophers, professors of English literature – come to believe not only that it is mightier than the sword, but that it actually writes such things as swords into existence. Whatever the case, the recent history of literary theory is not short of those who believe that the men and women of the world and their actions and experiences are 'mere symbols to juggle with in books and heavy registers'. (It should perhaps be added that although Conrad's words express disdain for the 'man of pen and ink' who reduces those who grapple directly with physical realities to 'mere symbols', it is possible to detect an antithetical prejudice in the quoted passage: only a direct engagement with the physical world is real, while those who engage with the physical world indirectly, through books and heavy registers, are themselves ghosts. It is of course the case that the reality of the ships of Conrad's life and books is constituted both by their physical identity and also by their incorporation in nets of economic, social, and political negotiations mediated through symbolic transactions. It is further the case that Conrad's views would not have come to us were not he also a 'man of pen and ink'.)

When, back in 1982, Richard Rorty coined the terms *textualism* and *textualist*, he commented ironically that while in the nineteenth century there were those who believed that nothing existed but ideas, 'In our century there are people who write as if there were nothing but texts' (1982, p139). Rorty listed a number of names on his charge-sheet; those accused of being card-carrying textualists or their fellow-travellers included Harold Bloom, Geoffrey Hartman, J. Hillis Miller, and Paul de Man; post-structuralist French thinkers such as Jacques Derrida and Michel Foucault, historians such as Hayden White, and social scientists such as Paul Rabinow. All of these, according to Rorty, held both an antagonistic attitude towards natural science and a belief that human thought or language can never be directly compared to 'bare, unmediated reality'. For the textualist, the prison-house is constructed from texts. I will return to look at the particular theories of some of those named by Rorty at a later point; for the time being I want to look at the theoretical roots of this alleged common belief that human thought and language are cut off from direct apprehension of an extralinguistic reality.

IV
Structuralism, Deconstruction and Decontextualization

The title of Fredric Jameson's influential study of structuralism, *The Prison House of Language* (1972), serves as a useful negative characterization not just of structuralism, but of a range of recent theories influential among literary critics. Language, for Jameson's structuralist, is a prison because it is allowed no direct purchase on the non-linguistic world. Like a monarch allowed only to converse with his lords and never with his subjects, according to the structuralists a sign can refer only to a signifier, a concept, and can never engage with a world untouched by language. Moreover, in many versions of structuralism the lord is similarly limited to intercourse with his monarch: the signifier has no more purchase on a world outside language than has the sign. *Reference*, present intermittently in Saussure's work, disappears completely from that of many of his followers.

This general position has been subjected to extended critiques by a range of recent writers, critiques made from a number of different discipline bases. But to my mind the most telling of these criticisms is the evolutionist one that such structuralist arguments fail utterly to explain where language comes from and why it has developed. For the non-structuralist, language is the product and enabler of human evolution. The acquisition and development of language gives human beings enormously increased power over nature, far more than is possessed by any animal. If language really were a prison-house, really were incapable of bringing human beings into contact with one another and with the world in which they live (a world over which, before the emergence of language, prehominids had far less control than their speaking successors were to enjoy), then it is hard to see for what possible reason language emerged and developed (Woolfson [1982] provides much relevant argumentation on this subject). Emergence and development are, of course, topics explicitly ruled out of court once the synchronic is allowed to obscure the diachronic; modern structuralism is thus able to deny its most potent objectors theoretical legitimacy.

Language is not the only prison-house in the realms of recent literary-critical theory, and structuralism is far from being the first theory to posit a pluralist reality in which individual systems – language games, ideologies, or whatever – are hermetically sealed from all the other systems which, together, constitute what is. But it is the most recent of such theories, and, together with its close relatives or offspring, post-structuralism and deconstruction, perhaps the most influential. It is not surprising that if the world of language could be seen as a prison-house, then the world of texts might be established as a rival penal system. In the world of contemporary theory, much as in contemporary Britain and USA, private prisons are very fashionable. Richard Rorty has suggested that there is a direct link between structuralism's prison-house of language and the newly fashionable prison-house of texts:

> There are, alas, people nowadays who owlishly inform us 'philosophy has *proved*' that language does not refer to anything nonlinguistic, and thus that everything one can talk about is a text. This claim is on a par with the claim that Kant proved that we cannot know about things-in-themselves. Both claims rest on a phony contrast between some sort of nondiscursive, unmediated vision of the real and the way we actually talk and think. Both falsely infer from 'We can't think without concepts, or talk without words' to 'We can't think or talk except about what has been created by our thought or talk.' (1982, pp154–5)

Perhaps the best-known statement of what Rorty refers to as *textualism* is Jacques Derrida's famous, or infamous, declaration that 'Il n'y a pas de hors-texte' – translated, alternatively, as either 'There is nothing outside the text' or 'There is no outer text'. The second alternative is perhaps weaker than the first; if there is no outer text there may even be an outer reality of a non-textual or non-linguistic sort. What Derrida, or his statement, actually means or meant is something that at least many of Derrida's followers believe could never be established, given their conviction that the play of signifiers is ceaseless and unstoppable. But in the hands of his followers, such statements have frequently provided *carte blanche* for an unfettered textualism. Indeed, many have seen textualism as a logical extension of deconstruction. Is not Derrida's aphorism tantamount to claiming that for us the past exists only in texts, and that there is no way of deciding between rival textual versions of the past, as there is no extratextual evidence to which one can appeal?

Lee Patterson has argued that it is not, and that deconstruction bequeaths to us a more nuanced view of such matters:

> Thus deconstruction, far from either denying the reality of history or its availability to knowledge, is a critical practice that seeks to understand how 'reality' is put in place by discursive means. When Derrida notoriously says that 'there is nothing outside the text', he is restating the position, held by many sociocultural historians, that reality is culturally or discursively produced, that – in Jonathan Culler's words – 'the realities with which politics is concerned, and the forms in which they are manipulated, are inseparable from discursive structures and systems of signification.' While of course such a program *could* lead to the neglect of the social, economic, and political institutions by which power is enforced, it need not; and while of course it *could* lead us to submerge agency into structure, nothing requires that it do so. Indeed, if we locate deconstruction within historiographical practice rather than in opposition to it, then it can be seen as a style of analysis directed towards understanding the production of cultural meanings. (1993, p71)

It seems to me that Patterson's prose, for all its carefulness, still hesitates between two irreconcilable positions: first, that it is texts (or culture, or discourse) which *produce* reality, and second, that texts *mediate* between us and reality. 'The reality of history [and] its availability to knowledge'; 'Reality is culturally or discursively produced': these two formulations seem first to posit a history which is separate from knowledge, and then one which is produced by forms of knowledge. It is also worth pointing out that whereas Patterson starts by talking of 'reality' (scare-quotes are very popular when many modern theorists come to write this word), he ends by referring to 'the production of cultural meanings'. This is perhaps a significant slippage: reality can clearly involve rather more than just the production of cultural meanings. To thus limit reality is to prepare for a subsequent step in which all of reality, rather than just that part of it that consists of cultural meanings, is produced by human beings.

This may be suggest that textualism is the child of philosophical or theoretical beliefs. But we know from Dickens as well as Conrad that many individuals have a weakness for seeing the whole world in terms of their own profession, and while we laugh at characterizations of such as Captain Cuttle we need to remember that the profession of academic literary critic is no different from any other in this respect; if the whole world is an extended ship for Captain Cuttle, perhaps we should not be surprised if for some literary critics the whole world is a collection of texts: textualism may owe as much to professional myopia as to a fully thought-out philosophy. Scholars and theorists have always had a weakness for forgetting about the existence of the world outside the study or library, and Yeats's splendid little poem 'The Scholars' reminds us that this is no less the case when the pages they are reading in the study or library refer very evocatively to that world. If you spend all your time reading about things, there is always a danger that, like Conrad's shore-official, you may come to believe that things are the product of reading. At any rate, twentieth-century literary theory has many examples of such beliefs, some of which restrict themselves to claiming that literary works have no connection – genetic or referential – to the extraliterary world. Others more ambitiously claim, first, that in this respect literary texts are no different from other ones, and second, that there is, anyway, no extratextual world for texts to come from or refer to, as our world is textually produced – is, in short, purely textual.

V
The Textualism of Postmodernism

Patricia Waugh has suggested that one thing post-structuralism and post-modernism have in common is a belief in the impossibility of a metacritical position – although she then goes on to outline a number of differences between the two as well (1992, p71). The differences should not be under-estimated: the term 'postmodernism', as Waugh suggests, can denote many different things: 'a mood or style of thought which privileges aesthetic modes over those of logic or method', 'an aesthetic practice with an accompanying body of commentary upon it', and 'a cultural epoch which has facilitated the rise to prominence of such theoretical and aesthetic styles and which may or may not constitute a break with previous structures of modernity' (1992, p7). Nonetheless, the fact that commentaries on post-structuralism and postmodernism (especially hostile ones) not infrequently lump the two together doubtless owes much to their shared rejection of universal, objective or extrasystemic guarantees of truth. If for post-structuralism there is nothing outside the text, a fundamental tenet of post-modernist faith is, as Jean-François Lyotard puts it, 'incredulity towards metanarratives' (1984, pxxiv). Both positions result in a multiplicity of monadic and self-identical 'truths' or systems which can be considered only in terms of their own, internal standards of validity.[3]

Lyotard's best-known work is, amongst other things, a sustained attack on realist theories of truth. Throughout *The Postmodern Condition* he argues repeatedly that the grand narratives of the past, 'such as the dialectics of Spirit, the hermeneutics of meaning, the emancipation of the rational or working subject, or the creation of wealth' (1984, pxxiii) – grand narratives

---

[3] Adherents of such a position are rarely completely consistent; their monadic worlds normally contain secret passages to more public discourses so that messages can be brought back to those outside.

that underpinned metadiscourses which legitimated sciences – hold no sway in the postmodern world. As a result, our accounts of the world – our stories, or narratives – can seek no legitimation from outside themselves:

> It is therefore impossible to judge the existence or validity of narrative knowledge on the basis of scientific knowledge and vice versa: The relevant criteria are different. All we can do is gaze in wonder at the diversity of discursive species, just as we do at the diversity of plant or animal species. (1984, p26)

Although such a position may appear new it closely resembles those many recent variants of traditional idealism which allow the academic or intellectual the power to observe, but not to intervene in, life. D. J. Manning's study *Liberalism*, for example, distinguishes between ideologists (who can so intervene) and academics, who 'can change minds', but who 'are incapable of calling for action', and who, according to Manning, refer to what is and not what ought or may be. Manning concludes his book with an attack on the liberal belief that the academic can so intervene in the extra-academic world:

> The price the academic must pay for being able to demonstrate the intellectual precision of his explanations is political impotence. He can say no more to those who find ideological argument distressing than could de Gaulle, who, in a rare liberal mood, said to his wife as they flew over Africa and she had just complained that she had seen elephants making love below: 'Laisses les faire' – 'Let them be.' (1976, p157)

When the example is elephants making love the assertion is amusing, but when one calls to mind that it could just as easily be applied to discussions about war or world starvation, it is less so.

Such idealism, whether it presents itself as postmodernist or not, condemns the writer to a textual or academic prison-house: the teller of tales, whether novelist or historian, is demoted to the task of cultivating his or her garden. Indeed, 'cultivating' might be too strong a term, suggesting as it does the possibility of intervention and control, a possibility clearly ruled out of court by Lyotard's preferred verb: 'to gaze'. Science, according to Lyotard, 'plays its own game: it is incapable of legitimating the other language games' (1984, p40). Lyotard's use of Wittgenstein's term here expresses a clear belief in the *spectatorial* nature of intellectual activity: the games have their own rules which we may learn, but these rules cannot be changed, nor can a knowledge of these rules allow us to intervene other than in the one game for which they are relevant.

Truth is no longer absolute or objective, but merely local. In the absence of the grand narratives, we are left with a succession of little narratives, gardens which we can cultivate (or gaze at), but gardens with very high walls round them. In his essay, 'Answering the Question: What is Postmodernism?', which is printed as an appendix to the English edition of *The Postmodern Condition*, Lyotard is even more blunt:

Finally, it must be clear that it is our business not to supply reality but to invent allusions to the conceivable which cannot be presented. And it is not to be expected that this task will effect the least reconciliation between language games (which, under the name of faculties, Kant knew to be separated by a chasm), and that only the transcendental illusion (that of Hegel) can hope to totalize them into a real unity. But Kant also knew that the price to pay for such an illusion is terror. The nineteenth and twentieth centuries have given us as much terror as we can take. We have paid a high enough price for the nostalgia of the whole and the one, for the reconciliation of the concept and the sensible, of the transparent and the communicable experience. (1984, pp81–2)

It is not a long step from this belief that the task is not to 'supply reality' but rather to 'invent allusions to the conceivable which cannot be presented', to the belief that, for example, the historian's task is not to expose the reality of what has occurred, but rather to present alternative *stories about* what has occurred which all share the same truth value (that is, none). As we will see when we turn to the theories of Hayden White, postmodernist ideas blend in very comfortably with other views of the impossibility of deciding between varying accounts of 'reality'. Lyotard's admittedly admirable desire to avoid the terrors of forced agreements can, ironically, lead to a terror of a different sort, in which a language game which denies that the Nazi holocaust ever took place is allowed its own territory within which to exist without fear of invasion from those who feel a moral commitment to seek, if not to supply, a reality that is more than just a 'nostalgia of the whole'. Although morally quite distinct, there is a theoretical continuity between neo-fascist denials of the holocaust and Baudrillard's statement that the Gulf War did not take place (see the discussion in Norris [1992]); both rely on that denial of the possibility of reference that is at the heart of postmodernism, and both face theory with the morally urgent need to develop a concept of the text that has a place for such reference.

Patricia Waugh has argued that modernism represents not so much a collapse but 'a *proliferation* of value which, far from destroying our powers of self-determination, offers them new forms and contexts' (1992, p8), and she clearly believes that this judgement can be extended to postmodernism – drawing some telling comparisons between postmodernism and Romanticism in this respect. My own feeling is that although one may understand aspects of both postmodernism and Romanticism as defensive retreats to areas of local truth, 'gardens' to which those battling a powerful, centralized reactionary authority felt they could retire, the overwhelming emphasis of at least first-generation Romanticism was on an opposition to that centralized tyranny, whereas with postmodernism there is in contrast a far more celebratory mood which is, to put it at its most positive, indulgent towards central authority. There is, moreover, no doubt that postmodernism generally manifests a far sharper critique of precisely that tradition of reason and justice *opposed* to reactionary central authorities that we know as the tradition of Enlightenment, than it does of the reactionary central authority. Waugh argues that what unites Romanticism and post-modernism 'is a shared crisis mentality connected to a sense of the fragmentariness of the commercialised world with which Enlightenment reason is seen to be complicit: in both the aesthetic becomes the only possible means of redemption' (1992, p15). The claim seems to me to apply more to postmodernism than to Romanticism. The Romantics had their suspicions of science and of philosophy (which latter, claimed Keats in 'Lamia', could clip an angel's wings). But it is not hard to marshal evidence to demonstrate that the major Romantics felt themselves to represent a rational tradition opposed to the obscurantism and superstition of moneyed power. Moreover, the belief that Enlightenment reason is complicit with the fragmentariness of the commercialized world is one for which the Romantics may be forgiven but which postmodernists may not; the period in which postmodernism appears is one characterized by highly publicized battles against commercialism of various sorts; battles informed and underpinned by what we can term Enlightenment reason.

VI
Post-structuralism and Postmodernism

Another similarity between post-structuralism and postmodernism – it has been claimed – is their shared commitment to a view of all narratives as fictional. Thus in the following account by Elizabeth Ermarth of the textual prison-house, the term 'postmodern writing' could probably be replaced by 'post-structuralism' without the substitution causing too many raised eyebrows:

> We are always deciphering a text: the Republican convention, the intentions of a friend, Hiroshima, the emergence of mass media, *glasnost*, the behavior of a relative, the invasion of a country, the painting of Paul Klee – all are texts; all are constructs; all are readable inventions. To read is to interpret and to interpret is to reinvent, or coinvent, the text. To say such things are inventions, moreover, is not at all to deny their reality or their profoundly consequential and material existence; it is not mere aestheticism to say that life literally is art because postmodern writing collapses the dualism between what is real and what is made that supports aestheticism as well as historicism. (1992, p23)

It seems to me that this is a mixture of the acute and the confused. It is true that most of those reading Ermarth's words will – fortunately for them – know of Hiroshima only through the medium of texts: television programmes, fictionalized film accounts, magazine articles, books. Quite probably no one who actually experienced the atomic explosion will read these words; of all the people in today's world who refer to the atomic explosion in Hiroshima hardly any will have had some direct contact with survivors, will have visited the town while the devastation was still apparent, will have *witnessed* the explosion or its immediate physical effects in some direct, non-textual manner. Few of us are in the position of Saint Thomas, able to thrust our physical hands into the physical wounds.

Even so, I imagine that I am not the only reader worried by the suggestion that 'Hiroshima' is – like the painting of Paul Klee – a text, a construct, a readable invention. I believe that art and fiction have genetic and performative connections to a non-textual world, but I am still unwilling to accept that there is no ontological difference between a Paul Klee painting and the dropping of the atomic bomb on Hiroshima. When I read an account of Hiroshima I certainly have to use my imagination, certainly have to interpret what I read (and I *do* believe that the skills of analysis and interpretation that are fostered by the reading and criticizing of literature can be brought to bear on non-fictional texts – but that is another matter). While Ermarth suggests that to read 'is to interpret and to interpret is to reinvent, or coinvent, the text', I would prefer to argue that to read is to interpret, and to interpret is to engage in a process by which meanings and experiences are produced through a dialectical encounter between reader and text in a context or a set of interlocking contexts – meanings and experiences which may be more or less the property of the reader, and more or less the true or false renderings of aspects of a reality which is *apart from* the text or the reader.

Reading is a creative process – which is why it would appear that no two reading experiences of any substantial literary work, even by the same person, are ever exactly the same. With the exception of certain forms of highly instrumental reading (checking the dosage instructions on a bottle of aspirin, for example), reading is not the same as decoding; it is not just recent reader-response theory which has insisted upon the fact that any reading of a literary work involves a certain degree of reader creativity – what Wolfgang Iser (1974) has referred to as filling in the gaps in a work. It would be very hard to read *Anna Karenina* with no pre-existing understanding of the concept of marriage. That is how complex texts work: they rely upon our ability to fill out meanings which can never be comprehensively encoded in the work. Clearly, then, a crucial issue becomes that of deciding to what extent what we are putting into the reading of a literary work is legitimate – or of deciding whether it is possible to establish standards of legitimacy at all. (It may well be that a more productive direction in which to proceed involves considering the fruitfulness rather than the legitimacy of what we put into our readings.)

Most ordinary, non-academic readers of *Anna Karenina*, I suspect, never pause to worry much about what they put into their reading of that novel's opening lines: the lines propose an unqualified generalization, and modern readers do not, I think, hesitate to wonder whether they need more historical knowledge of the rôle, status, function and experience of marriage in nineteenth-century Russia in order to be able to read them. Much reading of texts is like this: it further develops that force of generalization that is implicit in language itself, the force that those scientists in Swift's *Gulliver's Travels* reacted against when they proposed that the use of nouns be replaced by direct reference to things – which in turn meant that they had to carry around with them all the things to which they were ever likely to want to refer.

But just as we are on occasions brought up sharply by our perception that certain word-usages can imply a generalization which reality cannot honour, so also our too-comfortable naturalization of certain texts can sometimes be arrested by something which reminds us that the world in which the text was born was in certain crucial respects different from our own. We are confronted by the *foreign-ness* of the text, its attachment to a world with which we are not familiar, a world which is *alien*. (Most modern readers are, I suspect, faced with the shock of an alien set of cultural assumptions at the end of Shakespeare's *Othello*, when the text appears to expect audiences to assent to the rightness of torturing Iago to death.) We are then forced to realize that our reading of texts can sometimes take their relative culture-independence too far.

It seems to me that it is for this reason that we must respond to Ermarth's argument by insisting that interpretation may involve the reader's creativity, but that it should never be merely invention – or co-invention. Furthermore, the texts by which we know of Hiroshima may be constructs and readable inventions, but this is a world away from claiming – as Ermarth almost appears to do – that Hiroshima itself is a construct and a readable invention. Would that it were. Ermarth clearly recognizes that there is something unsatisfactory about her formulation, which is why she feels impelled to insist of her listed texts that we must not deny their 'reality or their profoundly consequential and material existence'. But it seems clear to me that to collapse 'the dualism between what is real and what is made' *is* to deny the specific reality of, for example, Hiroshima. And this is neither to argue that contemporary readers can hope for a direct hands-in-wounds experience of the reality of Hiroshima which is unmediated by texts, nor that fictional texts have no connection with the non-textual world: it is just to subscribe to the common-sense notion that fictional texts engage with the non-textual world in ways different from factual texts. The danger of saying that Hiroshima for us is a construct and a readable invention is that it leads very easily to the claim that different versions of Hiroshima – because they are all constructs and readable inventions – all have the same truth value. And one thing which Ermarth's statement does not take fully into account is that in our world there *are* different versions of Hiroshima: I write this after having read in a daily newspaper this morning that the organizers of an exhibition featuring the aeroplane which dropped the atomic bomb on Hiroshima have been pressurized into removing material about the horrific effects of the explosion from display, after protests from American veterans who found such material gave 'too pro-Japanese a slant' to the exhibition. One person's Hiroshima is another person's Japanese propaganda. And if both are to be classed merely as constructs and readable inventions, then we would be left in a position in which we had to allow everyone their own Hiroshima, with no grounds for privileging one rather than another invention other than, perhaps, that of aesthetic preference.

VII
Textualism and Reference
Reality or 'Reality'?

It seems clear that an absolutely central point which is at issue in these debates is the familiar one of *reference*. Many of the debates with which these early sections are concerned are new versions of old debates, except that instead of asking whether human thought or consciousness actually create a reality which is then deemed to exist independently of such mental activity, *texts* are substituted for thought and consciousness. (Thus preparing the way for a further question about whether texts themselves are the product of thought, and so on.) In other words, what we are seeing rehearsed are some of the traditional debates between realists and idealists, with a sideways shift of emphasis from thought to text.

I do not think that an extensive recapitulation of these debates would be all that helpful here, but for the record I will briefly outline what my own position is. I am a realist to the extent that I believe that if the human race had never emerged, the universe would still exist – and that it will continue to exist when the human race (or any other beings with the capacity to perceive and reflect on the reality around themselves) has vanished. Furthermore, certain aspects of human experience have a reality which is independent of our understanding of them. At the same time, it is clear that without human thought certain aspects of what human beings experience as their reality would cease to exist. As David-Hillel Ruben puts it, 'there can be no knowledge in a world in which there are no individual men to have that knowledge' (1977, p155), and human knowledge is certainly real. In one sense, then, thought does create aspects of reality. In the same way, language does not just give human beings a knowledge of what is, it also creates new levels of reality. And so do texts – emplotments of what is or has been. Freud's analyses of the human psyche do not just tell us about what is the case, they also create that new element of reality which is a knowledge (or, if you prefer, a misunderstanding) of what is the case. A historical explanation is necessarily to some extent creative because it produces belief, and human beings act on their beliefs – however misguidedly and indirectly. Thus a history of the Second World War does not just tell us what was the case; even though the events *and beliefs* that constituted the war exist independently of it, it also produces patterns of understanding (or misunderstanding) which are real and have real effects. Thus it is true both to say that the reality emplotted by a text is prior to and independent of that text, and also that texts can be to a certain extent constitutive of reality. (As I will attempt to argue much later in this book, the issues raised by *fiction* complicate this picture because fictional texts have a more complex and mediated relationship to extratextual reality, but nevertheless what I have said about texts in general applies too, I believe, to fictional texts.)

As my comments on Hiroshima should make clear, at its most extreme textualism can deny or imply a denial of the existence of any extratextual reality – or, alternatively, can suggest that such a reality is unrecoverable. In an article published in a collection of essays on the representation of the Nazi holocaust, Christopher Browning draws attention to the fact that the development of such ideas by literary critics and theorists has on occasions been put to shocking use. Writing about the Canadian lawyer Douglas Christie who, according to Deborah Lipstadt (1994, p160), is 'the main legal defender of Holocaust deniers, antisemites, Nazi war criminals, and neo-Nazis in Canada', Browning shows how the seemingly ivory-tower theories of contemporary literary criticism can be made to engage with the real world in ways that are anything but unimportant:

> A related argument, dealing with documentary evidence rather than postwar testimony, was made by Robert Faurisson, a deactivated professor of literature at the University of Lyons. During each trial he was in constant attendance as an advisor to Christie and was certified as an expert witness in 'text criticism'. Invoking the authority of recent theories of literary criticism, he claimed that the meaning of such terms found in Nazi documents as *resettlement* and *special treatment* could not be established by historical context. Since their meaning was indeterminate, an interpretation taking such terms literally and not as official euphemisms or code words for murder was quite valid. For Faurisson, of course, such literal interpretation also corresponded to objective historical truth. Neither he nor Christie has shied from working both sides of the objectivist-relativist fence. (1992, p339, n12)

According to Deborah Lipstadt, Faurisson's area of specialization 'is the rather unique field of the "criticism of texts and documents, investigation of meaning and counter-meaning, of the true and the false"'. Lipstadt points out that Faurisson's 'expertise' has allowed him to claim that 'the "so-called gassings" of Jews were a "gigantic politico-financial swindle whose beneficiaries are the state of Israel and international Zionism." Its chief victims were the German people and the Palestinians' (1994, p9). Her comments on the context in which such views have flourished are, to say the least, food for thought:

> While Holocaust denial is not a new phenomenon, it has increased in scope and intensity since the mid-1970s. It is important to understand that the deniers do not work in a vacuum. Part of their success can be traced to an intellectual climate that has made its mark in the scholarly world during the past two decades. The deniers are plying their trade at a time when much of history seems to be up for grabs and attacks on the Western rationalist tradition have become commonplace.

This tendency can be traced, at least in part, to intellectual currents that began to emerge in the late 1960s. Various scholars began to argue that texts had no fixed meanings. The reader's interpretation, not the author's intention, determined meaning. Duke University professor Stanley Fish is most closely associated with this approach in the literary field. It became more difficult to talk about the objective truth of a text, legal concept, or even an event. In academic circles some scholars spoke of relative truths, rejecting the notion that there was one version of the world that was necessarily right while another was wrong. (1994, pp17–18)

This is not, of course, to suggest that Stanley Fish or others who have contributed to a more sceptical view of the possibility of isolating 'the objective truth of a text', as Lipstadt puts it, are in any way to be blamed for the activities of such as Faurisson. Indeed, Lipstadt makes it clear that in her view such a shift in attitudes had certain things to recommend it: it placed an important, though possibly overstated, emphasis on the rôle played by the reader's perspective in assigning meaning to a text, and it was a reminder that the interpretations of the less powerful groups in society have generally been ignored. Against this, however, had to be set the fact that

it also fostered an atmosphere in which it became harder to say that an idea was beyond the pale of rational thought. At its most radical it contended that there was no bedrock thing such as experience. Experience was mediated through one's language. The scholars who supported this deconstructionist approach were neither deniers themselves nor sympathetic to the deniers attitudes; most had no trouble identifying Holocaust denial as disingenuous. But because deconstruction argued that experience was relative and nothing was fixed, it created an atmosphere of permissiveness towards questioning the meaning of historical events and made it hard for its proponents to assert that there was anything 'off-limits' for this skeptical approach. (1994, p18)

Given such possibilities of grotesque misapplication (or application) of theories denying that textual evidence was always indeterminate, literary and other theorists were very clearly faced with a renewed moral responsibility to follow through the full implications that their ideas might have in extra-academic contexts.[4]

In his introduction to the volume of essays in which Christopher Browning's essay is published, Saul Friedlander puts the matter clearly:

notwithstanding the importance one may attach to postmodern attempts at confronting what escapes, at least in part, established historical and

---

[4] In his *Uncritical Theory: Postmodernism, Intellectuals and the Gulf War* Christopher Norris has a useful section on François Lyotard's attempt to refute Faurisson's arguments, an attempt which, Norris claims, fails because Lyotard falls 'back into the relativist trap of making truth-claims solely and exclusively a product of socio-linguistic convention' (1992, p72).

artistic categories of representation, the equivocation of postmodernism concerning 'reality' and 'truth' – that is, ultimately, its fundamental relativism – confronts any discourse about Nazism and the Shoah with considerable difficulties. I cannot but adopt Pierre Vidal-Naquet's . . . words: 'I was convinced that . . . everything should necessarily go through a discourse . . . but beyond this, or before this, there was something irreducible which, for better or worse, I would still call reality. Without this reality, how could we make a difference between fiction and history?' (1992, p20)[5]

'Something irreducible which, for better or worse, I would still call reality.' This is a conclusion drawn by others concerned with the holocaust. The word used by Deborah Lipstadt is 'irrefutable':

Each one tries to glean some new insight or understanding from a story already known, seeking some new way of interpreting the past to help us better understand the present. That interpretation always involves some constant 're-visioning' of the past. By its very nature the business of interpretation cannot be purely objective. But it is built on a certain body of irrefutable evidence: Slavery happened; so did the Black Plague and the Holocaust. (1994, p21)

Now it might be countered that this may be the way in which extreme textualism in the field of history can be assaulted, but it is hard to see how such a strategy could successfully be applied unadapted to the field of literary criticism. Literary interpretation is not built on a certain body of irrefutable evidence in quite the same way: 'slavery happened' and 'Darcy eventually marries Elizabeth Bennett' are statements which clearly differ in terms of their truth status. Deborah Lipstadt has noted that those genuine historians (rather than covert apologists for Nazism) investigating the holocaust have recognized that not all the stories told by the holocaust's victims are reliable. As a result, such investigators have adopted from anthropology a procedure known as 'triangulation', in which a survivor's testimony is matched with other forms of evidence, including documents and other historical data (1994, pp53–4).[6] Most literary critics recognize that literary interpretations can also be authenticated in different ways, but that these tend to be less precise, less straightforward than 'triangulation'. Moreover, as I will attempt to demonstrate, there are important (and common-sense) differences between works of literature which appear to

---

[5] For discussion of the idea that 'everything should . . . go through a discourse', see the section below on Foucault. Pierre Vidal-Naquet's views can be found in Vidal-Naquet (1992).

[6] Linda Ruth Williams documents a different meaning for 'triangulation' from its use in psychoanalytic theory, in which it refers to the way in which the subject's desire for the object is always mediated by a third term (1995, p29). She notes that the term has currency in orienteering, but perhaps its most important contexts are those of navigation and surveying.

refer to real events such as the sinking of the *Titanic*, and works of literature which present us with *fictions*.

One solution to some of these problems is to give up the attempt to combat textualism in literary studies, to concede that there is no basis for preferring one interpretation of a literary text to another, save on aesthetic grounds. Textualism in the field of history can then be opposed much in the way Lipstadt does, by reverting to a traditional distinction between literary and historical texts: historical texts relate to an independent reality which is pre- and extratextual and whose objectivity can test the truth or falsity of these texts. Such a solution is by no means new: Sir Philip Sidney declared that poetry could not tell lies because it affirmed nothing, and he was by no means the first to banish literary works to a limbo of practical impotence and political irrelevance.

Many of those recent critics and theorists involved in the 'turn to history' have thus had to define themselves in opposition to two limit-positions: on the one hand a textualism that denies that textual accounts of any sort can ever be ranked in terms of their relative truth or falsity, and on the other a traditionalism that accepts that historical texts can be so ranked by appeal to an objective reality which is seen to be relatively unproblematic, but which believes that the only grounds for preferring one interpretation of a literary text to another are aesthetic, and subjective – matters of personal taste and preference. The first of these solutions trivializes literary texts along with all other texts; the second restores the importance of historical texts at the cost of again trivializing literary ones.

It is for this reason that New Historicist literary critics (using this term as a blanket description to describe a range of different theoretical positions and critical practices) have been forced to find some new answers: because the existing answers of new textualists and of old historians (and old aesthetes) are found to be equally unacceptable. What is required of such answers is that they provide some means to justify the importance of literary texts which goes beyond that of providing documentary historical evidence. For most of the critics with whom I shall be concerned this has involved attempts to analyse and display the various and complex ways in which literature interlocks with social and historical realities. In particular, it has involved attempts to grapple with the complex ways in which literary works arise out of and engage with a reality that may be mediated through texts or discourses, but which also exists independently of them.

VIII
Michel Foucault's Theory of Discourse

Most commentators on the New Historicism agree that the writings of Michel Foucault have been an important element in the theoretical movements behind the 'turn to history'. Foucault is a writer whose work is difficult to summarize or to gloss; not only does it range over a large number of subjects but it also manifests a constant element of self-criticism and modification. Even within the space of a single book we can see Foucault reconsidering his methods and reassessing their relevance to the direction in which his argument is proceeding. Richard Rorty, as has been seen, names Foucault as one of his 'textualists', and yet Foucault is inconsistent when it comes to the issue of the relationship between texts and the non-textual. Foucault's influence on such groupings as the New Historicism is not then likely to be a simple matter.

In spite of this it seems fair to claim that Foucault's theory of *discourse* constitutes a major influence on those who have contributed to the 'turn to history'. 'Theory of' is perhaps too optimistic a way of putting it; even in his *The Archaeology of Knowledge* – the work in which Foucault addresses the problem of defining discourse most directly – he admits to considerable vacillation and inconsistency:

> Lastly, instead of gradually reducing the rather fluctuating meaning of the word 'discourse', I believe that I have in fact added to its meanings: treating it sometimes as the general domain of all statements, sometimes as an individualizable group of statements, and sometimes as a regulated practice that allows for a certain number of statements; and have I not allowed this same word 'discourse', which should have served as a boundary around the term 'statement', to vary as I shifted my analysis or its point of application, as the statement itself faded from view? (1972, p80)

This fluctuation notwithstanding, it is discourse as 'a regulated practice that allows for a certain number of statements' that has generally been taken to be central to Foucault's use of the term. The definition shows the influence of structuralist ideas in spite of Foucault's expressed reservations concerning structuralism: 'discourse' for Foucault focuses not upon the expressive force involved in a statement within a discursive formation, but on those rules that allow the statement to be made; not on meaning but on meaning-enabling rules and conventions. Later on in *The Archaeology of Knowledge* Foucault adds that a discursive formation is 'the principle of dispersion and redistribution, not of formulations, not of sentences, not of propositions, but of statements', and that 'the term discourse can be defined as the group of statements that belong to a single system of formation; thus I shall be able to speak of clinical discourse, economic discourse, the discourse of natural history, psychiatric discourse' (1972, pp107–8).

Such a theory of discourse is not without its problems – not least that of defining what a 'system of formation' is and how it can be recognized. But at its best (or, to put it another way, in certain of Foucault's formulations but not in others) it is arguably anti-monocular in the sense in which I used this term in my Introduction, for it focuses attention both on to the conditions of emergence of a text and also on to the text's developing life through history. The strongest statement of such a dialectical approach to be found in *The Archaeology of Knowledge* is perhaps the following one.

Foucault here refers to 'the statement', but his argument nonetheless has clear implications for texts – including literary works:

> The statement, then, must not be treated as an event that occurred in a particular time and place, and that the most one can do is recall it – and celebrate it from afar off – in an act of memory. But neither is it an ideal form that can be actualized in any body, at any time, in any circumstances, and in any material conditions. Too repeatable to be entirely identifiable with the spatio-temporal coordinates of its birth (it is more than the place and date of its appearance), too bound up with what surrounds it and supports it to be as free as a pure form (it is more than a law of construction governing a group of elements), it is endowed with a certain modifiable heaviness, a weight relative to the field in which it is placed, a constancy that allows of various uses, a temporal permanence that does not have the inertia of a mere trace or mark, and which does not sleep on its own past. (1972, pp104–5)

What is striking here is that Foucault underwrites neither a formalist or 'textualist' treatment of the statement as pure *énoncé* wholly free from the conditions of its creation and birth, nor an 'old historicist' view of the statement as a goldfish that must swim in the bowl of its originating context if it is not to die. Foucault's argument in this quotation avoids some of the more rash and extreme polemics against originary meaning of which he can be guilty, and instead balances the need to pay attention to those 'spatio-temporal coordinates of [the statement's] birth' with which the statement cannot be 'entirely identifiable', against the need to recognize the statement's 'modifiable heaviness'. 'Modifiable heaviness' strikes me as a fine description of the literary work's paradoxical identity: 'heavy' – that is, resistant to being shifted around by us, distinct, not reducible to its origins or the uses to which we would put it – but at the same time possessed of a heaviness that does get modified from reading to reading, from historical period to historical period. Discourse, Foucault argues, 'must not be referred to the distant presence of the origin, but treated as and when it occurs' (1972, p25) – including, presumably, its first appearance.

Foucault's position here is, then, an anti-essentialist one. For him, the 'frontiers of a book are never clear-cut; beyond the title, the first lines, and the last full stop, beyond its internal configuration and its autonomous form, it is caught up in a system of references to other books, other texts, other sentences: it is a node within a network' (1972, p25). Indeed, as his later comments make clear, the book is a node within many networks – not just at the time of its first publication but also subsequently. This is not just an anti-essentialist position but also a dialectical or relational one; the book is not just 'caught up' in systems of reference, but these systems of reference actually bring the book into existence – not in a physical but in an interpretative sense: '[T]he object does not await in limbo the order that will free it and enable it to become embodied in a visible and prolix objectivity; it does not pre-exist itself, held back by some obstacle at the first edges of light. It exists under the positive conditions of a complex group of relations' (1972, p45). There is more:

> These relations are established between institutions, economic and social processes, behavioural patterns, systems of norms, techniques, types of classification, modes of characterization; and these relations are not present in the object; it is not they that are deployed when the object is being analysed; they do not indicate the web, the immanent rationality, that ideal nervure that reappears totally or in part when one conceives of the object in the truth of its concept. They do not define its internal constitution, but what enables it to appear, to juxtapose itself in relation to them, to define its difference, its irreducibility, and perhaps even its heterogeneity, in short, to be placed in a field of exteriority. (p45)

Clearly, then, when 'institutions, economic and social processes, behavioural patterns, systems of norms, techniques, types of classification, modes of characterization' change, then the relations between them and the object must change, and thus the object itself will alter. Hence Foucault's position has built into it a conception of the *historical life* of the object, a life which will be richer the more complex the object's relations are. With a literary work whose relations to 'economic and social processes' are extremely complex we can expect to see an extremely complex historical life:

> The affirmation that the earth is round or that species evolve does not constitute the same statement before and after Copernicus, before and after Darwin; it is not, for such simple formulations, that the meaning of the words has changed; what changed was the relation of these affirmations to other propositions, their conditions of use and reinvestment, the field of experience, of possible verifications, of problems to be resolved, to which they can be referred. (p103)

If this is true, then think how much *more* development and alteration there must be in the life of a literary work through history.

What implications does such theoretical work have for the literary critic? As one might expect from the man who wrote 'What is an Author?' (1980), Foucault is not especially interested in directing attention back to the origins of a literary work in an authorial consciousness:

> Now, the function of enunciative analysis is not to awaken texts from their present sleep, and, by reciting the marks still legible on their surface, to rediscover the flash of their birth; on the contrary, its function is to follow them through their sleep, or rather to take up the related themes of sleep, oblivion, and lost origin, and to discover what mode of existence may characterize statements, independently of their enunciation, in the density of time in which they are preserved, in which they are reactivated, and used, in which they are also – but this was not their original destiny – forgotten, and possibly even destroyed. (1972, p123)

Even when Foucault is interested in a statement's first appearance in public, then, it is in terms of the network of relations which gives it its identity and not the originating consciousness of its human parent. As the above statement makes quite clear, Foucault is not interested in *énonciation* as against *énoncé*. Moreover, although it is apparent that it is possible to find statements in Foucault's writings which are what I have termed 'non-monocular' in their view of statements and texts, it is necessary to admit that it is also easy to find other statements in which one of his critical eyes is less than fully open. For if at one point Foucault admits to a recognition of the 'heaviness' of the statement or text and the (admittedly limited) interpretative relevance of 'the spatio-temporal coordinates of its birth', at other times he is happy to allow the statement to drift away from the 'flash' of its birth, and he is unwilling to challenge its drifting away from its origin in a sleep that he treats more like an awakening, an awakening to potentialities impossible unless it achieves independence of its enunciation and is allowed to be 'reactivated, and . . . forgotten, and possibly even destroyed'.

Thus although Foucault's work undoubtedly encourages a complex view of a statement as having a 'heaviness' which is certainly related to the conditions of its birth while (presumably) modifying or losing some or all of this heaviness in the sleep of its existence in times other than those in which it was born, the emphasis of his work seems more on the sleep than the weight. If we gloss the traditional function of *scholarship* as being that of awakening literary works from their present sleep and reminding them or their readers of who or what they 'really are', then it must be said that the emphasis of Foucault's work is likely to find favour not with the traditional scholar, but more with the literary sociologist investigating the 'sleep' of literary works through a range of different interpretative contexts. To this extent it may appear odd that Foucault is more often cited as an intellectual patron of the (largely) American New History than of the (largely) British cultural materialism – odd, because it is the latter rather than the former group of critics and theorists which has laid more emphasis on the need to pursue the literary work through its 'sleep' in cultures different from that in which it first saw the light of day.

The oddity diminishes somewhat, however, when we note the distance between Foucault's theoretical positions and those of traditional Marxism – a distance that seems likely to have contributed to making his work more palatable to American New Historicists than to British cultural materialists. Both Foucault and (probably all) Marxists agree that a statement cannot be examined 'in itself' in terms of a self-identical meaning, but must be understood to produce a meaning through its relations to 'institutions, economic and social processes, behavioural patterns, systems of norms, techniques, types of classification, modes of characterization'. Marxists, however, have gone beyond this to arrange such determinants and other factors in particular *hierarchies of determination,* and thus have believed themselves to have had a clearer view of whether (for example) an economic process is more or less fundamental in this hierarchy of determination than is a system of norms. This is not to say that Marxist analyses have no gaps of their own (for example: in the life of a statement over time what respective weight do we give to the 'economic basis' of the society in which the statement was made, and what to the 'economic basis' of the societies within which it survives?). But it does leave Foucault's discursive formations seeming very vague in contrast to the components of a Marxist analysis of society, not least when they are used as a guide to interpretative action. Foucauldian discourse, then, has little in common with the Marxist concept of ideology – itself one of the more problematic and controversial of Marxist analytical terms. Indeed, Foucault's description of literature as both something which bases itself on, and is, 'true discourse', is very far removed from many Marxist accounts which place literature among the ideologies.[7]

Consider a statement to which I have already referred. 'The frontiers of a book are never clear-cut; beyond the title, the first lines, and the last full stop, beyond its internal configuration and its autonomous form, it is caught up in a system of references to other books, other texts, other sentences: it is a node within a network' (1972, p23). There is nothing here to suggest *where one should start* in tracing this system of references, these networks – references and networks which, presumably, change from reading situation to reading situation. Thus in a long account of the 'associated field' that turns a sentence or a series of signs into a statement, Foucault lists the following components:

- the series of other formulations within which the statement appears and forms one element;
- all the formulations to which the statement refers (implicitly or not);
- all the formulations whose subsequent possibility is determined by the statement, and which may follow the statement as its consequence, its natural successor);
- all the formulations whose status the statement in question shares (adapted from 1972, pp98–9).

With no guidance as to which of these factors is determining, which are primary and which are secondary, an investigator could spend a lifetime researching a single statement from, say, a play by Shakespeare without exhausting his or her potential material. One would like to know: where

---

[7] The comments come in Foucault's lecture 'The Discourse on Language', which is printed as an appendix to *The Archaeology of Knowledge*. 'For, even with the sixth century Greek poets, true discourse – in the meaningful sense – inspiring respect and terror, to which all were obliged to submit, because it held sway over all and was pronounced by men who spoke as of right, according to ritual, meted out justice and attributed to each his rightful share; it prophesied the future, not merely announcing what was going to occur, but contributing to its actual event, carrying men along with it and thus weaving itself into the fabric of fate' (1972, p218). 'I am thinking of the way Western literature has, for centuries, sought to base itself in nature, in the plausible, upon sincerity and science – in short, upon true discourse' (1972, p219).

does a particular discursive formation begin and end, and what are, typically, its determining elements?[8]

Unfortunately, these are questions which Foucault rarely addresses, and to which he seems not to give consistent answers. At this point his shifting definitions of what a discourse is ('treating it sometimes as the general domain of all statements, sometimes as an individualizable group of statements, and sometimes as a regulated practice that allows for a certain number of statements') becomes a problem for the investigator concerned to set – say – a literary work in the context of its relevant discursive practice or practices:

Foucault writes of 'systems of formation' of a discourse, but these are not really defined in such a way as to make clear what the 'laws' which lie behind their formation are.

> [A]nd by discourse, then, I meant that which was produced (perhaps all that was produced) by the groups of signs. But I also meant a group of acts of formulation, a series of sentences or propositions. Lastly – and it is this meaning that was finally used (together with the first, which served in a provisional capacity) – discourse is constituted by a group of sequences of signs, in so far as they are statements, that is, in so far as they can be assigned particular modalities of existence. And if I succeed in showing, as I shall try to do shortly, that the law of such a series is precisely what I have so far called a *discursive formation*, if I succeed in showing that this discursive formation really is the principle of dispersion and redistribution, not of formulations, not of sentences, not of propositions, but of statements (in the sense in which I have used this word), the term discourse can be defined as the group of statements that belong to a single system of formation; thus I shall be able to speak of clinical discourse, economic discourse, the discourse of natural history, psychiatric discourse. (1972, pp107–8)

It cannot be said that the reader of *The Archaeology of Knowledge* is offered much unambiguous advice as to how to settle boundary disputes between different discourses; Foucault's discourses are given an autonomy and self-sufficiency on the theoretical plane which parallels that granted language games by Wittgenstein, while in practice (as, it will be seen, Foucault admits) reality is a lot more messy. Foucault suggests that discursive

---

[8] A refusal to *rank* determining factors in hierarchies is common to a number of otherwise very different theorists of the last few decades. In my next section I will refer to Hayden White's view of non-narrativized reality as constituted by 'chains of mechanical causes and effects', and later on I will argue that Raymond Williams's rejection of the Marxist base–superstructure model in favour of his concept of 'structures of feeling' leaves him, in like manner, with a multiplicity of determining relationships any one of which may be dominant. I will go on to suggest that this common refusal to espouse a theory which involves ranking determinants in hierarchies is reflected in the woolliness of much American New Historical discussion of social determination, and I will refer to Iain Wright's telling criticism of Stephen Greenblatt's concept of *circulation* on just these grounds.

formations are recognized through a 'system of dispersion' such that 'between objects, types of statement, concepts, or thematic choices, one can define a regularity (an order, correlations, positions and functionings, transformations)' (1972, p38). The trouble is that, as Foucault implies elsewhere, one can define all sorts of rival systems of dispersion between these different elements.

There is also the problematic issue of the relation of discourse to the non-discursive. Take the following statement:

> The determination of the theoretical choices that were actually made is also dependent upon another authority. This authority is characterized first by the *function* that the discourse under study must carry out *in a field of non-discursive practices*. The General Grammar played a role in pedagogic practice . . . (1972, pp67–8)

From this it would appear that pedagogy is not a discursive practice, although why pedagogy should be distinguished from medicine in this way is not at all clear.

IX
Hayden White: History as Text

Narrative theory – sometimes called narratology – has played a significant part in the development of the New Historicism, and has helped to undermine the comfortable assumption that the academic disciplines of history and literary criticism are fundamentally distinct in terms of their methodologies. Both historians and novelists (and literary critics) tell stories, and the *way* in which they tell stories has been the starting-point for attempts to demonstrate that the narratives of the historian have far more in common with those of the novelist than had previously been supposed – especially by historians themselves. The debates engendered by such arguments have had, not surprisingly, their greatest impact within the discipline of history. But a more long-term effect has been that of forcing literary critics to look afresh at 'the historicity of texts, and the textuality of history', as Louis Montrose has expressed it.

Without much doubt Hayden White's book *Metahistory: The Historical Imagination in Nineteenth-Century Europe* (1973) was instrumental in setting an agenda for much subsequent debate. The radical nature of White's challenge to established historiography was apparent from the start of his book; instead of accepting that the writing of history is to be distinguished from other writing by means of its factual subject matter, White started off from an emphasis of a very different sort, on the work of history as 'a verbal structure in the form of a narrative prose discourse'. There is a clear *textualist* emphasis here, an emphasis not on the object of historical writing but on its textual form. Such an emphasis has the potential of drawing attention not to what distinguishes historical writing from other forms of writing, but to what it shares with other narrative discourses:

> In this theory I treat the historical work as what it most manifestly is: a verbal structure in the form of a narrative prose discourse. Histories (and philosophies of history as well) combine a certain amount of 'data', theoretical concepts for 'explaining' these data, and a narrative structure for their presentation as an icon of sets of events presumed to have occurred in times past. In addition, I maintain, they contain a deep structural content which is generally poetic, and specifically linguistic, in nature, and which serves as the precritically accepted paradigm of what a distinctively 'historical' explanation should be. This paradigm functions as the 'meta-historical' element in all historical works that are more comprehensive in scope than the monograph or archival report. (1973, pix)

Now it should be noted that White's interest in narrative structure is here limited to the *presentation* of both 'data' and theoretical concepts for explaining these data; there is no suggestion at this stage that historical events are in any way themselves created by their narrative presentation. But White does then go on to outline three kinds of strategy by means of which historians are able to gain different kinds of 'explanatory effect':

> I call these different strategies explanation by formal argument, explanation by emplotment, and explanation by ideological implication. *Within* each of these different strategies I identify four possible modes of articulation by which the historian can gain an explanatory affect of a specific kind. For arguments there are the modes of Formism, Organicism, Mechanism, and Contextualism; for emplotments there are the archetypes of Romance, Comedy, Tragedy, and Satire, and for ideological implication there are the tactics of Anarchism, Conservatism, Radicalism, and Liberalism. A specific combination of modes comprises what I call the historiographical 'style' of a particular historian or philosopher of history. . . .
>   In order to relate these different styles to one another as elements of a single tradition of historical thinking, I have been forced to postulate a deep level of consciousness on which a historical thinker chooses conceptual strategies by which to explain or represent his data. On this level, I believe, the historian performs an essentially *poetic* act, in which he *pre*figures the historical field and constitutes it as a domain upon which to bring to bear the specific theories he will use to explain 'what was really happening' in it. (1973, px)

White outlines four types of such prefiguration: metaphor, metonymy, synecdoche and irony, and is soon ready to confirm that by disclosing the linguistic ground on which a given idea of history was constituted, he has attempted to establish 'the ineluctably poetic nature of the historical work' (1973, pxi).

Crucial to White's approach, then, is a distinction between different 'levels of conceptualization' in the historical work, which he enumerates as follows: '(1) chronicle; (2) story; (3) mode of emplotment; (4) mode of argument; and (5) mode of ideological implication' (1973, p5). For our purposes it is the distinction White makes between the first three of these categories that is of interest: while a chronicle is a mere list of events with no beginning and no end, a chronicle is organized into a story 'by the further arrangement of the events into the components of a "spectacle" or process of happening, which is thought to possess a discernible beginning, middle, and end' (1973, p5). Finally, when the historian provides a 'meaning' for his story 'by identifying the *kind of story* that has been told' (a tragedy or a comedy, for example), then he has provided an 'explanation by emplotment' (1973, p7).

It is fair to say that White does not appear to be wholly clear and consistent in the distinctions he makes between, for example, 'organizing into a story', and 'emplotment' – and this should not surprise us as the distinction between story and plot in narrative theory, although enormously productive, has proved to be far more complex and problematic than was once supposed. In a later article, for example, White attempts to distinguish between a historical discourse that *narrates*, and one that *narrativizes*. Thus a discourse that narrates 'openly adopts a perspective that looks out on the world and reports it', whereas one which narrativizes 'feigns to make the world speak itself and speak itself as a *story*' (1981a, pp2–3). This would certainly seem to suggest that the narrating of events (what one would normally refer to as telling a story) can be such as to avoid imposing an order on to the chaos of events, for in normal usage the verb 'to narrate' is not normally applied to the recounting of a chronicle (a sequence of events not linked by some sort of causality or other). If a historical discourse can narrate a story that just 'looks out on the world and reports it' and imposes no order on it, then this would suggest that it is possible for the historian to discover an order in the world, in the sequence of events. But later on in the same article White makes it quite clear that stories are always *imposed* by human beings *on* events in the world:

> [T]his value attached to narrativity in the representation of real events arises out of a desire to have real events display the coherence, integrity, fullness, and closure of an image of life that is and can only be imaginary. The notion that sequences of real events possess the formal attributes of the stories we tell about imaginary events could only have its origin in wishes, daydreams, reveries. Does the world really present itself to perception in the form of well-made stories, with central subjects, proper beginnings, middles and ends, and a coherence that permits us to see 'the end' in every beginning? Or does it present itself more in the forms that the annals and chronicle suggest, either as mere sequence without beginning or end or as sequences of beginnings that only terminate and never conclude? (1981a, p23)

In all this there seems to be some hesitation concerning the extent to which stories can or cannot be innocent of emplotment, and also concerning the extent to which stories are, or are not, to be found in the unnarrated world, the actual flow of historical events. Such issues, as we will see, are by no means unimportant, and form the basis of much later controversy around White's work. There is however no doubt that White's characterization of stories as fundamentally different from the world which they ostensibly describe, and with which they profess to engage, has the effect of trivializing them. From White's perspective, stories have much the same function as that which Marx attributed to religion – the heart of a heartless world, the opiate of the people. Stories for White are 'wishes, daydreams, reveries' – and White seems less convinced than is Freud that our wishes, daydreams and reveries are produced by, and have a productive function in, the lives that we lead.

In particular, White's clear belief that *explanation* and *persuasion* when practised by the historian have more to do with rhetoric than with fact – have, perhaps, *only* to do with rhetoric – are clearly extremely controversial. For it is apparent already in *Metahistory* that White believes *order itself* to be something which is imposed on events rather than something which is discoverable in them and their interrelations. 'Unlike the novelist, the historian confronts a veritable chaos of events *already constituted*, out of which he must choose the elements of the story he would tell' (1973, p6, n5). This leads White, ineluctably, to view *different* historical emplotments as enjoying a parity of accuracy and truth. (More precisely, that matters of accuracy and truth are relevant only when dealing with monadic events, and not when considering the virtues of different emplotments.) Not surprisingly, then, White admits that

> My method, in short, is formalist. I will not try to decide whether a given historian's work is a better, or more correct, account of a specific set of events or segment of the historical process than some other historian's account of them; rather, I will seek to identify the structural components of these accounts. (1973, pp3–4)

In consort with such an approach, then, when discussing the work of Karl Marx, White is not prepared to assess whether Marx's account of history is better or worse, more or less true or false, than the work of another historian:

> My aim is to specify the dominant style of Marx's thought about the structures and processes of history-in-general. I am interested in Marx primarily as a representative of a specific modality of historical consciousness, a representative who must be regarded as neither more nor less 'true' than the best representatives of other modalities with which it contended for hegemony in the consciousness of nineteenth-century European man. In my view, 'history', as a plenum of documents that attest to the occurrence of events, can be put together in a number of different and equally plausible narrative accounts of 'what happened in the past', accounts from which the reader, or the historian himself, may draw different conclusions about 'what must be done' in the present. With the Marxist philosophy of history, one can do neither more nor less than what one can do with other philosophies of history, such as those of Hegel, Nietzsche, and Croce, even

> though one may be inclined to do different *kinds* of things on the basis of a belief in one's philosophy's truth. (1973, p283)

I find it curious that the historian is allowed talk of 'the best representatives of other modalities' – that is, to rank *within* a modality – but is not allowed to rank modalities themselves. I must also confess to a stunned inability to imagine what the world would now be like had the theories of Nietzsche had as much effect on the course of the twentieth century as have those of Marx.

White concludes that

> The Marxist view of history is neither confirmable nor disconfirmable by appeal to 'historical evidence', for what is at issue between a Marxist and a non-Marxist view of history is the question of precisely what counts as evidence, and what implications for the comprehension of the present social reality are to be drawn from the evidence thus constituted. (1973, p284)

It is worth noting that in the two above quotations White is quite happy to see a cause-and-effect relationship between Marxism and 'a specific modality of historical consciousness', while simultaneously denying that the logic of a Marxist account of history can possibly be said to be more or less true than any rival account. If one denies that one historical account in any way can be said to represent any reality higher or more complex than that of the individual events of history, what stronger evidence is there for seeing that historical account to represent a specific modality of historical consciousness? The answer would seem to be that as a (self-confessed) formalist, White – like all formalists – is happier seeing relations between formal structures (linguistic, intellectual, academic) than between such formal structures and the non-textual events of history.

Significantly, White sees history to be quite different from science in terms of its falsifiability:

> We have no choice with respect to the principles of knowledge we must adopt for effecting transformations in, or for exercising control over, the physical world. We either employ scientific principles of analysis and understanding of the operations of nature or we fail in our efforts to control nature.
>
> It is different with history. There are different possible ways of comprehending historical phenomena because there are different, and equally plausible, ways of organizing the social world which we create and which provides one of the bases of our experience of history itself. (1973, pp283–4)

I find this to be significant for two reasons. First, because it makes clear that White and Lyotard are in complete agreement that science and history proceed according to completely different rules – that they constitute different language games. Second, because it makes it clear that for White the purposes of history do not include that of 'effecting transformations in, or for exercising control over, the physical world' – or, presumably, over the social world. Attempts to control the social world in a manner comparable to the way in which the scientist controls the physical world are categorized by White as *ideological*:

> By the term 'ideology' I mean a set of prescriptions for taking a position in the present world of social praxis and acting upon it (either to change the world or to maintain it in its current state); such prescriptions are attended by arguments that claim the authority of 'science' or 'realism'. (1973, p22)

If, then, attempts to change the world by reference to a theory of history cannot be underwritten by an appeal to the events of history themselves, and if different historical accounts are – in like manner – equally valid when judged by reference to historical events, then why should historical accounts ever be written? According to White, 'the best grounds for choosing one perspective on history rather than another are ultimately aesthetic or moral rather than epistemological' (1973, pxii). But can one claim that one is making a moral (for example) choice when that choice can make no appeal to a non-subjective truth or to any possibility of bettering the world? It seems clear that such an attitude degrades moral and aesthetic choice to the level of – as Wordsworth put it in the Preface to the *Lyrical Ballads* – having 'a taste for Poetry . . . as if it were a thing as indifferent as a taste for rope-dancing, or Frontiniac or Sherry' (de Selincourt 1944, p394).

White clearly does not see it thus. According to him,

> I would contend that the world has a specifically moral, as well as a determinative physical, meaning. Story forms, or what Northrop Frye calls plot structures, represent an armory of relational models by which what would otherwise be nothing but chains of mechanical causes and effects can be translated into moral terms. (1981b, p253)

The comment is revealing to the extent that it shows that White *does* believe that there are chains of cause and effect in the world; it would be interesting to know why the historian is unable to represent such processes and use them as the structuring principle of a historical narrative. But White's causes and effects are of course *only* mechanical: human history here seems to be reduced to precisely the level of the physical world from which White has declared he wishes it to be distinguished. Are there no chains of cause and effect in history which have a moral dimension? According to White,

> It is only by virtue of what it teaches about moral wisdom, or rather about the irreducible moralism of a life lived under the conditions of culture rather than nature, that narrative can claim cognitive authority at all. (1981b, p253)

Surely human beings live both in culture and nature? Is not culture built on, in, and around nature? White here presents us with a monastic vision of the moral world as parallel to but separate from the natural world.

At this point I would like to underline what seem to me to be the two key elements in White's arguments. First, that order exists in our *accounts of* events, and not in those events or their interrelations or succession themselves. In brief: no patterns of cause-and-effect can be attributed to events in history, which form a chaos quite different from the implied order of the physical world.[9] Second, that attempts to *find* such an order are actually attempts to *impose* an order on the chaos of events by means of a sort of selective quotation; because of this, it is not possible to demonstrate the superiority of one such attempt over another, one story over another story, by appeal to the facts, the events of history.

It is this refusal to recognize any reason to prefer one historical emplotment to another (other than moral or aesthetic) which has been most controversial in White's work – and not least when this work has touched upon sensitive issues relating to Nazism and the Second World War. In the same collection of essays on representations of the holocaust to which I referred earlier, Carlo Ginzburg takes White to task for extending his belief that different historical emplotments of the same events cannot be ranked by reference to the events with which they deal:

> The Zionist historical explanation of the Holocaust, [Hayden] White says, is not a *contra-vérité* . . . but a truth: 'its truth, as a historical interpretation, consists precisely in its *effectiveness* [my italics] in justifying a wide range of current Israeli political policies that, from the standpoint of those who articulate them, are crucial to the security and indeed the very existence of the Jewish people.' In the same way, 'the effort of the Palestinian people to mount a politically *effective* [my italics] response to Israeli policies entails the production of a similarly *effective* [my italics] ideology, complete with an interpretation of their history capable of endowing it with a meaning that it has hitherto lacked.' We can conclude that if Faurisson's narrative were ever to prove *effective*, it would be regarded by White as true as well. (Ginzburg 1992, p93; for Faurisson see p26)

[9] In an article criticising White's article 'Historical Emplotment and the Problem of Truth', Martin Jay points out that although he denies it, White employs a tripartite division of the process of history writing which consists first of facts or events, the 'content' of history, which are understood to be prelinguistic phenomena; these then become the stuff of stories, which are emplotted narrations about the significance of the first-level events, and finally, at the third level, we find interpretations about the meaning of the stories. Jay argues that White's first level of facts and events, which according to White includes such things as wars, revolutions, earthquakes and tidal waves, is highly problematic: wars and revolutions are certainly not prelinguistic. Jay concludes that there is 'virtually no historical content that is linguistically unmediated and utterly bereft of meaning, waiting around for the later historian to emplot it in arbitrary ways'. See Jay (1992, pp97–9).

The perhaps predictable result of arguing that one can decide between rival historical accounts of the same set of events only on moral or aesthetic grounds, and never in terms of their greater or lesser truthfulness, has by now degenerated into a rather squalid instrumentalism: we concoct fictions about the past (ideologies) so as to be able more effectively to get what we want in the present. I might add that I fail to understand how it is that narratives can help us to get what we want in the world but cannot reflect that world in an accurate manner.

Such problems emerge even more clearly in White's comments on the German revisionist historian Andreas Hillgruber, who controversially argued that the struggle of German soldiers on the eastern front during the Second World War was worthy of respect in terms of their perception of what they were fighting for. White acknowledges that this point of view is controversial, but counters:

> Yet Hillgruber's suggestion for emplotting the story of the defense of the eastern front did not violate any of the conventions governing the writing of professionally respectable narrative history. He simply suggested narrowing the focus to a particular domain of the historical continuum, casting the agents and agencies occupying that scene as characters in a dramatic conflict, and emplotting this drama in terms of the familiar conventions of the genre of tragedy. (White 1992, p42)

So much the worse for 'the conventions governing the writing of professionally respectable narrative history'. White seems unable to grasp the fact that 'narrowing the focus to a particular domain of the historical continuum, casting the agents and agencies occupying that scene as characters in a dramatic conflict, and emplotting this drama in terms of the familiar conventions of the genre of tragedy' (in other words, perhaps, ignoring that the tenacity of German soldiers on the eastern front was prolonging the war and allowing for the more complete murder of the Jews of Eastern Europe) is morally unacceptable precisely because it renders the particular emplotment in question inadequate to those historical events which demand to be taken into account because they are causally linked to 'a particular domain of the historical continuum'. What I am saying, then, is that an 'emplotted story' of the Second World War which sees the murder of the Jews and the military dedication of German east-front soldiers as unconnected *is untrue*; it can and must be rejected precisely because it inadequately measures up to 'what really happened'. It is not merely one possible emplotment among many, all equally true, if more or less morally or aesthetically pleasing. Such an interpretation, indeed, *is* morally unacceptable – but because it is not true, because it lies by omission.

In his introduction to the volume of essays to which I have been referring, Saul Friedlander offers a useful summary of White's position:

> White's by now familiar position aims at systematizing a theory of historical interpretation based on a fundamental redefinition of traditional historical understanding: Language as such imposes on the historical

narrative a limited choice of rhetorical forms, implying specific emplotments, explicative models, and ideological stances. These unavoidable
choices determine the specificity of various interpretations of historical
events. There is no 'objective', outside criterion to establish that one
particular interpretation is more true than another. In that sense White is
close to what could be termed a postmodern approach to history.
(Friedlander 1992, p6)

Why should White's work be of interest to literary critics? Why indeed *have*
works such as *Metahistory* started to appear on the reading lists pinned up
in departments of English as well as departments of history? What
influence has White's work had? I think that a number of answers to these
questions can be volunteered.

First, it will be noted that White uses a certain model and conception of
literature to underpin his arguments. In referring to 'the ineluctably poetic
nature of the historical work', White engages in a concealed categorization
of the poetic work as one which cannot be judged in terms of the truth or
falsity of its account of the world. Such a categorization feeds off views of
literature as a sort of invention or feigning which belongs to a world of the
imagination quite distinct from the real world of fact and event. White's
work thus presents us with what in many ways it is fair to describe as the
transposition of formalism from literary criticism to historiography. Given
the clearly postmodernist elements in White's work (mentioned by Friedlander), White's work has drawn attention to the formalist and anti-realist
elements in postmodernism, and has presented literary critics with a view
of what such elements can lead to. Literary critics are not normally asked
to explain what implications their theories have for depictions of (or even
the existence of) the holocaust.

Second, that if there is no '"objective", outside criterion to establish that
one particular interpretation is more true than another', as Friedlander's
account of White has it, then this undercuts much of the competitive
energy of literary-critical argument during (at least) the present century,
which has famously striven to determine which interpretations of literary
works are the most true, and which are either inadequate or wrong.
Literary critics have, therefore, a vested interest in determining whether or
not White's view of the parity of interpretations is correct.

Third, White's work has drawn attention to what one may call the
ideological dimension of emplotment, the fact that accounts of the world
– whether histories of the Second World War or interpretations of *Anna
Karenina* – inevitably organize their depictions in ways that have philosophical and ideological implications. Thus many of those recent critics who are
least sympathetic to the formalist and anti-realist elements in White's work
(myself included) have found much that is thought-provoking in the way
he infuses an ideological dimension into the analysis of narrative and
rhetorical techniques. Narratology, it should be remembered, grew out of
structuralism, and its enormously important categorizing of narrative
techniques and strategies was initially highly formal and technical in
nature. White's work had the perhaps unexpected effect of drawing

attention to the fact that narrative techniques – techniques of emplotment – are never ideologically neutral. This lesson has had a considerable impact on the way in which recent theories view the history of literary works' reception. It has, in other words, drawn attention to the ideological elements in literary criticism itself.

Another way of expressing this point is by saying that White has forced researchers in a number of fields to consider the extent to which interpretations are already explicit in reports, such that there are very few neutral 'facts'. In the critique of White to which I have already referred, Martin Jay takes White's two levels of 'nonnarrativized chronicle' and 'the historian's imposition of plot and meaning', and suggests that these be seen, rather, as first- and second-order narratives:

> For although not absolutely everything that historians fashion into their own stories is already emplotted by the actors, enough is to make it more than unformed raw material available as mere fodder for the historian's imagination. There is instead a process of negotiation that goes on between the two narrative orders, which prevents historical representation from being an utterly arbitrary concoction. (Jay 1992, p104)

The proposal is strikingly reminiscent of what a number of New Historical literary critics have argued concerning literary interpretation. The work of literature is not just fodder for the critic's imagination – but neither is it merely self-identical, carrying its own fully formed and final meaning within itself. Its meaning and significance for successive generations have to be regularly renegotiated. There is, following Bakhtin, a necessary dialogue between the critic and the work or the author, and between the twentieth-century critic and the nineteenth- or eighteenth-century one. If White's work dramatically exposes the inadequacy of a post-structuralist *mise-en-abyme* of self-generated interpretations by transposing it to the arena of history, it nevertheless draws attention to the impossibility of seeking refuge from such interpretative play in a simplistic realism. Thus if White's argument for preferring the more 'effective' emplotment meets with many of the same problems as Stanley Fish's 'interpretive community', like Fish's work it nonetheless forces the unconvinced to come up with some way of preferring one emplotment to another which is not that of a simplistic realism which ignores the saturation of facts by interpretation in human history and culture.

Finally, White's work has, I think, forced literary critics to think more of the problems of recapturing the past – problems faced both by the author and by the critic. The fact that White is primarily concerned with the discourses of the academic discipline of history but has utilized many theoretical insights from literary critics has helped this process.

If we move to a brief consideration of Howard Felperin's 1990 book *The Uses of the Canon: Elizabethan Literature and Contemporary Theory*, it is very quickly apparent that recent literary criticism such as Felperin's which is engaged in productive dialogue with New Historical ideas is throwing up some very similar topics to those we have seen emerging from Hayden White's work. Felperin sees much post-structuralist criticism to have ended up in a sort of conventionalist impasse:

> The weakness of this new 'conventionalism', then, is a new vulnerability to the charge of relativism, in so far as its claim to objective validity or verifiability has been abandoned. Having insisted on the textuality of history and culture, what *extra*textual grounds are left on which to mount the claim that one's own interpretations are correct or privileged, or to meet the charge from a resurgent 'right' that they are not? The deconstructive aporia beyond which the new historicism was supposed to have moved us thus returns in the form of a relativism that goes to the heart of its own project. Having left behind an older 'empiricist' or 'realist' historical narrative constituted by 'facts' and connected by 'cause and effect' for a 'conventionalist' historical hermeneutics consisting only of 'texts' and 'discourses', there is nothing solid to fall back on when its 'knowledge' is relativized as only a matter of opinion or interpretation. (1990, pvii)

This is surely no bad description of central problems in White's work; White has himself declared, for example, that 'There is an inexpungible relativity in every representation of historical phenomena' (1992, p37). White's work has put in sharp focus a dilemma faced by many contemporary literary critics influenced by post-structuralism, one expressed with plain directness by Felperin:

> [The] relapse into 'realism' is particularly embarrassing for post-structuralist interpreters of all schools, whose commitment to what Catherine Belsey terms 'discursive knowledge' and Louis Montrose 'the textuality of history' has effectively deprived them of the right of appeal to an outmoded or unsustainable objectivity, or, in Montrose's elegant phrasing, 'the historicity of texts', to substantiate their historical readings and clinch their political points. Short of bracketing everything one writes between inverted commas, there is no avoiding the relapse into a residual interpretive realism from which we have all taken leave – at least in theory. And even if one were to bracket everything thus, one would then be exposed to the opposite and no less vitiating charge of interpretive relativism. (1990, ppviii–ix)

If deconstruction achieved a limited notoriety outside the academy through Derrida's 'There is nothing outside the text', textualism seems set to achieve the same goal through Louis Montrose's 'the historicity of texts, and the textuality of history'. Montrose has attempted to explain what he meant by this chiasmic and gnomic utterance as follows:

> By *the historicity of texts*, I mean to suggest the cultural specificity, the social embedment, of all modes of writing – not only the texts that critics study but also the texts in which we study them. By *the textuality of history*, I mean to suggest, firstly, that we can have no access to a full and authentic past, a lived material existence, unmediated by the surviving textual traces

of the society in question – traces whose survival we cannot assume to be merely contingent but must rather presume to be at least partially consequent upon complex and subtle social processes of preservation and effacement; and secondly, that those textual traces are themselves subject to subsequent textual mediations when they are construed as the 'documents' upon which historians ground their own texts, called 'histories'. (1989, p20)

We see here, I think, the same double emphasis which we have found in the claims of other 'textualists', but in a less extreme form. On the one hand there is the argument that human beings are forced recurrently to reinvent the past through textual interpretations, and on the other the argument that 'we can have no access to a full and authentic past, a lived material existence, unmediated by the surviving textual traces of the society in question'.

Few (if any) have ever really gone so far as to claim that such access is possible. Nonetheless I call this a less extreme form because here Montrose does not attempt to obliterate the distinction between fictional and non-fictional texts, nor does he reject the possibility of preferring one historical account to another by means of an appeal to extratextual evidence. (I am not saying that this applies to all that Montrose has written on this subject, but it does apply to this particular statement.) Montrose here leaves open the question as to whether we can have access to a less than full, less than completely authentic past, but one which has an at least partially non-textual existence which is *mediated* to us by texts, and not *created* for us by texts. Nonetheless, I draw attention to the familiar double emphasis of textualism: no direct, non-textual access to the past; continual remaking of the past through 'subsequent textual mediations'. It will be noted that this double emphasis has equally important implications for the disciplines of history and literary criticism, and for their relationship with each other. Perhaps one of the most important legacies of textualism has been that of shattering the Berlin wall between these two disciplines, leaving excited but nervous individuals wandering into recently out-of-bounds territory and meeting with those who live next door but who are strangers, while musing about the implications of this territorial revolution.

The recent turn to history (in literary studies and elsewhere) is then both a reaction against textualism *and* in part a product of it. It is a reaction against textualism inasmuch as it seeks to assert very strongly that there *is* something outside of the text which both produces the text and produces responses to it. At the same time the turn to history owes a debt to textualism inasmuch as it draws on textualist ideas to explore the complex and multifaceted life of the text in history.

3

CONTEXTS

History and Histories

Historical literary criticism is, by general consent, a form of contextual criticism that is opposed to and distinguished from what I have referred to as textualism. For contextualists, the relationship between text and context is more than accidental, although its precise nature may vary: it may be constitutive or defining, it may be enlightening, or it may be modifying. Thus the term 'context' in literary studies has, in the past, been used to imply or invoke a range of different possible relationships to the literary text. Studying a literary work's context may, it has been argued at different times, help us to understand *why* it is as it is, *what* it is, or *how* it should be understood differently from the way it appears to be when considered 'out of context'. Contextual criticism thus comes in many different varieties, but before looking at some of these – and at some of the innovations associated with those recent varieties of contextualism which are gathered under the umbrella term of 'New Historicism' – it is worth reminding ourselves of the range that these varieties can cover. It is not just that there are different *sorts* of context, but also that what is understood by the term 'context' in literary-critical usage can vary very considerably.

It needs also to be remembered that the very distinction between text and context is a problematic one. I have, earlier, defined texts as 'fixed arrangements of signs designed to have a certain independence of time and space'. That self-containedness and mobility which we associate with a text because of that 'certain independence of time and space' should not blind us to the fact that to function as a text these 'fixed arrangements of signs' rely upon certain umbilical connections to the extratextual world. These different connections can be, for example, linguistic, generic, institutional, social and cultural, ideological, aesthetic, documentary and distributive/transmissive. Without these connections our fixed arrangement of signs is no longer a text, as it has no communicative or expressive potentiality. We very often obscure such connections by assuming that they are constants which are always 'there'; thus not even the most formalist of critics has ever argued that the meanings of the words in a poem are defined by that poem in the manner in which they are defined in a dictionary. (And given that the words in a dictionary are themselves defined by other words in that same dictionary, it is apparent that the dictionary is, in the last resort, no more self-sufficient than the poem.) If you do not understand English you cannot read *Pride and Prejudice* in Jane Austen's words – a point whose obviousness has not always ensured that it has been remembered. 'English' is, however, neither completely homogeneous nor absolutely unchanging: it is an entity which is fissured and volatile – although this should not obscure the existence of underlying continuities and fixities.

In practice, then, what is textual for one reader or one generation may be contextual for another reader or generation. Shakespeare's audience did not need to read books with titles such as *The Elizabethan World Picture* before enjoying a performance of *King Lear*.

For literary critics there is a traditional if conceptually ill-defined way of stressing the dependence of our 'fixed arrangements of signs' on an interlocking continuum of determining and defining contexts: the distinction between 'text' and 'work'. It is to this tradition that Jerome J. McGann appeals when he refers to 'those profoundly nondialectical forms we call texts' (1988, p22), to which he pointedly contrasts 'literary "works" [which] *continue* to live and move and have their being' (1988, p125). One might almost submit that a text becomes literary only when it is seen as a work, that is, when it starts to *live* (or to work) in a context. For McGann it is clear that 'we must reconceive the literary "text" as the literary "work", i.e. as a related series of concretely determinable semiotic events that embody and represent processes of social and historical experience'. He sees this as an essential first part of 'a general theory of historical criticism', and continues:

> Second, and following from this, is the concept of a critical methodology as embracing two large and related fields: the history of the literary work's textualizations and the history of its reception. Both of these histories occupy themselves with three important heuristic distinctions: between the work at its point of origin, the work through its subsequent transmissions, and the work situated in the immediate field of a present investigation. (1985, p10)

As I will go on to suggest, McGann's proposal sums up much of the innovatory thrust of New Historicist work, and represents a significant broadening and sophistication of more traditional historicist or contextualist literary criticism.

I
The Aims of Contextualism

As I have already suggested, very different aims can lie behind the impulse to read literary works in contextually informed ways. Recent criticism has tended to assume that behind such an impulse there lies an interpretative imperative: we contextualize works of literature so as to be able to produce better (more accurate, more all-embracing) interpretations of them. But there are other possibilities: the desire to demonstrate that a particular literary work performed a particular function in a given historical context may be pursued without any belief that such a demonstration will generate any new interpretative possibilities. In like manner, explaining that a literary work could not have been written independent of a particular complex of determining personal and social factors and forces may not be intended to imply that such an understanding has any relevance when one comes to interpreting or evaluating that work – as Samuel Johnson pointed out a long while ago in his *Preface to Shakespeare*:

> Every man's performances, to be rightly estimated, must be compared with the state of the age in which he lived, and with his own particular opportunities; and though to the reader a book be not worse or better for the circumstances of the author, yet as there is always a silent reference of human works to human abilities, and as the enquiry, how far man may extend his designs, or how high he may rate his native force, is of far greater dignity than in what rank we shall place any particular performance, curiosity is always busy to discover the instruments, as well as to survey the workmanship, to know how much is to be ascribed to original powers, and how much to casual and adventitious help. (Bronson 1958, p258)

Contextualization, therefore, *may* be believed to have aesthetic or interpretative implications – but this is not necessarily the case. It is possible to be an aesthetic or interpretative monist but a functional relativist, and to believe that although a literary work's aesthetic value is fixed and unchanging, the functions which the work performs or can perform vary from one social and cultural context to another. Contextualism can, in other words, have a sociological imperative behind it, or (as in Johnson's case) it can be undertaken as part of an inquiry into human potentialities rather than interpretative accuracy or aesthetic truth. Alternatively, it is possible to believe that the aesthetic is relative rather than absolute, but that it is relative not to the enabling context of a work's genesis but to the contexts of a work's reception and use.

II
Varieties of Contextual Information
Modes and Relations

In distinguishing between *modes* and *relations* of contextual information I wish to draw attention to the difference between *what sort of information* is being looked for, and *what sort of relationship* is argued to exist between this information and a work of literature. Information about language-use contemporary with the writing of a literary work I define as *modal*, while information about the way in which, say, the publication of a literary work entered into a current political struggle I define as *relational*. It is palpable that there is no hard-and-fast dividing line between these two.

Among the most important modes I would list the following: linguistic, generic, institutional, social/cultural, ideological, and documentary/transmissive. To put it another way, a range of different categories of information can be deemed to constitute relevant material for the study of a literary context. These include information about language use, information about the generic constraints or possibilities which governed the writing of a work, information concerning the rôle of the institution of literature in a given culture, information about a society or culture from which a work emerges or within which it is read, information about ideological formations which inform the work, and information about the material form in which the work appears and the manner in which it is distributed.

Among the most important relations are those of *determination* or *conditioning*. To take determination first, we can say that the fact that a work is written and published, or the form in which it is written and published, can be related to extratextual forces operating through direct or mediated processes which can be mapped by the critic. Such forces may be highly general or very specific: the effect of changes in the economic base as seen by traditional Marxists, the ideas and the personal experiences of the author, the ways in which an author stays alive (Virginia Woolf's £500 a year, patronage, book sales, etc.). So far as conditioning is concerned, we can list a number of possible relevant factors: *reference* (a work cannot be properly appreciated without an understanding of that to which it refers); *engagement* (certain works do not just refer to aspects of the world, they try actively to intervene in matters social, religious, political, and so on); *transformation* (a work is read in the light of those various forces which determine and condition a reader's or audience's 'framing' of a work), and so on. These are crude categories, and finer distinctions can be drawn. As I have already suggested, for example, what we can term genetic forces can be either enabling or constitutive: thus a sudden windfall (such as Virginia Woolf's inheritance) may enable a novel to be written sooner than it would otherwise have been, without its in any significant way altering *what* is written. On the other hand, the existence of a patron may not just allow a book to be written; it is very likely also to lead to a different book from the one that would or could have been written in the absence of a patron. In like manner, changes in a given culture may affect the continued life of a literary work in different ways. The closing of theatres will lead to a different sort of life for dramatic works, whereas changing attitudes towards colonialism are likely to lead to different ways of reading certain works, different evaluations of their moral and (perhaps) aesthetic value.

In the pages that follow, then, I want to outline some of the key ways in which a family of linked but not necessarily cohesive theoretical positions which are often lumped together under the term 'New Historicism' have revolutionized attitudes towards the use of contextualizing information by literary critics, and in particular to show how certain historicist literary-critical traditions have been radically transformed by these recent developments. I have chosen to present these changes by focusing upon a number of specific theoretical shifts. This procedure enables me to present brief summaries of more traditional or 'old historicist' standpoints, while showing how more recent work has built upon, extended, qualified or rejected such traditional standpoints.

I have attempted to impose a certain order on the sequence of different theoretical shifts upon which I focus by moving from questions of literary genesis through to issues associated with reception and interpretation. Given that traditional historicist criticism very often limited itself to questions of literary genesis, this order reflects the order of a development within literary criticism itself, at the same time that it mirrors a logical chronological progression in the historical life of the literary work – from genesis to reception and interpretation.

III
From World Picture and Background to Faultline

My subheading makes reference to a number of influential critical texts – both old and new. E. M. W. Tillyard's *The Elizabethan World Picture* (first published 1943), Basil Willey's *The Seventeenth Century Background* and *The Eighteenth Century Background* (first published 1934 and 1940), and Alan Sinfield's *Faultlines: Cultural Materialism and the Politics of Dissident Reading* (1992). Restricting oneself to these titles alone, one can hardly fail to be struck by the older critics' confident use of the singular, a usage which contrasts markedly with Sinfield's more tentative use of plural forms. If we look around at other recent books which can be broadly grouped under the umbrella of New Historicism the pattern seems to become clearer: Stephen J. Greenblatt's *Shakespearian Negotiations*, Howard Felperin's *The Uses of the Canon*, Thomas Healy's *New Latitudes: Theory and English Renaissance Literature*, Dominick LaCapra's *Rethinking Intellectual History: Texts, Contexts, Language*, Jerome J. McGann's *Social Values and Poetic Acts* – modern historicist critics seem much more comfortable with plural forms and the suggestion that they are dealing with a historical reality which is certainly not monolithic and may not even constitute a continuous whole. As Jeffrey N. Cox and Larry J. Reynolds put it in the introduction to their own collection of New Historicist essays, the New Historicism 'rejects the idea of "History" as a directly accessible, unitary past, and substitutes for it the conception of "histories", an ongoing series of human constructions, each representing the past at particular present moments for particular present purposes' (1993, p4). In the same volume, in an essay entitled 'Figures, Configurations, Transfigurations', Edward Said argues that it is necessary 'to speak of our element as secular space and humanly constructed and interdependent histories that are fundamentally knowable, but not through grand theory or systematic totalization' (1993, p325).

In such comments we can, I think, perceive the influence of *textualist* ideas: the belief that the past is available to us only, or primarily, in textualized form, and that we represent it in a sequence or series of different projections which are as much a reflection of our contemporary needs and concerns as of a vanished reality or set of realities. But there is also a clear shift towards the belief that even *were* we to have direct access to the past, it would not prove to be, in the words of Jeffrey N. Cox and Larry J. Reynolds, a 'unitary past'. It is very hard to imagine that the following words could be written by a modern historicist critic. They are taken from the openings of the third and fourth chapters of Tillyard's *The Elizabethan World Picture*, and from the openings of the three sections of the fifth chapter of the same book.

> The conception of world order was for the Elizabethans a principal matter; the other set of ideas that ranked with it was the theological scheme of sin and salvation. (1972, p26)
> The Elizabethans pictured the universal order under three main forms: a chain, a series of corresponding planes, and a dance. (1972, p33)
> It will be convenient to describe the Elizabethan scheme of creation from top to bottom. (1972, p45)
> It has been well said that for the Elizabethans the moving forces of history were Providence, fortune, and human character. (1972, p60)
> Whether or not every educated Elizabethan had it well in his mind that the ether, according to Aristotle, had its native and eternal motion, which was circular, he took the motions and properties of the four elements very much for granted. (1972, p68)

Generations of students (myself included) have worked their way through these generalizations, making careful notes which will allow them to convince their examiners that their understanding of *King Lear* or *Hamlet* is based upon a properly historical understanding of the assumptions shared by Shakespeare, his contemporaries, and their audiences. And generations of students have indeed found that the information provided by Tillyard's book often is helpful and illuminating for those attempting to obtain a historical perspective on Elizabethan life and literature. But long before the term 'New Historicism' was ever uttered, many students must have wondered about the contrast between a set of immensely powerful plays focused upon struggle, confrontation and *difference*, and Tillyard's picture of the culture from which these plays emerged: one seemingly based on a near-unanimity of belief. Tillyard himself feels the need, in his second chapter, to deal with the fact that if the Elizabethan age is 'ruled by a general conception of order', at first sight the 'drama is anything but orderly'. His answer to this contradiction is that the conception of order in the Elizabethan age 'is so taken for granted, so much part of the collective mind of the people, that it is hardly mentioned except in explicitly didactic passages' (1972, p17).

This explanation has by no means satisfied more recent historicist critics. Stephen J. Greenblatt himself, in an early (1982) comment on 'what we may call the new historicism', contrasts it to the *monological* nature of the earlier historicism:

> that is, concerned with discovering a single political vision, usually identical to that said to be held by the entire literate class or indeed the entire population. . . . This vision, most often presumed to be internally coherent and consistent . . . has the status of a historical fact. It is not thought to be the product of the historian's interpretation, nor even of the particular interests of a given social group in conflict with other groups. Protected then from interpretation and conflict, this vision can serve as a stable point of reference, beyond contingency, to which literary interpretation can securely refer. (1982, p5)

More recently, Graham Holderness has accused what he terms the 'authoritarian school of criticism' (which according to him includes Tillyard, was anticipated by L. C. Knights and G. Wilson Knight, and was extended by J. Dover Wilson), of constructing its model of Elizabethan culture

> from a highly selective range of sources, arbitrarily privileged and tendentiously assembled. The sources drawn on are either works of government propaganda or of Tudor apology from the more conservative 'organic intellectuals' of the state (Tillyard asserts for instance that the Machiavellian school of Italian humanist thought had no impact on English culture); or convenient details arbitrarily stripped from works which are by no means as reductively orthodox as Tillyard implies. These materials constitute a fair description of the dominant *ideology* of Elizabethan society: in no sense do they represent a complete or even adequate picture of the true complexity and contradictoriness of culture and ideology in this rapidly changing, historically transitional period. (1992, p4)

On the one side, then, we have an ordered set of interlocking conceptions which are common to 'the Elizabethans', and which include few points of tension or debate, and on the other side a culture marked by complexity and contradiction that includes but is not limited to a dominant ideology – a dominant ideology which, it is argued, Tillyard mistakes for an all-embracing 'Elizabethan world picture'. What is perhaps even more representative of recent historicist theory is Holderness's argument that we can learn as much about Tillyard's world picture from his book as about that of the Elizabethans (always accepting that Tillyard's views are representative of a particular ideological configuration current at the time his book is written, and are not purely personal). Holderness links Tillyard's work to a range of other studies published in the 1940s and 1950s,[10] and argues that whatever diversities of argument and approach differentiate these interventions from one another,

> they all derive from a common problematic: the ideological crisis of British nationalism precipitated by the events of the 1930s and 1940s: the Depression, the crisis of Empire and particularly of course the Second World War. What these critics said of 'order' in Elizabethan England can easily be read at this distance as a coded address to immediate problems of political authority in their contemporary Britain. (1992, p22)

Raymond Williams – a key influence on many of the present generation of historicist critics – has argued for the existence of a common process whereby an 'effective dominant culture' is passed off as '*the* tradition', '*the* significant past' (1980, p39). According to him the 'real social process' upon which an 'effective and dominant culture' depends is that of *incorporation*, an incorporation which selects for emphasis certain meanings and practices from a whole possible area of past and present, while neglecting and excluding other meanings and practices from consideration (1980, pp38, 39). For Williams, then, studying the past (or its art or culture) thus needs to involve a concern with 'those practices, experiences, meanings, values which are not part of the effective dominant culture'. These, according to him, can be either oppositional or alternative, that is to say they can either be ignored or tolerated by the dominant culture, or they can be in overt opposition to it (1980, p40). Finally, Williams notes that both oppositional and alternative elements can be divided into residual and emergent forms (1980, p40).

This is a world away from Tillyard's homogeneous and stable 'Elizabethans', whose disagreements, conflicts and tensions are all matters of the surface which fail to ruffle a common base of agreement and harmony. In his revealingly titled *Faultlines: Cultural Materialism and the Politics of Dissident Reading*, Alan Sinfield has paid tribute to this aspect of the work of Raymond Williams:

---

[10] Holderness argues that the following studies had 'essentially similar approaches' to that of Tillyard: Lily B. Campbell, *Shakespeare's Histories: Mirrors of Elizabethan Policy* (1947), and G. Wilson Knight, *The Olive and the Sword* (1944), and that this approach was then promulgated more widely to different publics by J. Dover Wilson through the popular revised 'complete works', *The New Shakespeare* (1953), and by critics associated with F. R. Leavis's journal *Scrutiny* such as D. A. Traversi in *Shakespeare from 'Richard II' to 'Henry V'* (1957).

> Much of the importance of Raymond Williams derives from the fact that at a time when Althusser and Foucault were being read in some quarters as establishing ideology and/or power in a necessarily unbreakable continuum, Williams argued the co-occurrence of subordinate, residual, emergent, alternative, and oppositional cultural forces alongside the dominant, in varying relations of incorporation, negotiation, and resistance. (1992, p9)

It is not just that recent historicist theorists see the culture from which a literary work emerges, to which it refers, and with which it engages as fissured and volatile, but that the writing or publishing of a work of literature may itself constitute an act of social or cultural struggle. 'Paradise Lost' is not just (in part) the product of, or 'about', the struggles of Milton's time: its writing and publication are themselves aspects of these struggles.

IV
From Reflection to Production and Engagement

Such a view is by no means limited to those who can be called – or who call themselves – New Historicists. J. Hillis Miller – a critic who has not objected to being called a formalist – puts the matter concisely:

> Works of literature do not simply reflect or are not simply caused by their contexts. They have a productive effect in history. This can and should also be studied. To put this another way, the only thing that sometimes worries me about the turn to history now as an explanatory method is the implication that I can fully explain every text by its pre-existing historical context. But the publication of these works was itself a political or historical event that in some way or another changed history. I think that if you don't allow for this, then literature is not much worth bothering with. (1991, pp152–3)

This does not of course commit Miller to a view of cultures as internally divided between dominant and oppositional/alternative forces, but it does testify to the extent to which contemporary critics are far more likely to grant literature an interventionist rôle in history, rather than restricting it to the ivory tower or to the office of spokesperson for the dominant culture. Indeed, once one accepts a view of history such as Williams has proposed, one which although it may stop short of underwriting the Marxist motto that history is the history of class struggle certainly sees history as the history of struggles between different groups and interests, then it is hard to see how the writing and publication of literary works *could* escape from these warring interests into a realm of calm neutrality.

The critic who has done most to draw this *performative* aspect of literary production to the attention of present-day readers is, unquestionably, Jerome J. McGann. Once again, a significant thrust of McGann's work can be indicated by citing the title of one of his recent books: *Social Values and Poetic Acts: The Historical Judgment of Literary Work*. A poem, for McGann, is in an important sense an *act* or a series of acts: its writing and publication can never be seen merely as neutral and routine adjuncts completing an inspirational process which belongs to a world different from that of quotidian reality; they are, rather, acts of engagement with a reality for which such involvement can never be non-partisan. As McGann puts, it, poetic texts hold a mirror up to the world, but they do this as a challenge, and not just as a picture to be observed (1988, p9).[11] From this perspective, the events following the publication of Salman Rushdie's *The Satanic Verses* are an extreme form of what is normal, rather than a qualitatively different sort of reaction from that which we associate with the publishing of literary works. Indeed, for McGann even the decision *not* to publish a work or sequence of works has meaning, a meaning which infects or informs the text from that point on:

> The retreat of Emily Dickinson is eloquent with social meaning, and her poetic methods – the refusal to publish, the choice of album verse forms, the production of those famous manuscript fascicles – are all part of a complex poetic statement which is explicated in the context of her world, and which carries significance into our day when we are able, not to enter, but to face and come to terms with that world. (1988, pp48–9)

In the everyday world, of course, we frequently assume that texts are coloured by the circumstances of their publication. A proposal of marriage is not the same delivered in person by a kneeling man as it is uttered over the telephone – especially if the person telephoning has every possibility of performing the act in person. But there is a long tradition in literary studies which has attempted to set literature aside from this fact of everyday life. For McGann, in contrast, '[t]he price of a book, its place of publication, even its physical form and the institutional structures by which it is distributed and received, all bear upon the production of literary meaning, and hence all must be critically analyzed and explained' (1985, p4). Recent attempts to divorce the literary work from the conditions of its composition, publication and continued historical life can thus be seen as the latest examples of textualist and formalist attempts to consider works of literature as monadic and suprahistorical, unchanging self-identical verbal complexes which may engage with the world but which, like non-stick pans, are somehow unaffected by this engagement.

---

[11] Consciously or unconsciously, McGann's point here is reminiscent of that scene near the end of Virginia Woolf's *Between the Acts* at which the performers at the pageant hold up mirrors and force their audience to see themselves. The act is (correctly) taken to be one of, in part, aggression.

During the last two decades McGann has mounted a sustained attack on such assumptions. For him, a literary work is not just marked by but is in part *constituted* through its documentary manifestations[12] and publishing history. McGann has typically focused most attention on to these factors as they inform the *first* emergence of the work into the world, but he has not limited himself to this stage of the public life of the work. For McGann, the failure to incorporate documentary studies into modern hermeneutics 'has obscured that horizon of the poetic where the work's ideological dimensions are clearest'. He continues:

> The options that writers choose in the areas of initial production, as well as in printing, publishing, and distribution – the options that are *open* to them in these matters – locate what one might call the 'performative' aspect of the poetic: what poems are *doing* in saying what they say. (1988, pp74–5)

Thus from Godwin's *Political Justice* through Lawrence's *Lady Chatterley's Lover* and Salman Rushdie's *The Satanic Verses*, whether a book is or is not available in a cheap edition can have very significant social, political and legal consequences – and whether an author chooses to avail him- or herself of this possibility has a meaning-constituting force to anyone who believes that a literary work's meaning is wholly or partly constituted by authorial intention. Accordingly, information concerning such matters can be believed to have very significant interpretative force.

Later on in this book I will be looking in some detail at McGann's discussion of one particular poem – John Keats's 'To Autumn'. For the time being I would argue that although McGann makes a strong case for the importance of evidence concerning the literary work's documentary identity (and I will also discuss this issue with reference to Thomas Hardy's 'The Convergence of the Twain' and W. H. Auden's 'Spain'), I would add that it is possible to take such documentary contextualization too far. A good example of this seems to me to occur in the introductory chapter of McGann's book *Black Riders* (1993), in which he considers Yeats's reference to the 'foul rag-and-bone shop of the heart' in 'The Circus Animals' Desertion'. McGann asks why Yeats chose 'to associate the "heart"' of poetry with that particular image of commercial activity, the rag and bone shop', and answers his question with an extended essay on the use of rags to produce the paper used in fine-press printing – a craft to which Yeats was strongly attached both emotionally and ideologically. The chapter needs to be read in its entirety to assess the strength of McGann's

---

[12] McGann uses more than one set of terms to describe the literary work's different forms of public embodiment. Earlier in this section I quoted a comment of his in which he refers to the work's *textualizations* – by which he appears to mean more than just its physical manifestations as a text but also the cultural and ideological implications of different forms of publication. A narrower term is *documentary*, by which McGann refers to the physical form of a work's appearance 'in print', along with, again, the cultural and ideological implications carried by this form.

argument, but I have to report that I remain unconvinced, and that here McGann's case seems to me to serve to demonstrate that it is possible to emphasize the documentary over the textual aspects of a literary work to excess.

V

Base and Superstructure,
or Structures of Feeling?

The most powerful contextualist tradition in literary criticism in the present century has undoubtedly been the Marxist one. The force of Marxist criticism has much to do with the fact that Marxist critics have been committed not just to a belief in the determining force of social and economic factors in the production of literary works, but to the necessity of differentiating between dominant and secondary determining elements among these factors. The classic distinction between base and superstructure in Marxist theory, and the manner in which this distinction is applied to the understanding and interpretation of literary works, have never been uncontroversial – especially in recent years. But it is important to recognize that the reason why this much-maligned distinction has retained the interest of theorists, many of whom have tried to refine it and sophisticate its application rather than merely to cast it out, is that it does provide a means whereby causal and conditioning forces active in (especially) the period of a literary work's genesis, can be ranked. It allows, therefore, a myriad possible determining factors to be ordered in terms of their relative importance. Terry Eagleton puts the case for Marxism's hierarchizing of determining factors by contrasting it to a fashionably non-hierarchizing theory:

> The Marxist objection to the poststructuralist 'expansionistic' concept of power is not that it is false but that it is quite often politically unhelpful. It gives us no indication of whether children's quarrels are more or less helpful than, say, the struggles of revolutionary nationalist movements. Poststructuralism, at least in some of its variants, is shy of such discriminations because they appear 'hierarchical' . . . (1985, p115)

The base–superstructure distinction is nothing if not hierarchical; Karl Marx's *A Contribution to the Critique of Political Economy* contains what is probably the classic formulation:

> In the social production of their existence, men inevitably enter into definite relations, which are independent of their will, namely relations of production appropriate to a given stage in the development of their material forces of production. The totality of these relations of production

constitutes the economic structure of society, the real foundation, on which arises a legal and political superstructure and to which correspond definite forms of social consciousness. The mode of production of material life conditions the general process of social, political and intellectual life. It is not the consciousness of men that determines their existence, but their social existence that determines their consciousness. (1971, pp20–21)

The great bulk of Marxist literary-theoretical and literary-critical work has been concerned with – and limited to – study of the literary work's genesis. Most traditional Marxist critics have defined literature as clearly superstructural, thus requiring them to understand literary works as in some way 'corresponding' to a primary or determining 'economic base'. As is well known, the work of tracing such 'correspondences' can involve either great sophistication or no sophistication at all. At the latter end of the continuum we can locate the view of Zhdanov, Stalin's cultural hack, who in the 1930s committed himself to the view that as the Soviet Union had the most advanced economic structure, it must also have the most advanced literature. Of more sophisticated versions there is no shortage. To take one well-known example, Lucien Goldmann's important study *The Hidden God* starts out, Goldmann announces,

from the fundamental principle of dialectical materialism, that the knowledge of empirical facts remains abstract and superficial so long as it is not made concrete by its integration into a whole; and that only this act of integration can allow us to go beyond the incomplete and abstract phenomenon in order to arrive at its concrete essence, and thus, implicitly, at its meaning. (1964, p7)

Goldmann goes on to argue that this process of integration must proceed along a particular route: ideas must be seen in the context of 'the whole, living man', the man must be seen as 'an element in a whole made up of the social group to which he belongs' (1964, p7), and the most important of such groups is that of social class – defined, it is implied, in a traditional Marxist manner by reference to 'relations of production appropriate to a given stage in the development of their material forces of production' as Marx puts it. Goldmann's subsequent study of French seventeenth-century tragedy involves a sophisticated analysis of the relationship between certain writers and a particular social fraction with which they were associated, one which enjoyed a doomed social position analogous – the argument runs – to that tragic vision in Goldmann's chosen writers of which it was a highly mediated expression. Goldmann argues that

In a few cases – and it is these which interest us – there are exceptional individuals who either actually achieve or who come near to achieving a completely integrated and coherent view of what they and the social class to which they belong are trying to do. The men who express this vision on an imaginative or conceptual plane are writers and philosophers, and the more closely their work expresses this vision in its complete and integrated form, the more important does it become. (1964, p17)

This, it will be perceived, does not condemn writers to being the passive means whereby an economic base is 'reflected', and it also provides some means whereby the 'importance' of a writer's work can be measured in terms not of a *direct* reflection of 'the economic base', but in terms of its expression of a vision that is both that of an individual and a social class, a vision which is a personal and social expression and reworking of a more fundamental or foundational force.

On Goldmann's death Raymond Williams published an important account and celebration of the importance of such work, which is reprinted in his *Problems in Materialism and Culture* (1980). There is no doubt that Goldmann's work was valuable for Williams not so much because it sophisticated the base–superstructure distinction, but because it actually called it into question. According to Williams, 'in ordinary hands' the base–superstructure distinction

> converted very quickly to an interpretation of superstructure as simple reflection, representation, ideological expression – simplicities which just will not survive any prolonged experience of actual works. It was the theory and practice of reductionism – the specific human experiences and acts of creation converted so quickly and mechanically into classifications which always found their ultimate reality and significance elsewhere – which in practice left the field open to anybody who could give an account of art which in its closeness and intensity at all corresponded to the real human dimension in which works of art are made and valued. (1980, p18)

We have to ask whether it is helpful to judge the theory in terms only of what it converts to 'in ordinary hands'; that a theory can be crudified by mechanical application does not constitute a damning indictment of the theory. Williams however went on to claim that after a period of initial belief that the base–superstructure distinction constituted a useful analytic tool, he came to realize that he had to give it up in favour of an

> attempt to develop a different kind of theory of social totality; to see the study of culture as the study of relations between elements in a whole way of life; to find ways of studying structure, in particular works and periods, which could stay in touch with and illuminate particular art-works and forms, but also forms and relations of more general social life; to replace the formula of base and superstructure with the more active idea of a field of mutually if also unevenly determining forces. (1980, p20)

In particular, Williams reports that at this point he found that he had to develop 'the idea of a structure of feeling' – a concept which he suggests has something in common with Goldmann's concept of structure, 'which contained, in itself, a relation between social and literary facts' (1980, p22). Williams's 'structure of feeling' was developed 'to indicate certain common characteristics in a group of writers but also of others, in a particular historical situation' (1980, p22).

My response to this is, again, to question whether or not the base–superstructure model necessarily rules out a study of culture which involves 'the study of relations between elements in a whole way of life'. What it seems to me the model *is* concerned to do is not to rule out any of the elements of a whole way of life, or the forms and relations of a more general social life, but to make it possible to *rank or order* these different elements, to distinguish between primary and secondary, causal and adventitious influences and forces. Terry Eagleton puts this point well when he suggests that

> We can best distinguish between these two 'levels' [= base and superstructure, J. H.] not 'vertically,' as the model itself misleadingly suggests, but 'horizontally' – a matter, so to speak, of time scale. To say that the changes you have effected in a particular form of social life are only 'superstructural' is less a philosophical doctrine than[13] a political warning and reminder: it is to argue that you have not yet run up against that outer limit or horizon which will prove most resistant to transformation – for Marxism, the property system – and that therefore not only is there more to be done, but until your political practice bumps up hard against that limit, what changes you *have* managed to bring about are not as radical as they might look. You have not yet tackled the 'acting', the forms of material practice, whose transformation is a necessary if not sufficient condition for the transformation of our very categories of thought. (1985, pp120–21)

Now to say all this is not of course to demonstrate that the model distinguishes correctly between such primary and secondary causes – nor is it to demonstrate that such a distinction can actually be made at all. And it is certainly the case that there is much force behind Williams's charge that traditional Marxist literary criticism very often signally failed to 'stay in touch with and illuminate particular art-works and forms'. But I do think that it is important to stress that the force of the base–superstructure model is not to *exclude* any element in the analysis of culture and society but to *rank and order* these elements, because in rejecting the model Williams leaves unanswered the question of whether the study of society *can* draw on a more general theory which distinguishes between those factors which have a dominant effect on the movements of history, and those which do not. What is implied in Williams's account is a much more pragmatic approach which assumes that any factor may assume a dominant importance, and that so far as the literary critic is concerned, one starts from the work with no preconceptions at all. I am nothing if not sympathetic to the idea that study of, as Williams puts it, a work or a period must involve enormous sensitivity to its actuality, and that the critic must beware of that Procrusteanism that forces the work (or the period, or whatever) to conform to his or her preconceived model. But total open-mindedness is impossible. If one believes that the colour of Henry James's socks is as likely to have determined the content of his novels as the larger society to

---

[13] The printed text has 'that', which is clearly a misprint.

which he belonged, then the definitive account of the determining and constitutive forces behind the composition or initial reception of *The Turn of the Screw* will be a long time in the writing.

Now it can be argued that Williams's yoking together of 'particular works and periods' is itself unwise and tends towards falsification. A whole historical period, runs the argument, because it is the product of innumerable interacting forces over a very broad social and temporal canvas, will inevitably have allowed for the victory of those structurally stronger forces which may be defeated in the very short term or in very limited arenas. A literary work, on the other hand, is normally the product of one writer, a person who typically lives on the margins of society and is him or herself a demonstration of the fact that art is founded on the accidental, the tangential, the unusual. For this reason – again, the argument I am concerned to consider runs – while it may make sense to study broad social movements, historical periods, even literary institutions and genres, in terms of a model which distinguishes between primary and secondary influences, it makes no sense to proceed in the same way when investigating or interpreting individual literary works.

I am certainly prepared to concede that this argument has some force. But I would add that the argument fails to take account of a number of important points. First, that however marginal the position of the writer may be (and very often it is not), canonical literary works circulate widely among large numbers of people – usually but not exclusively people who belong to the writer's own society. Second, that however marginal the writer, he or she normally has to make use of – and, importantly, anticipate making use of – less marginal institutions such as theatres, publishing houses, libraries, schools and journals. Institutions such as patronage and subscription also have the effect of binding that free soul, the writer, to what Marx calls 'definite relations, which are independent of their will, namely relations of production appropriate to a given stage in the development of their material forces of production'. Thus to argue that the writing of a literary work is so private that it cannot be subject to more general social laws is like arguing that making love is too personal, private and individual a thing for the laws of biology to apply to it. (Which is not, I hasten to add, to suggest that there is *nothing* personal and idiosyncratic either in writing a poem or in making love.)

Thus while Williams's rejection of the base–superstructure model certainly goes far to head off the danger of reductionism, perhaps in doing so it walks backwards into the rather different weakness suggested by Eagleton's critique of post-structuralism – that by failing to distinguish between primary and secondary influences or determinants it ends up being simply unhelpful. Williams's formulations are certainly undogmatic, but it is also arguable that they offer little help to the scholar or critic who requires some basis for looking here rather than there in the search for that which has caused, conditioned or influenced a work's production, identity or reception. 'The real human dimension in which works of art are made and valued', 'a different kind of theory of social totality; to see the study of culture as the study of relations between elements in a whole way of life', 'forms and relations of more general social life', 'the more active idea of a field of mutually if also unevenly determining forces' – well yes . . . but don't all these formulations beg the question? What *is* 'the real human dimension in which works of art are made and valued'? *Which* relations between *what* elements in 'a whole way of life'? If the forces determining the field do so 'unevenly', then are there *any* more general rules as to which forces are more likely to be predominant or subservient – or are we back to purely empirical research from literary work to literary work? Does 'uneven' mean random? If so, then we may safely reject the base–super-structure model, but in that case there is no point in replacing it with any alternative model – including that of the structure of feeling.

Of course, a key difference between the base–superstructure model and Williams's structure of feeling is that, as Marx made clear, the former has no necessary parallel with what human beings *thought* they or their society were controlled by, whereas Williams's structure of feeling is based upon, as the words suggest, what individuals actually feel. (Although 'feel' is, one suspects, a carefully chosen word; it does not necessarily imply 'conscious-ness of'. I can feel uneasy without thinking, 'I feel uneasy'.) Williams's formulation, then, seems chosen in part to grant human consciousness – or experience – a more important rôle in the constitution of a historical period or the production of a literary work. I say 'in part' because there is this half-implied passivity about 'feeling', one which becomes apparent when one contrasts it with a word such as 'understanding' or even 'conscious-ness'. 'Structures of feeling' is a term which, whether deliberately or not, radically restricts the rôle of analytical intelligence. 'Structures of feeling' are responses to a given situation or a precise set of forces; they do not by themselves constitute a determination to change either situation or forces.

Williams does in fact claim that at the time he decided to give up any reliance upon the base–superstructure model he 'did not want to give up my sense of the commanding importance of economic activity and history' (1980, p20). But that commitment to the *commanding* importance of anything seems to disappear once we get to more precise formulations of the meaning of 'structure of feeling'. In a different essay entitled 'Base and Superstructure in Marxist Cultural Theory', while discussing those concepts of oppositional and alternative cultures I have mentioned earlier, Williams talks of the need to 'think again about the sources of that which is not corporate; of those practices, experiences, meanings, values which are not part of the effective dominant culture' (1980, p40). One may concur that all these things are of great importance and should certainly be studied, while, at the same time, feeling that this constitutes an impossibly large check-list so long as there is no indication as to which 'practices, experiences, meanings, values' are likely to be the more influential. Put another way: are these 'practices, experiences, meanings, values' to be studied because they are interesting in themselves, or because they are important in terms of what they represent, initiate, make possible? And if they *are* deemed to be intrinsically interesting and valuable, is it not then obvious to ask why that which is valuable is not 'part of the effective dominant culture', or to ask how it can indeed be made so? And does this not lead on, inexorably, to the need to develop some sort of theory of historical causality and cultural power? Something which, like the base–superstructure model, indicates what it is that is dominant in a particular social or cultural formation, and what has to be changed if a social and cultural formation is to be altered?

Iain Wright has criticized a similar refusal to hierarchize in the work of Stephen J. Greenblatt. He quotes the following passage from Greenblatt's chapter 'The Circulation of Social Energy', in his *Shakespearian Negotiations*:

> For the circulation of social energy by and through the stage was not part of a single coherent, totalizing system. Rather it was partial, fragmentary, conflictual; elements were crossed, torn apart, recombined, set against each other; particular social practices were magnified by the stage, others diminished, exalted, evacuated. What then is the social energy that is being circulated? Power, charisma, sexual excitement, collective dreams, wonder, desire, anxiety, religious awe, free-floating intensities of experience [Wright comments at this point: 'A pretty comprehensive catalogue isn't it? All human life is there.']: in a sense the question is absurd, for everything produced by the society can circulate unless it is deliberately excluded from circulation. Under such circumstances, there can be no single method, no overall picture, and exhaustive and definitive cultural poetics. (Greenblatt 1988, p19)

Wright sees this as 'a representative slice of new-historicist rhetoric', and describes it as 'Engaging, but a little slippery, don't you think?' (1994, p4). Earlier, he has compared Greenblatt's attack on the monological nature of the old historicists with Foucault's attack on 'totalitarian periodization' in his *The Archaeology of Knowledge*, and one needs to ask whether the combined debt to Raymond Williams, Michel Foucault, and Hayden White (of whom more below) does much to explain why some (primarily American) New Historicists seem unable or unwilling to rank determining factors at all. So far as Williams is concerned, the key problem is not that he rejects the particular hierarchical ranking of determinants which he associates with the base–superstructure model, but that in doing so he appears to abandon *any* attempt to rank determinants at all. Wright continually insists that the most valuable insights of the New Historicists are often linked to the weaknesses of their work, work that breaks down the fixed categories and rigid hierarchies of old historicism but which runs the risk of degenerating into 'mere anecdotage, bricolage; tumbled collectors' cabinets of curios' (1994, p6). In particular, he warns of three dangers. First, that we will lose sight of the fact that different symbolic systems have different modes of operation. Second, that texts will become so permeable and polyvalent that they will decompose altogether into a heap of shards in the critic's hand. And third, that historical process, too, will become mere inexplicable jumble (he refers to what he terms Greenblatt's obsession with the word 'contingency') (1994, p6). Such warnings need to be heeded; we need, too, to ask to what extent the vulnerabilities of such New Historicist work are at least partly implicit in the work of their spiritual parents – including Raymond Williams.

Williams devotes a separate chapter of his *Marxism and Literature* to the base–superstructure model, and claims that it was the 'transition from Marx to Marxism' that led to the way in which 'the words used in the original arguments were projected, first, as if they were precise concepts, and second, as if they were descriptive terms for observable "areas" of social life'. He goes on, further, to observe that it is ironic to remember that Marx's original criticism 'had been mainly directed against the *separation* of "areas" of thought and activity (as in the separation of consciousness from material production) and against the evacuation of specific content – real human activities – by the imposition of abstract categories'. He concludes that the 'common abstraction of "the base" and "the superstructure" is thus a radical persistence of modes of thought which he attacked' (1977, p78). Williams does, however, make a significant concession:

> That in the course of other arguments he gave some warrant for this, within the intrinsic difficulties of any such formulation, is certainly true. But it is significant that when he came to any sustained analysis, he was at once specific and flexible in his use of his own terms. (1977, p78)

It seems to me that Williams's mistake, here, is to imply that there is a contradiction between, on the one hand, Marx's continued 'warranting' of the base–superstructure model, and his 'specific and flexible' use of his terms on the other. One cannot help thinking that in Williams's mind any theoretical model which aims to distinguish between primary and secondary determining and determined elements in a social formation is inimical to specificity and flexibility in a sustained analysis – but this is surely not the case.

Thus he goes on to quote from Marx's *Introduction to the Critique of Political Economy*, in which Marx, (in the translation cited by Williams) observes that 'As regards art, it is well known that some of its peaks by no means correspond to the general development of society; nor do they therefore to the material substructure, the skeleton as it were of its organization' (1977, p78). Williams gives no source for his translation, and in other translations an importantly different emphasis can be noted: the translation by Lee Baxandall and Stefan Morawski reads: 'It is well known that certain periods of highest development of art stand in no direct connection with the general development of society, nor with the material basis and the skeleton structure of its organization' (Marx and Engels 1974, p136).

But however one interprets the detail of this particular statement, what seems to me to be indisputable is that the whole thrust of Marx's discussion in the *Introduction* is towards establishing a means whereby the base–superstructure model (not named but clearly implied) can be preserved and reconciled with the empirical fact that 'certain periods of highest development of art stand in no direct connection with the general development of society, nor with the material basis and the skeleton structure of its organization'. And the way in which this is achieved is by use of the concept of unequal development – the example Marx gives before he mentions art at all is that of Roman civil law and modern production. In developing this theory of unequal development, Marx stresses the *mediated* nature of the base–superstructure relationship, a mediation that takes place in part on a temporal plane (thus leading to uneven development). Ancient Greek society includes a mythological relationship to nature, and it is on the basis of this myth that art flourishes. The mythology is not produced by the economic base, but it thrives and survives in a particular form – as Marx says, not 'any mythology taken at random', but (clearly implied) one appropriate to the society in which it performs a function.

As Marx himself notes, 'But the difficulty does not lie in understanding that the Greek art and epos are bound up with certain forms of social development. It rather lies in understanding why they still afford us aesthetic enjoyment and in certain respects prevail as the standard and model beyond attainment' (1974, p137). Here Marx takes the argument beyond the issue of artistic genesis, an area in which, unfortunately, much Marxist discussion of literature has remained confined, and opens up the (to him) more challenging set of problems associated with the trans-historical survival of art, with the problem of an aesthetic value that seems to outlive successive revolutions in the economic and social structure of society. I will return to this issue once I have considered some other theoretical debates connected to the genesis of literary works.

VI
From Ideology to Critique of Ideology

If, as I have argued earlier, the problems of defining exactly what is meant by 'discourse' in the non-Marxist tradition (or even in the work of Michel Foucault) are considerable, they are more than matched by the problems of defining 'ideology' in traditions which are mainly but not exclusively Marxist. 'Ideology' is a term that almost everyone writing in historicist or contextualist traditions agrees is used in a variety of confusingly different ways, but which few seem to be willing to dispense with. The reason for this, I suggest, is that anyone working in a historicist or contextualist tradition needs to be able to refer not just to ideas or sets of ideas, but to *systems* of ideas which have some connection to *relations of power* in a society. Indeed, in the course of tracing a range of other arguments I have already made reference to the use made of this term by a number of different theorists.

Thus when Graham Holderness asserts that Tillyard's 'Elizabethan world picture' was actually a dominant ideology (1992, p4), the argued difference is that although both concepts involve a system of interlocking ideas, Holderness's categorization implies that this system has been con-

structed by or for, and serves the interests of, a dominant *class* in Elizabethan society rather than – as Tillyard implies – reflecting the beliefs and
interests of a whole culture. And when Jerome J. McGann claims that it is
at the documentary level that 'the work's ideological dimensions are
clearest' (1988, pp74–5), he means to imply that the material details of a
work's initial publication are those which throw most light on a writer's
desired engagement or disengagement with systems of ideas important in
the maintenance of or opposition to political power in his or her society.
And when Geoffrey Hartman contends that 'To Autumn' is an ideological
poem 'whose very form expresses a national idea and a new stage of consciousness' (McGann 1985, p50; see the discussion on pp170–79), the intention is once more to suggest that the ideas and arguments of the poem
need to be seen in relation to a system of ideas that reach outside art and
which have wider social and political pretensions. In his book *Social Values
and Poetic Acts* Jerome J. McGann quotes a definition of ideology from John
B. Thompson's *Studies in the Theory of Ideology* (1984): 'the forms and ways
"in which meaning (signification) serves to sustain relations of domination"' (1988, p113). Finally, I have already quoted Hayden White's
definition of the term:

> By the term 'ideology' I mean a set of prescriptions for taking a position
> in the present world of social praxis and acting upon it (either to change
> the world or to maintain it in its current state); such prescriptions are
> attended by arguments that claim the authority of 'science' or 'realism'.
> (1973, p22)

Thus far the matter seems relatively unproblematic. But a bit further the
ambiguities and differences of definition of which I have spoken begin to
become apparent. An influential tradition within Marxism holds that an
ideological belief is one marked by *false consciousness* – i.e. that although
held as truth it in fact reflects only class interests. But other Marxists have
argued that all that is required for a system of ideas to count as an
ideology is that it represent the interests of a given social class. If it is in
the interests of that class to perceive the physical and social world
objectively, then an ideological belief may also be true. Both views can find
support in the canonical writings of Marx and Engels.

During the 1970s the writings of Louis Althusser were the focus of much
debate around the concept of ideology. Althusser's view of ideology
juxtaposed it to *science*, a science which escaped from the false consciousness within which ideology was trapped. Althusser tended also to talk of
ideology in the singular, seeing it as all-embracing and as inescapable in
social life as is breathing. More recent debates about ideology have shared
in that shift from singular to plural to which I referred earlier, preferring
to see a society as the site of contending ideologies, fissured by ideological
division. It is the Althusserian tradition to which Raymond Williams is
almost certainly referring in the following comments:

The main error of this solution [= 'one powerful modern variant of Marxism', J. H.] is that it substitutes Ideology (a general, coherent and monopolizing practical consciousness, with its operative functions in institutions, codes and texts), for the complex social relations within which a significant (including dominating and subordinated but also contesting) range of situations, were being at once expressed, produced and altered, in practice in contradictory as well as in coherent, directive ways. These could in any case not be seen as a superstructure, or as simple ideological manipulation, in a period in which the process involved quite large-scale primary production, in publishing and broadcasting, and in which, also, what was seen by capitalist institutions as a market often contradicted what was seen by bourgeois ideologists as a culture. (1980, p245)

It is this aspect of Raymond Williams's work to which more recent theorists such as Alan Sinfield have paid explicit tribute; for them, a model which allowed for opposition, struggle, ideological faultlines, got closer to the reality which they perceived in the cultures they studied.

Other areas of debate involve questions about first, whether ideologies are or are not a part of the superstructure in the Marxist tradition and second, whether literature is or is not purely ideological – however defined.

Now these sound, perhaps, as if they are arguments which are of little interest to non-Marxists, to whom they may well be as pressing as the question of how many angels can dance on the head of a pin. But in the work of certain recent theorists – historicist and non-historicist – other questions have been asked concerning the relation of ideology and literature which are of more than purely sectarian interest. It may be remembered that in my account of the Foucauldian concept of 'discourse' I made mention of Foucault's belief that literature was a form of 'true discourse' (1972, pp218–19). For Jerome J. McGann, such a claim is tantamount to arguing

> that poetry does not traffic in ideology – at any rate, poetry before the coming of Plato (which presumably means, for subsequent periods, 'authentic' poetry, or poetry as such). Whatever in poetry is ideological is *ipso facto* not poetry. (1988, p21)

Although he uses a different terminology, and although like Foucault he does not use the word 'ideology', Frank Kermode argues for the historical importance of poetry in terms which, on the surface at least, seem to have a lot in common with those of Foucault:

> We know that we have to read [poetry] against the grain of the manifest, and because of that requirement *good* poems about historical crises speak a different language from historical record and historical myth. Poems we judge not to be good will usually be poems which quickly sank into one or the other. The poems I have discussed here have not done so, whether we care much or little about the record of myth of the crises they celebrate. They make history strange and they are very private in their handling of the public themes. They can protect us from the familiar; they stand apart

from opinion; they are a form of knowledge. Quite simply they are better poems than the myths provide, and much harder to interpret. Which is why the interaction between them and their historical contexts is a subject calling for subtlety and caution. (1990, p67)

Kermode's distinction between historical record, historical myth and poetry is thought-provoking. *Do* literary works deal with the past in ways that are different from those of history and myth – or can historical record and myth form a part of the discourse of literature? Does major literature distance itself from ideology, or can it be in part ideological – in part actually constituted by ideology? According to Marjorie Levinson, 'there is no reason why ideology should operate more self-critically in art than anywhere else' (1988, p51). Does ideology 'work in' art, or is art antithetical to ideology; does art actually work against, rather than in, ideology?

Jerome J. McGann ends up stating directly what is implied more than stated by Foucault and Kermode: that major art is not composed of or situated amongst the ideologies: it *is* literature to the extent that it distances itself from ideology, to the extent that it in some way or other exposes ideology to view:

> Whatever the historically specific character of its ideologies, however, authentic literary work, both productive and reproductive, has always mediated the contradictions which ideology necessarily both represses and, in virtue of that fact, sustains. This truth about literature explains why conservative and reactionary work – or even work which may simply appear past and irrelevant – is able to maintain a 'critical instance.' Whether seen from a mimetic or a mediative position, poetry carries – and carries out – social contradictions. (1988, p112)
> Why are we committed to these things [= 'our inherited cultural materials', J. H.]? The brief answer is: because they represent, and themselves enact, programmatic goals which simultaneously display their own insufficiencies, alienations, self-contradictions. Only imaginative work does this: *et tout le reste est idéologie.* (1988, p114)

Later on in this book I want to test out some of these claims in practice by seeking to find exactly what relations certain specific works have to ideology, and by further asking how the aesthetic and the ideological are or are not connected.

VII
From Essentialist Humanism to the Human in History

One of the striking characteristics of much of the recent theory that can be described as politically radical is its break with traditional humanism.

Before the 1960s left-wing literary critics, whether Marxist or not, could generally be expected to subscribe to some belief in the transhistorical identity of the human race – a belief that was seen to be as fundamental to a progressive view of the world as a commitment to racial and sexual equality. Indeed, one of the apparent (and perhaps real) paradoxes of radical thought in the last three or so decades has been that as a radical commitment to transcultural and inter-gender solidarity increased, a belief in the transhistorical unity of the human race has come under increasing attack. Michèle Barrett has pointed out that this process has been so marked that in some circles it is taken for granted that the term 'humanist' is derogatory (1991, p93).

In twentieth-century Anglo-American critical theory, a commitment to humanism generally carried with it a number of central items of belief. First, that while customs, techniques and manners might change, there was nonetheless an unchanging core of 'the human' which was transhistorical and which comprised a set of fundamental emotions, impulses, needs. The individual human being was born with this human core, and confronted the changing demands of the natural and social world from the security of this sense of what being human involved. Changing social customs were only the surface form through which the unchanging human manifested or disguised itself. Second, that human beings made their own history in the light of a knowledge of what they were and what they needed. Human beings were, in other words, the centre of history, and they were this *consciously*: the world outside might be complex and unknown, but inside, a warm world of the known, of familiar humanity, offered a secure refuge. Third, human reason was bit by bit building a better world, one which would match the innate aspirations of the human race.

What happened to change all this? I have elsewhere argued that recent anti-humanism has more than one source – or, to use contemporary jargon, is an overdetermined phenomenon. First among these sources is probably the writing of a theorist to whom I have already referred: the French neo-Marxist Louis Althusser. In Althusser's book *For Marx* (first published in French 1966), Althusser declares that his aim is to oppose 'Marxist humanism' and the '"humanist" interpretation of Marx's work' (1969, p10). In his essay 'Marxism and Humanism' (1963; included in *For Marx*), Althusser makes clear that a key opposition for him is that between the insistence on the end of *class* exploitation (the Marxist goal), and the attainment of human freedom (which, he implies, is the goal of humanism) (1969, p221). Althusser locates a non-Marxist humanism in the works of the early Marx, in which, according to Althusser, 'the proletariat in its "alienation" represents the human essence itself, whose "realization" is to be assured by the revolution' (1969, pp221–2). For Althusser this positing of a human essence lies at the heart of humanism, and many subsequent theorists have accepted his emphasis. For them such a posited human essence is beyond history and beyond society, and is, consequently, essentially idealist rather than realist, often involving the projection of the characteristics of one form of society on to human beings at large (thus one often finds reference to *bourgeois humanism* or *liberal humanism*). Furthermore, (the argument continues), humanism typically situates the human essence in individual human beings rather than in social structures or cultural formations: humanism is thus idealistic, ahistorical and individualistic.

Another significant sources of contemporary anti-humanism is to be found in a range of different attempts to 'demystify the subject and subjectivity', seeing subjectivity as something constructed and secondary rather than unified, homogeneous and primary. Michel Foucault offers a useful summary of a range of different ways in which the subject has been moved from centre-stage, has been demoted from the rôle of source and unifying factor of history, to that of product and captive of history:

> Lastly, more recently, when the researches of psychoanalysis, linguistics, and ethnology have decentred the subject in relation to the laws of his desire, the forms of his language, the rules of his action, or the games of his mythical or fabulous discourse, when it became clear that man himself, questioned as to what he was, could not account for his sexuality and his unconscious, the systematic forms of his language, of the regularities of his fictions, the theme of a continuity of history has been reactivated once again . . . (1972, p13)

Foucault's comment has the virtue not only of drawing attention to some of the sources of contemporary anti-humanism, but also of some of its implications. We can say that a set of traditional humanist assumptions lay behind a range of different attempts to understand the past. Within the field of literary criticism, for example, the formalism of the New Critics typically depended upon a belief in an essential and unchanging human nature: scholarly research into the social and cultural context of a literary work was very often deemed to be unnecessary precisely because all that it could uncover were surface details; underneath, the same essential human emotions, needs, experiences were to be found. Reading a poem written four centuries ago we might need to be filled in on matters of contemporary social custom, on the detail of now-forgotten habits and ceremonies, but this was only in order to make contact with a core of unchanging humanity.

All this is now changed. The subject is no longer the centre of history, but a being shivering on its margins, not even understanding what he or she is, and set absolutely apart from whatever it was that was *determining* the course of history. As Michel Foucault puts it in *The Order of Things*:

> One thing in any case is certain: man is neither the oldest nor the most constant problem that has been posed for human knowledge. Taking a relatively short chronological sample within a restricted geographical area – European culture since the sixteenth century – one can be certain that man is a recent invention within it. It is not around him and his secrets that knowledge prowled for so long in the darkness. (1994, p386)

And he concludes that if the 'change in the fundamental arrangements of knowledge' which, a century and a half previously, had made it possible for the figure of man to appear, were now to disappear, 'then one can certainly wager that man would be erased, like a face drawn in sand at the edge of the sea' (1994, p387). These are the closing lines of *The Order of Things*, and their elegiac wistfulness does not seem to include any sense of profound regret for the possible end of what we can see as the humanist conception of mankind. Indeed, it is clear from much of Foucault's writing ('What is an Author?', for example) that he sees the sea already swirling round that face in the sand, lessening its sharpness and reducing its hold on our consciousness.

What effect does such an intellectual shift have on the activities of the literary critic? Looking at our four-century-old poem now, after the tide has started washing away at the face in the sand, we are faced with something with which we can no longer automatically claim kin, something which comes from and reflects or expresses realities which are not ours. Now that the laws of our desire, the forms of our language, the rules of our action, or the games of our mythical or fabulous discourse are different from what they were, *we* are different too. Moreover, where the traditional humanist scholar could take human aspirations and stated aims at face value, the new anti-humanist believes that such things are epiphenomenal, delusional products of a set of determining forces which were unperceived by those on whom they worked. In brief, the rejection of humanism (especially during the past decade and a half) has been very much identified with deconstruction and its denial of the existence of any absolute meaning-confirming centres of authority. The renunciation of humanism has involved a rejection of the idea that 'the human' can constitute a fixed reference point, and thus anti-humanism is very much tied up with a commitment to the belief that no determining centre or centres exist to interrupt or condition the free play of the signifier. And although such a position has a very different pedigree from the Foucauldian belief that the laws of a discourse are specific to itself, or from Hayden White's argument that different historical emplotments of a set of events cannot be measured against any objective standard of truthfulness, or from a postmodernist playfulness that reduces truth to a question of aesthetics, all of these different positions have tended to produce similar results: an unfettered relativism that gives the interpreter – whether of history or of Shakespeare's sonnets – free play.

Is humanism necessarily premised upon a suprahistorical bourgeois view of an unchanging human essence, as those who have led the assault on it in recent years have argued? I have expressed my own view elsewhere that it is not, and must crave indulgence for repeating some of my arguments here.

First, it has to be pointed out that Althusser's view of the early Marx is not uncontroversial. In the early *Economic and Philosophical Manuscripts of 1844* Marx does, it is true, refer to 'man's' (by which he means the human individual's) *'essential* being', but he also says that this is what man makes from his 'life activity'. He also argues that man is a being that treats its species as its own essential being – that treats itself 'as a species being' (1970, p113). None of these arguments, it will be noted, posits an essence that is outside of history, and indeed Pauline Johnson has presented evidence to suggest that Marx's theory of a human essence does not imply any 'natural' human attributes, but 'refers specifically to the process of transformation and development which characterizes the history of the species' (1984, p36). Johnson claims that this is certainly how both Lukács and Adorno interpreted Marx's 'human essence' (1984, p100).

Second, there is the more empirical argument that humanist ideals and beliefs have, generally, been ranged on the side of those wishing to oppose reactionary, élitist and oppressive centres of power. As Laurence Lerner points out, the 'picture of a black slave with the subscription "Am I not also a man and a brother?" is a reminder that radicalism often appeals to an idea of humanity that, instead of articulating existing power relations, deliberately offers itself in contrast to them' (1993, p275).

Moreover, there are humanist traditions that can by no means be accused of basing themselves on a view of an unchanging, suprahistorical human essence. A relevant example for our purposes comes from the Marxist literary critic Arnold Kettle in his essay 'The Progressive Tradition in Bourgeois Culture', which was first published in 1954. Kettle argues that the positives in Shakespeare's work are neither the feudal values nor the bourgeois ones, nor are they the values of the masses, which at this time do not yet constitute a conscious class. What then are these positive values? Kettle concludes: 'I can only say that they are the values of *humanity*.' This, he recognizes, is a problematic statement:

> There is, I know, a danger in thus formulating humanity as the positive value behind the plays. Humanity, abstracted from actual situations, becomes an idealistic conception of no validity. Humanity does not exist in the abstract; Man is always a particular man. What I mean then by humanity in this context is *man in his fullest aspirations realizable in the concrete situation of England of the sixteenth and seventeenth centuries*, remembering always that England of the sixteenth and the seventeenth centuries is the England not only of the feudal landowners and the Puritan businessmen but of Sir Thomas More and Francis Bacon and the New Model Army. (1988, pp25–6)

The same point is expressed in Alan Sinfield's comment that, so far as cultural materialists are concerned, 'our "humanity" is not an essential condition towards which we may aspire, but what people have as a consequence of being socialized into human communities' (1992, p291), although it is certainly not accidental that Sinfield's formulation is expressed in the passive voice and Kettle's in the active – itself a revealing marker of a shift in attitudes.

Sinfield's understanding of 'humanity' leaves us with the need to determine what one human community has in common with another: if the answer in some cases is 'Nothing', then clearly in that case one person's humanity may have nothing in common with that of another person. However, if the answer varies from case to case, while always including a statement to the effect that all human communities have something in common with one another, then even a view of humanity as formed through changing sociohistorical forces can find room for an element of continuity in human experience. This at any rate directs us towards the sort of enquiry that is involved in the current radical reaction against anti-humanism, an enquiry that does not posit a transhistorical human essence but which does seek to expose specific continuities in 'the human' as it is formed in and through different historical conjunctures. Such enquiries are also very likely to be informed by a renewed sense of the positive contribution that humanist ideas have made to our history; as Pauline Johnson puts it, to assume that the term can and should be dispensed with

is historically a great injustice, in that it ignores the immensely progressive role that humanism – as an 'ideology' – has played. In particular, one can point to the honourable tradition of humanism as a secularising force and, indeed, to its enormously important role in contemporary politics. (1984, p93)

I want to stress that when I argue for a recognition of 'an element of continuity in human experience' I am not suggesting that this is to be found only on a biological rather than a social or cultural level. It seems to me that this is a false turn made by Raymond Williams in his essay 'Problems of Materialism', in which, following Sebastiano Timpanaro, he addresses the problem of why works of art survive through very different cultures and societies by suggesting that 'certain kinds of art' relate more clearly to 'elements of our biological condition, often much more strongly than to elements of our socio-historical experience'. Even though Williams goes on to stress that 'these elements of the biological condition are mediated by socio-historical experience and by its cultural forms' (1980, p113), the reduction of a shared humanity to the biological level seems to me to sell out to contemporary anti-humanism. I will return to make my own case against anti-humanism at a later stage, but will remark at this stage that given our control of our biological nature through modern medicine, a humanism that pins its flag to sub-sociocultural elements seems on very shaky ground.

VIII
From Travel to the Past to
Dialogue with the Past

By no means all historicist literary criticism produced today is new – or New. J. R. de J. Jackson's *Historical Criticism and the Meaning of Texts*, published in 1989, exemplifies a conception of historicist criticism which has a long pedigree. Jackson offers the following definition: 'historical criticism is criticism that tries to read past works of literature in the way in which they were read when they were new' (1989, p3). For Jackson, the time which has elapsed since first a work of literature was published or performed has but one effect: that of diminishing the work for reader or spectator:

> When we are fresh from attending a play by Shakespeare or reading a novel by Jane Austen we have no sense of our inadequacy or of being less fully competent readers than we once were. Nevertheless, as readers of past literature we are demonstrably decayed because we do not bring to it the experience that is required for its imaginative or intellectual realization in its own time; instead we bring the experience that is required for the realization of literature in our own time, an experience in which only fragments of the earlier experience survive. The consequence is in several respects analogous to the antique statues' loss of limbs. (1989, p38)

Jackson's statement seems to be to be vulnerable to two separate and seemingly contradictory criticisms. First, that the experience of attending a play by Shakespeare or reading a novel by Jane Austen *can* and very often *does* give us a sense of inadequacy as readers – although this is by no means all that it involves. And second that readers are not like atomic waste, decaying slowly as their radiation level decreases over time. Jackson never seems to consider that an author's intended audience may have included individuals not yet born in his or her own time: the passage of time can carry with it both gains and losses for the reading of a literary work. The experience brought to a performance of *King Lear* by a modern spectator may include elements which are artistically or aesthetically productive, even though they could not possibly have been possessed by an Elizabethan, or expected in members of his audience by Shakespeare. *Response* as well as *communication* is fundamental to the way in which art functions: artworks are items to which different individuals bring different expectations, experiences, knowledge – and, as a result, from which different responses result. This is not to say that there are no elements of 'decay', as Jackson puts it, in a modern individual's ability to profit from a novel by Jane Austen or a play by Shakespeare. And it is certainly the case that part of the task of historicist criticism as I see it is to attend to these elements and to attempt to alleviate their effect. But as I suggested earlier, when talking about recent criticisms of Tillyard's views of the Elizabethan world picture, no culture is utterly homogeneous – and no contemporary readership or audience is either. I really cannot believe that members of Shakespeare's audience did not discuss performances of his plays with one another, and argue about them. One of the most frequently obscured but nonetheless essential aspects of artistic experience is the way it allows groups of people to explore their differences from one another. Literary criticism is thus quite unlike, say, chemical analysis, which attempts to isolate from human contamination that on which it is focused.

Literary criticism is, among other things, an exploration of human variety (and similarity) through responses to and interaction with literary works.

Much recent critical theory has been devoted to exploring the implications of some of the issues discussed above. Howard Felperin, for example, offers convincing reasons why a historicism such as Jackson's reduces, rather than restores, the full potentiality of a literary work. Felperin does not refer to Jackson; he is responding to an essay by Francis Barker and Peter Hulme (1985) in which they argue that colonial discourse is structurally 'dominant', the 'articulatory *principle* of *The Tempest*'s diversity'. Felperin argues that this claim should not go unchallenged:

> For the critical and political consequences of such a claim, pre-emptive as it is of the very resources of inscription available to the play, of the enabling structures of its signifying potential, are far-reaching indeed. Such a claim would mark the text from the beginning and for all time as decisively structured by an historical discourse beyond the power, because beyond the reach, of any contemporary re-inscription to recuperate. (1990, p129)

Felperin's argument includes some careful formulations that I would like to use in a somewhat expanded form. While the historicism recommended by Jackson restricts the reader or spectator to the 'resources of inscription available to the play' at the time of its first performance, Felperin does not wish to limit these resources to this one time, and indeed sees 'the enabling structures of [the play's] signifying potential' to be very much wider. A key word here is 'potential': readers and spectators bring an enormous multiplicity of varying subjectivities to play on literary works – although these are not without their common elements. This potential responsive diversity cannot be limited to the time of first publication or performance – important as information about the possible responses of such initial readers or spectators is for subsequent readers and spectators. Jerome J. McGann points out that literary works *continue* to live and move and have their being; 'meaning' in literary works cannot be isolated from the uses to which persons and social organizations put those works (1988, p125).

Seen from this perspective, Jackson's brand of historicism is ill-suited to the complexity of the way works of art function – to the way in which they continue to live as new readers and spectators bring new life and experiences to them. Put another way: do we want merely to situate texts in the context of their production and first publication, or do we want to *read* them – with all that that entails?

None of this, however, addresses the problems attendant upon the fact that while works of art emerge out of and are formed by a particular context, readers carry with them their own experiences and expectations – experiences and expectations which are generated by what are often very different contexts. Reading Jane Austen or experiencing a performance of *King Lear* is much more than a process of passive absorption: it is an active process which involves grappling with difficulties, reconciling contradictions, choosing between mutually exclusive alternatives. It is not so much that Jackson's view is wrong, as that it is incomplete. The reader and critic must be as open to the literary work's historical identity as is possible, while at the same time (or subsequently) *interacting* with the work. I have elsewhere argued that there is no better description of the simultaneously active and passive nature of literary engagement than that provided in Keats's sonnet 'On Sitting Down to Re-read *King Lear* Once Again'. Throughout this poem the poet alternates between a sense of passive opening up to the identity of Shakespeare's work on the one hand, and a commitment to the need more actively to 'burn through' the play – an alternation which I believe to be typical of the manner in which readers engage with complex literary works.

Stephen J. Greenblatt has used the term 'negotiation' to describe the process whereby 'collective beliefs and experiences were shaped, moved from one medium to another, concentrated in manageable aesthetic form, offered for consumption' (1988, p5). Greenblatt's use of the term is generally limited to processes taking place within a given culture, but 'negotiation' takes place too when readers or spectators in one culture attempt to make contact with and use collective beliefs and experiences through the mediation of art. Others have suggested that *dialogue* is a more appropriate term,[14] and given Greenblatt's desire to talk with the dead it is not unlikely that he might agree. At the same time, however, textualist ideas have led to the proposal of a very different model of the relationship between modern readers and older works of literature. Just as the textualist historian gives up the idea of recapturing the past, arguing that all the historian can do is to offer different emplotments of past events which all have equal (that is, no) truth value, so too a parallel argument in the field of literary criticism involves the argument that all the modern reader or critic can do with the literary works of the past is to reinvent them, to give them new life in a range of modern readings which, like emplotments of past events, all share an equal validity.

Now there is no doubt that there is a world of difference between the view that the modern reader negotiates or holds a dialogue with the literature of the past, and the belief that modern readings of such literary works are constructions or inventions which can be ranked only aesthetically – that is, only in terms of the pleasure they give to readers, a pleasure that cannot be linked to their truth or falsity or their conformity to any historical standard. In practice, however, the same critic can talk in one breath about holding a dialogue with the past and, in the next breath, about inventing or constructing this past in a reading. I have already quoted Jerome J. McGann's comment that 'meaning' in literary works is a function of the uses to which persons and social organizations put those works (1988, p125). It should be clear that such a view has a textualist ring

---

[14] Current use of the word 'dialogue' normally suggests the influence of the writings of Mikhail Bakhtin, and this has certainly been active in attempts to theorize the interaction of modern readers and older literary works. But others proposing that we consider this relationship as a form of dialogue have cited the influence of the German aesthetician Hans-Georg Gadamer and the American Dominick LaCapra.

to it – even though McGann is generally very critical of most of the standard textualist arguments. In his introduction to the critical anthology *New Historicism and Renaissance Drama*, Richard Wilson highlights the fact that behind the ostensible agreement amongst New Historicists that modern readings of older literary works involve an element that comes from the present rather than the past, there lies a fundamental disagreement. Wilson assumes that behind the New Historicism are to be found two starting points: first that 'man' is a construct and not an essence, and second that

> the historical investigator is likewise a product of his history and never able to recognize otherness in its pure form, but always in part through the frame work of the present. This last point leads one to what is perhaps the crux of any 'new' historical criticism, and that is to the issue of what one conceives history to be: a realm of retrievable fact or a *construct* made up of textualized traces assembled in various configurations by the historian/interpreter. Hayden White points to the central question in dispute when he argues that history is produced, not discovered, and when he shows how those synthesizing histories which attempt to describe a period are *someone*'s historically-conditioned constructs. (Wilson and Dutton 1992, pp26–7)

I have already indicated that White's arguments about the production of the past seem to me to be seriously flawed. But this was in the context of a discussion about historical events rather than literary works, and it might be argued that a reader's response to and experience of, say, a novel, is necessarily less constrained by 'fact' than is a historian's attempt to set a historical event in an explanatory context. Surely – the argument might continue – literary criticism and history constitute separate academic disciplines for a number of good reasons: one is that literary works are designed not just to be understood but to be responded to, and while historians are not expected to be totally devoid of the ability imaginatively to respond to the events with which they are concerned, this faculty is not integral to the work of the historian in quite the way which it is to that of the literary critic. A literary response is not subject to the ultimate test of 'either this happened or it did not', or that of 'either this happened for these reasons or it did not'.

Such a view can only be sustained on the basis of a view of literary response as subjective, idiosyncratic, unconstrained by matters of fact, and incapable of being assessed in terms of its legitimacy or falsity – which is, more or less, the view expressed by W. K. Wimsatt and Monroe Beardsley in their attack upon the 'affective fallacy' (1949). More recent theorists have been less sure about this, and have refused to consider the subjective and personal elements in literary reading as either purely idiosyncratic or as inaccessible to reasoned inquiry.

The involvement of the present in our response to literature (or in our judgement of the significance of historical events, come to that) does not mean that the pastness of literature (or of historical events) is reduced to being merely a function of the present, a construction or an invention. Since the end of the New Criticism's period of general hegemony in the 1960s, much theoretical energy has been expended in the attempt to construct a model of literary reading which recognizes the fact that literary response involves a creative input from the reader, but which denies the reader the right to do anything he or she likes with the work. Thus Wolfgang Iser, for example, talks of those gaps in the literary work which have to be filled in by the reader, and he uses the metaphor of the fixed stars in the sky which can be formed into different shapes by different perceivers (1974, p280). In a complicated formulation Jerome J. McGann appears to be trying to find some means whereby the identity or 'there-ness' of the literary work – that which, according to Howard Felperin, is manifested by its 'resistance' to the reader; Foucault's 'modifiable heaviness' – can be preserved while leaving space for a work of creative addition on the part of the reader in the composite process of reading, interpretation, and response:

> One of the special graces of poetic works – probably their chief social value – is that they are conceptual forms which operate at a high level of generality, on the one hand, and at an equally high level of particularity on the other. The particulars, the 'matters-of-fact', are subjected to a general organizing structure which precisely *does not* reduce those particulars to conceptual finishedness, but instead preserves them in a state of (as it were) freedom. The particulars are grains of sand in which the world may be seen – may be seen again and again, in new sets of relations and differentials. (1988, pp126–7)

McGann's efforts here can be compared to those of recent historians who wish to respond to the challenge posed by Hayden White and others while stopping short at reducing sequences of historical events to functions of a historian's mode of emplotment. It is revealing, I think, that McGann's comments come in a chapter of *Social Values and Poetic Acts* entitled 'The Scandal of Referentiality' – a title McGann takes from a passing reference made in a lecture by Geoffrey Hartman. Writing in the wake (or perhaps at the wake) of the New Criticism, McGann's awareness of the 'lack of conceptual finishedness' of 'poetic particulars' and of the way in which a never-ending sequence of completions is given to these unfinished particulars by successive readings, is tempered by an understanding of the perils involved in cutting literary works off from the defining contexts of their first emergence into public life. The reaction against the sort of historicism advocated by J. R. de J. Jackson need not, then, lead to an unfettered textualism in which the reader feels no pull from the past, encounters no resistance from the works he or she is reading.

It has, however, convinced many that if the reader cannot become a contemporary of the author, and if a reader's own situation necessarily impacts upon his or her reading of a literary work, then readers should perhaps start to see if they cannot marshal the resources of their own time and situation in the most productive manner. Earlier I cited John Frow's view that the text's naturalization within its genetic context should be countered through a process of 'unframing' by which it becomes 'subversive of its own legitimacy' (1986, p228). Without necessarily going that far (the reader or critic may well feel that the text derives its legitimacy from a laudable engagement with the life of its own time, and may thus not wish to subvert this), recent theory has been far more receptive to the idea of reframing than were the critics of a previous generation, to the extent, as we have seen, of suggesting that perhaps literary response is necessarily premised upon reframing processes. While he does not actually use terms such as 'reframing', Jerome J. McGann goes so far as to suggest that the question is not *whether* the reader should reframe the work but, given the inevitability of some such recontextualization and use, *how* the reader completes or uses the work by bringing his or her personal, cultural and historical experience into contact with the world encapsulated in the work:

> The tales told in the *Oresteia* are certainly happening here today, and will happen again tomorrow. The question is: how will we choose to read these tales – objectively, or in terms of their own (and our own) celebrations and self-conceptions? (1989, p94)

The question is a challenging one, not least because it confronts and rejects our perhaps unthinking belief that to read a literary work in the exclusive light of its own assumptions – the context of its own time and its author's beliefs and intentions – is *more* rather than less objective a way of proceeding. McGann reminds us, though, that if objectivity means anything it means taking all available relevant information into account – an imperative as applicable to the reader or critic of literature as to the historian. This is not to *replace* but to *temper* and *qualify* the work's own celebrations and self-conceptions with our own. Unlike J. de R. Jackson, then, McGann does not see the modern reader as 'demonstrably decayed' in his or her ability productively to engage with a work such as the *Oresteia* – although McGann would certainly be very ready to grant that the more the modern reader can acquaint him- or herself with the knowledge and expectations of those who first experienced this work the better.

IX
Towards a Historical Aesthetic

I have, earlier, noted that a familiar historicist or Marxist reaction to formalist or essentialist claims that works of art possess a value which is autonomous, unchanging, and apart from history and culture, is to collapse the aesthetic back into history. The technique is to demonstrate that the work of art could not have emerged other than at the time and in the context it did, and that both at the time of its genesis and later, its use and function are by no means innocent of ideological and political interest.

But to demonstrate that aesthetic value needs determinate conditions for its production, and that it can be yoked to non-aesthetic interests, does not in itself prove that there is a historically volatile element in the aesthetic itself.

In the *Introduction to the Critique of Political Economy*, Marx's own proposed solution to the problem posed to historicism by an apparently transhistorical aesthetic value has not generally been found at all convincing. Marx suggests that just as an adult enjoys the naïve ways of a child, so too 'the historical childhood of humanity' exerts 'an eternal charm as an age that will not return' (1974, p137). This is unsatisfactory for several reasons. First, it does not explain why Greek or Elizabethan art still serves as an aesthetic model whereas other aspects of the societies that produced the art are certainly not considered as models and unattainable ideals. The 'charm of childhood' argument, in other words, offers no explanation for the fact that it is in the aesthetic alone that this supreme transhistorical value appears to reside. Second, as many commentators have observed, one could hardly find a less suitable analogy for the perceived value of Greek (or Elizabethan) art than that of the charm of childhood. *Oedipus Rex*? *King Lear*?

A solution which avoids such problems while perhaps introducing others is suggested elsewhere, in a letter to Ferdinand Lassalle (22 July 1861), in which Marx notes that

> the three unities, as the French dramatists under Louis XIV theoretically construe them, must surely rest on a misunderstanding of the Greek drama (and of Aristotle, its exponent). On the other hand, it is equally certain that they understood the Greeks in just such a way as suited their own artistic needs which is why they still clung to this so-called 'classical' drama long after Dacier and others had correctly interpreted Aristotle for them. Thus, too, all modern constitutions rest in great part on the *misunderstood* English constitution, for they take as essential precisely that which constitutes the decadence of the English constitution – which now exists only *formally, per abusem* in England – e.g. a so-called responsible *Cabinet*. The misunderstood form is precisely the general form, applicable for general use at a definite stage of social development. (1974, p98)

Is it also possible that, say, Greek art survives in 'misunderstood' form, reapplied to or reinterpreted in the light of, changed conditions? Such an application of Marx's comments here would bring us rather disturbingly close to Hayden White: the history of a work of art's reception is a history of misunderstandings, of self-interested emplotments.

But it is possible to propose a less textualist and more dialectical application of Marx to the issue of the transhistorical survival of the aesthetic. In the *Grundrisse* Marx argues that the anatomy of the human being is the key to the anatomy of the ape, although 'the intimations of the higher animal in lower ones can be understood only if the animal of the higher order is already known' (McLellan 1971, p39). He goes on to make the important qualification that

The bourgeois economy furnishes a key to ancient economy, etc. This is, however, by no means true of the method of those economists who blot out all historical differences and see the bourgeois form in all forms of society. One can understand the nature of tribute, tithes, etc., after one has learned the nature of rent. But they must not be considered identical.

Since, furthermore, bourgeois society is only a form resulting from the development of antagonistic elements, some relations belonging to earlier forms of society are frequently to be found in it, though in a crippled state or as a travesty of their former self. (McLellan 1971, pp39–40)

The passage is reminiscent of Jerome J. McGann's discussion of the, as it were, posthumous 'reach' of the *Oresteia*. In reading the literature of the past we need to immerse ourselves in the actualities of its historical life, while, at the same time, informing the experience of such immersion with the benefits of our own historical vantage point. Such a model of literary reading proposes an activity which oscillates or tacks between immersion and alienation, a dialectical process that tests the past and the present against each other.[15]

It seems fair to say that recent theorists working in traditions which, if not conventionally Marxist are certainly influenced by Marxist categories and concepts, have taken one of three possible directions when confronted by this general problem. We can, I would suggest, distinguish between the 'adapters', the 'transhistoricists', and what I would name the 'dialectical historicists'. The adapters argue along lines that are reminiscent of the work of Hayden White that art survives because every generation, every new culture, every transformed society, adapts works of art to its own needs, models them in its own image. The transhistoricists argue in some form or other that historical change does not rule out historical continuities, and that, say, although it is unthinkable that *King Lear* could have been produced by any other time, culture or society than those from which it did emerge, it nevertheless deals with a set of issues that have a purchase in subsequent times, cultures and societies – albeit in different forms. The dialectical historicists agree with Jerome J. McGann that the aesthetic effect of literature is radically if paradoxically related to the reader or viewer's sense of history. Commenting upon Marx's inadequate categorization of the attraction of the art of the past as 'charm', McGann stresses that Marx's comments reveal his profound sense of the pastness of the past, and of the importance which this differential has for all aesthetic experiences:

Aesthetic effect depends upon the distancing of the art work, the estrangement of it, its isolation from our immediacy. We say that it seems to occupy a place outside of time, as it were. But this is merely a way of saying that art works are forever placed *in* history, that is, in the vertical and horizontal circumstances which define human events. . . .

---

[15] In my first book, *Identity and Relationship* (Hawthorn 1973), I took the concept of 'tacking' – 'from evidence to hypothesis to further evidence to renewed hypothesis' – from Allan Rodway (1970, p94).

The celebrated estrangement effect of art is simply the reign of art's own inherent historical dimension *vis-à-vis* its audience. To analyse, in literature, this deeply felt distance between us and our pasts requires the precise specification of historical details – from the merest facts picked up in a gloss, to the most sharply defined categories of ideological order. (1985, p64)

But to become *dialectically* historicist, such an investigation must also focus upon the interaction between our own historically situated selves and the art of the past; it must take full measure of the fact that as we read the literature of the past and the past in literature, we are also read by literature. As we seek to find out the hidden details of the work's historically situated identity, the work seeks out, finds, and even in part produces our own. Such interaction does not diminish aesthetic value: it is its necessary precondition.

Part Two

INTERROGATIONS

4

IDEOLOGY, MYTH, HISTORY

The Literature of the Titanic *Disaster*

Early in the morning of 15 April 1912, the White Star Line steamship *Titanic* sank after striking an iceberg while on her maiden voyage from Europe to the United States. Over 1500 men, women and children perished as a result of the disaster, most because the ship carried insufficient lifeboats; had all the available lifeboats been properly launched and filled to capacity (which they were not) the death toll would still have been very large.

It is likely that there are few reading the present book who have never heard of the *Titanic* and its fate. The disaster has a fame that is out of all proportion to its actual size. In his 'My Country Right or Left' George Orwell observed that 'If I honestly sort out my memories and disregard what I have learned since, I must admit that nothing in the whole [First World] war moved me so deeply as the loss of the *Titanic* had done a few years earlier' (Orwell and Angus 1968, p536). In the 1970s I was shocked to discover that in a group of British undergraduates there were more who knew about the *Titanic* than who were aware of the significance of Auschwitz. A July 1995 article on the biggest of six British companies which sell old newspapers, reports that by 'far and away' the most requested editions are those dealing with the *Titanic* (Rogers 1995, p53).

Why has the disaster entered into such near-universal public awareness? It seems likely that the fame of the *Titanic* and its fate is linked to something more than the physical horrors suffered by its ill-fated passengers – especially so long after the disaster, when these horrors seem less extreme than many that the twentieth century provides for our consideration. Nearly eight decades after the sinking, a book about the discovery of the wreck, complete with underwater photographs, became a world bestseller. Eric Hobsbawm has pointed out that disasters such as the loss of the *Titanic* or the burning of Karltheater in Vienna in 1881 during a performance of Offenbach's *Tales of Hoffmann*, in which almost 1500 lives were lost, tend to be remembered while the much greater catastrophes which affect the lives of the poor, such as the 1908 earthquake in Messina which, Hobsbawm notes, was much vaster and is more neglected than the more modest 1905 San Francisco tremors, do not (1989, p328). The death of the rich makes more of a mark than the death of the poor.

But many ships have sunk in many different periods of time, and have sunk much more quickly than the *Titanic* (for example the *Lusitania*, and the *Britannic* – one of the *Titanic*'s two sister ships of which most people have never heard). It seems as if the foundering offered itself as a perfect symbol for a variety of things: over-confidence and complacency, the end of an era, a presage of the collapse of British invincibility and of the changes that would be wrought by the First World War.[16]

As news of the ship's loss reached Britain, the United States and the rest of the world, the *Titanic* began a new life in popular myth. Almost before the bubbles had stopped rising to the surface, rival *emplotments* of this event – to use Hayden White's terminology – began to be circulated and to compete with one another. The disaster acted much like a lightning-rod through which different ideological battles were mediated; the disaster was quickly transformed into what we can call ideological capital, ideological capital which different interest groups competed to possess. In time this battle waned – although it has never entirely ended – and the disaster started a new life as myth, one in which it would permeate through to the furthest reaches of British (and not just British) culture. I think – although I am not sure – that I first became aware of the ship and its fate through a piece of graffiti on a contraceptive dispenser in a men's room somewhere. Part of the information displayed on the machine was a reassuring statement to the effect that the product offered for sale was tested in accordance with the requirements of the appropriate British standard. Underneath this declaration someone had scrawled, 'So was the *Titanic*'. It will be noted that this piece of irreverence feeds off a confident belief that its readers will understand that the loss of the ship has, today, a clearly established *meaning*: that it serves as an example of British over-confidence – in technology, in established standards, in 'official' reassurances, in British superiority, and so on. Such a meaning seems to me to have both an ideological and a mythic dimension (I will try to explain, below, how I understand the distinction between ideology and myth); it is a meaning that rests upon a historical event (as Hayden White would define an event), but an event mediated through ideology and myth.

Since 15 April 1912, however, the disaster has spawned a whole library of articles, historical accounts, technical studies, films – and literary works. It thus offers us a perfect opportunity to explore a number of the claims detailed in the opening part of this book. (For reasons of space I have

---

[16] Robert Serling's 1990 popular novel, *Something's Alive on the Titanic* has a character wonder (in the 1970s) about the continued fascination with the ship. The character concludes that 'The *Titanic* was something special – a symbol of nobility, arrogance, bravery, stupidity, of beauty transformed into an ugly, mutilated metal corpse; of proud, indestructible power and strength suddenly drained by a hidden stiletto of frozen water' (Serling 1993, pp75–6). It will be noted that the symbolic significance of the disaster is here depoliticized and dehistoricized – as is no doubt appropriate for the genre 'thriller/ghost story'.

decided to pass over a number of very interesting film versions of the event. And a multi-media study of artistic responses to the disaster would also have to include a musical elegy entitled *The Sinking of the Titanic*, by British composer Gavin Bryars, which according to a report in *Time* magazine [Walsh 1995, p110], weaves together a clanging ship's bell, 'the shuddering impact of steel meeting solid, razor-sharp ice', sounds representing buckling bulkheads, rushing water, disembodied voices of survivors, and repeated renderings of the hymn *Autumn* – now believed to be the last music played by the ship's musicians.)

Literary responses to the disaster range from Hardy's poem 'The Convergence of the Twain', which was produced for a 'Dramatic and Operatic Matinée in aid of the Titanic Disaster Fund', held on Tuesday 14 May 1912, at 2 o'clock, through (among other examples) a scene in Noël Coward's 1930 play *Cavalcade*, a long narrative poem finished in 1935 by the Canadian E. J. Pratt and a 1937 novel in German entitled *Titanensturz*, recent popular fiction such as Clive Cussler's 1976 'action' novel *Raise the 'Titanic'!* (later filmed – fortunately for the film's sponsors – just before the discovery of the wreck revealed that the ship was in two pieces and could never be raised)[17] and Robert Serling's 1990 thriller/ghost story *Something's Alive on the Titanic*, to Hans Magnus Enzensberger's poem 'The Sinking of the Titanic' (begun in 1969 and finished eight years later) and a modernist/surrealist play *Le Titanic* written by the French-Canadian Jean-Pierre Ronfard, published in 1986, which boasts a cast of characters including the actual captain of the *Titanic*, along with (among others) Isadora Duncan, Charlie Chaplin, Adolf Hitler and Sarah Bernhardt. The disaster has even reached into high-investment children's literature. Daisy Corning Stone Spedden's *Polar the Titanic Bear*, written from the perspective of her son's toy bear (mother, son and bear all survived the disaster), was written for her son Douglas and given to him as a Christmas present in 1913. (Douglas, alas, died shortly afterwards in an automobile accident.) It was discovered by a relative and published in a very lush edition first in 1994.

[17] Lord Grade, whose company financed the disastrous film, claimed that 'It would have been cheaper to have lowered the Atlantic' (Davie 1987, p218). Clive Cussler's novel, on which the film was based, is standard cold-war fare: the sunken ship contains a rare element ('byzanium') which can help the Americans construct a secure Star Wars defence against Soviet missiles. The book ends with the system reassuringly in place, but the film version leaves the byzanium where no one can touch it – the result, perhaps, of a decade of détente. Cussler's dialogue, on occasions, deserves to be placed in the *Titanic*; here is a sample. '"Give it up," she repeated, tears forming in her eyes. "No one is indispensable. Let Mel Donner take your place." He shook his head. "No." he said firmly. "I created this project from nothing. My gray matter was its sperm. I must see it through to completion."' (Cussler 1976, pp20–21)

I
The *Titanic* as Ideological Capital and Mythic Meaning

The loss of the *Titanic* was one of the first international media events. News of the disaster reached North America by radio before survivors arrived in New York, and discussions in press and pulpit hardly waited for the accounts of those who had been involved in the tragedy. It was clear that there had to be much to discuss. The *Titanic* was not only the largest but also the most luxurious ship afloat. Even today, it is hard to get a sense of its immense size into one's head without setting it against landmarks such as St Paul's Cathedral. Before the disaster, the White Star Line used such enormous size as a selling point, illustrating it by means of a picture of an up-ended *Olympic* (the *Titanic*'s sister ship) set against – and exceeding in height – a range of well-known buildings such as the Washington Monument and the new Woolworth Building in New York.

The level of luxury on board included provision for a swimming pool, a gymnasium and a level of décor in the first-class section which was unparalleled – even by its sister ship the *Olympic*. And even the conditions for steerage passengers were far better than those in other ships. The *Titanic* was on its maiden voyage, and it had been heralded as unsinkable; Geoffrey Marcus cites the account of the journal *Engineering*, that the ship 'was the product of the fullest experience, alike in design and construction, of one of the premier ship-owning companies and one of the most scientific and practical shipbuilding organizations in the world. She embodied all that judgment and knowledge could devise to make her immune from disaster', and he reports the story that during the week while the leviathan lay in the Ocean Dock one of the seamen observed complacently, 'God Himself could not sink this ship' (1969, p31) – a statement that was widely circulated after the disaster, although in a suspiciously varied set of accounts.[18] Marcus notes that

> Some years earlier Captain Smith had publicly stated that he could not conceive of any vital disaster happening to one of these great liners – 'I cannot imagine any condition which would cause a ship to founder. I cannot conceive of any vital disaster happening to this vessel. Modern shipbuilding has gone beyond that . . .' (1969, p80)

After the loss of the ship, those in search of evidence of hubris did not have too far to look.

---

[18] Hans Magnus Enzensberger, for example, in his poem 'The Sinking of the Titanic', describes this comment as the penultimate words of one portly gentleman to another portly gentleman, shortly before the *Titanic* set sail. (See Enzensberger 1989, twenty-first canto.)

The number of lifeboats carried by the ship had been reduced from that proposed during its construction, partly, it would appear, to improve the line of the ship, but also to save money (Wade 1979, p37), and the crew were unfamiliar with their operation (a statistic that is pretty damning in the light of hindsight is that out of a staff of 900, the ship had only eighty-three sailors: the rest were stewards, musicians, maids, cooks, waiters and so on [Wade 1979, p207]). Significantly, though, the number of lifeboats actually carried was in excess of those required by obsolete Board of Trade regulations which were still in force.

When details of the survivors were published it became apparent that the more expensive a ticket one had, the more likely one was to have survived. Many third-class women and children perished while many men from the first-class – including Bruce Ismay, the Managing Director and Chairman of the White Star Line – were saved.[19] In time evidence came to light that radio messages from other ships warning of ice were ignored, or never got to the captain (one was given, extraordinarily, to Ismay rather to a member of the ship's crew), that radio operators from other ships attempting to pass on such warnings were told to get off the air by the *Titanic's* operator, who was engaged in sending and receiving personal messages for passengers, that no binoculars were provided for those in the crow's nest and acting as look-out, and that the ship's speed was not reduced in spite of the fact that changed conditions clearly made this advisable.

Someone had to be blamed for all this – but who? The captain and crew, who had immediate responsibility for the ship? The company which had commissioned the *Titanic* and its two sister ships, providing a level of luxury unparalleled before and, some have argued, since? Those (primarily American) millionaires who had demanded such a level of luxury? (A special suite for the crossing to New York cost a spectacular $4350 – about £850 then [Lord 1955, p111].) The Board of Trade and the British, whose complacency and failure to keep regulations up to date had recklessly endangered passengers? The whole Edwardian era, the 'gilded age', which had embraced obscene private affluence and luxury? Human blindness and overconfidence in general? It was clear that the buck could be granted a variety of places to stop, each of which had a rather different ideological or political force.

---

[19] According to Walter Lord, 'the *Titanic's* casualty list included four of 143 First Class women (three by choice) . . . 15 of 93 Second Class women . . . and 81 of 179 Third Class women.' Of the children, 'Except for Lorraine Allison, all 29 First and Second Class children were saved, but only 23 out of 76 steerage children' (1955, p107). Lord points out that such indifference towards third-class passengers extended to the press and the two official inquiries, all of which seemed uninterested in the experiences of the third-class passengers. He also reports that 'when the White Star Liner *Republic* went down in 1908, Captain Sealby told the passengers entering the lifeboats, "Remember! Women and children go first; then the First Cabin, then the others!"' (1955, p109). Hans Magnus Enzensberger reprints the survival statistics class by class in the twenty-second canto of 'The Sinking of the Titanic' (Enzensberger 1989, p59).

What I want to argue is that the different emplotments of the disaster which were offered in the days and weeks following the sinking, all have as much to do with pre-existing ideological faultlines in British and American society as they have to do with more specific causes of the ship's foundering. This, however, does not rule out the possibility that there may be some connection between such ideological faultlines and the failures which led to the disaster. What are these faultlines? First, an officially sanctioned belief in a loving and omniscient God, whose presence apparently does nothing to prevent calamities such as the sinking. Second, a commitment to democracy and human equality in societies in which women are disenfranchised, and racial discrimination is institutionalized (especially in Britain and in the United States). Third, a commitment to a religion which claims that it is as easy for a rich man to enter heaven as it is for a camel to go through the eye of a needle, which in practice (as the *Titanic* microcosmically demonstrated) did not alter a society rigidly stratified on lines of class and wealth. Fourth, a belief in the ability of White Anglo-Saxons to subdue and control the natural world, while class and gender conflicts domestically, and ethnic and national conflicts on a world-wide basis, cast a shadow on this optimism. And fifth, an expressed belief in national unity at a time when the battle for Irish Home Rule and, on a lesser scale, church disestablishment in Wales, threatened to expose this claim as a sham.

We might expect, then, that those perceiving the disaster as ideological capital which was up for grabs might try to use it to demonstrate that, appearances notwithstanding, we are safe in the hands of God, that rich and poor are equal in the face of death (with the implication that class conflict should now cease and things should be left as they are), that the disaster allowed White Anglo-Saxons and the British to demonstrate their natural leadership and the national unity of both Britain and the United States, that the practice of 'women and children first' meant that women enjoyed great benefits without the vote, and should not be trying to change the established rôles of the sexes. At the same time, of course, Irishmen fighting for Home Rule, women fighting for the vote, and non-believers seeking to expose established religion as hypocritical, could be expected to challenge such emplotments.

Wyn Craig Wade's study *The Titanic: End of a Dream* (1979), one of the best books focusing primarily on the aftermath of the loss of the ship, provides the reader with a fine sense of the way in which the first reports of the event often seemed to betray special interests and secret agendas. As Wade points out, accounts of the last hours of the ship and many of its passengers and crew were, from the start, radically inconsistent:

Captain Smith had at least five different deaths, from heroic to ignomini-
ous. Seaman G. A. Hogg said, 'I saw Captain Smith in the water alongside
a raft. "There's the skipper," I yelled, "Give him a hand." They did, but he
shook himself free and shouted to us, "Good-bye boys, I'm going to follow
the ship." That was the last we saw of our skipper.' Others remembered
E. J. [Captain Smith] swimming with a child in his arms whom he

managed to deliver to a lifeboat before being swept away in a wave. Another claimed that Smith had shouted, 'Be British, boys, be British!' before going under with the ship. G. A. Drayton claimed that E. J. had simply been swept off the bridge when it lunged forward: 'I saw him swim back onto the sinking ship. He went down with it in my sight.' (1979, p53)[20]

There were also persistent rumours that the captain had used a pistol to commit suicide – and more convincing ones that an officer named Murdoch had shot himself. It seems clear that such stories were fuelled by ideological forces: the behaviour of individuals was taken as a token of the worth of institutions, classes, or nations.[21]

As in any disaster of this sort, some people behaved well and some displayed a range of serious or trivial weaknesses. Even before embarrassing information about who had survived – and how – was generally available, attempts were made to yoke the disaster to the ideological bandwagons of different interested parties. Six days after the ship went down, Wyn Craig Wade reports,

> Many ministers preached about the 'fact' that in the *Titanic*'s last moments, social caste had disappeared and all stood on the decks as equals. For example, Reverend Professor Eakin remarked: 'There was no distinction on the ground of wealth or any other of those barriers that we in our folly have raised so high . . . . The prospect of death levelled all distinction.' The extend of Reverend Eakin's own 'folly' would stand revealed when the statistics of the survivors were published. Eakin, incidentally, also disparaged the love of luxury, of which women were 'the greatest sinners in this regard.' (1979, pp66–7)

What is striking here is the immediate lunge made for what was perceived to be valuable ideological capital. Eakin's sermon seems clearly aimed both at doctrines which promoted or argued for the recognition of class conflict and, more generally, at women (Britain and America were both sharply divided by the battle for women's suffrage at this time).

Eakin was certainly wrong about the levelling of class distinctions: not only were there those disproportionate survivor statistics mentioned by Wade, but the treatment of survivors followed rigidly stratified lines. When surviving passengers were picked up by the *Carpathia*, they were allotted

---

[20] Walter Lord provides similar details of the contradictory stories told about the last moments of Archie Butt and John Jacob Astor (1955, p100).

[21] Some stories in particular achieved an almost immediate mythic status – especially that concerning the last tune played by the band. Wyn Craig Wade quotes tellingly from a sermon preached on 21 April by the Rev. F. W. Clampett in San Francisco. 'The brave captain was a sailor true,' Clampett intoned. 'Cannot we picture the last moment so that the message will come home to us all? The last boat was launched, the last grand plunge had begun. The strains of "Nearer, My God, to Thee" floated to the ears of those pulling away. And what was the cry? "Be British, boys, be British!"' (1979, p66). We are almost told that being British brings one nearer to God!

to areas according to the class of their tickets, and different doctors were assigned to look after the interests of each class (Lord 1955, p139).

Various commemorative books, newspaper supplements and magazine articles were rushed into print. Thus Marshall Everett's *Wreck and Sinking of the Titanic: The Ocean's Greatest Disaster* (1912) includes an introduction by Rev. Henry Van Dyke, DD, LL D entitled 'Women and Children First!' which is dated 13 May 1912 – just under a month after the sinking of the ship. Everett was, however, an old hand so far as cashing in on disasters was concerned; he had previously produced a book on the great Chicago Theatre disaster in 1904 and (in the same year) one entitled *Exciting Experiences in the Japanese-Russian War: Including a Complete History of Japan, Russia, China and Korea*. The year 1906 saw a book by him offering the complete story of the San Francisco earthquake with material on the eruption of Mount Vesuvius 'and other volcanic eruptions and earthquakes' thrown in for good measure. The commercial media exploitation of disasters hardly starts in the twentieth century – Defoe did after all write a journal of the plague year – but the establishment of what one can legitimately term a disaster *genre* is very much a modern phenomenon, and perhaps reflects both an attempt commercially to exploit a universal *Schadenfreude*, and also a more politically interested desire to attach ideological capital to one's own interests.

Even without the evidence of Van Dyke's introduction it is clear that *Wreck and Sinking of the Titanic* was put together very hurriedly. It represents something of a soup of ideological raw material, and resembles those statements by newly-apprehended felons who have not yet managed to get their story straight. Thus although the book includes a breakdown of losses and survivors detailed according to passenger class, it also includes statements such as the following – both from its first chapter entitled 'The Two Titans', written by Fred S. Miller:[22]

> When he builds and boasts of his *Titanics*, man may be great, but it is only when he is stripped of every cloying attribute of the world's pomp and power that he can touch sublimity. Those on the wreck had mounted to it from the time the awful impact came. The rise began when men of intellect and noted works, of titled place and honored station, worked as true yoke-

[22] Given the speed with which this volume was rushed into print, it would seem that the idea of seeing the iceberg and the *Titanic* as complementary equals doomed to collide with each another ('The Two Titans') occurred independently to Thomas Hardy and to the author of this chapter – and to others. The *Los Angeles Daily Times* of 17 April, 1912, prints a cartoon of a monstrous iceberg holding, and breaking, the doomed ship. The cartoon is labelled, 'The Real "Titanic"'. The Richmond (Virginia) *Times-Dispatch* of 21 April, 1912, prints a cartoon by John T. McCutcheon entitled 'The Rival Titans', showing a personified iceberg brooding over the sinking ship. The Everett volume contains further evidence that such a way of viewing the participants in the collision was common immediately after the disaster, although as I will suggest in my discussion of Hardy's 'The Convergence of the Twain', such conceptualizations could be informed by a variety of ideological interests.

fellows with the steerage passengers to see that all the women and their little ones were safely placed within the boats. (Everett 1912, p16)

But through all the time of terror the heroes of the *Titanic* remained true, nor yielded hearts to fear; and then, when all was done, when the last well-laden boat had safely put away, when the chill waters could be felt encroaching in the darkness, those who voluntarily awaited death, who has exemplified the sacred words: 'Greater love hath no man than this, that a man lay down his life for a friend' – then these put heroism behind them for humility, rose to the greater height, threw themselves on Him who walked the waters to a sinking ship, as they sang in ecstasy the simple hymn of steadfast faith: 'Nearer, my God, to Thee, nearer to Thee'! (Everett 1912, p17)

At the very point where a belief in a loving and omniscient God is most under challenge, the voices of those suffering from an apparent divine betrayal are enlisted to proclaim an undiminished faith. The London *Times* of 22 April, less than a week after the news of the disaster reached Britain, published the first verse of a hymn for the survivors of the *Titanic*, written by Hall Caine. Sung to the tune of 'O God, Our Help in Ages Past', the verse reads:

> Lord of the everlasting hills,
>   God of the boundless sea,
> Help us through all the shocks of fate
>   To keep our faith in Thee.

The ideological crisis is expressed very directly here.

The anonymous fifth chapter of Marshall Everett's *Wreck and Sinking of the Titanic: The Ocean's Greatest Disaster*, entitled 'The Rescue of the Survivors', carries the subhead: 'No Choice Between Classes', and bears witness to some failure on the part of its author to decide whether he or she wants to stress the democracy of death or the beastliness of non Anglo-Saxons:

> Men whose names and reputation were prominent in two hemispheres were shouldered out of the way by roughly dressed Slavs and Hungarians. Husbands were separated from their wives in the battle to reach the boats. Tearful leave-takings as the lifeboats, one after another, were filled with sobbing women and lowered upon the ice-covered surface of the ocean were heart-breaking.
>
> There was no time to pick or choose. The first woman to step into a lifeboat held her place even though she were a maid or the wife of a Hungarian peasant. (Everett 1912, pp47–8)

(One is forced to wonder whether the alleged lack of class precedence in the filling of the lifeboats was due to a casting away of earthly distinctions in the face of death, or to the fact that 'there was no time to pick and choose'. The writer seems not to have made up his mind.)

An insistence on the way in which class differences melted away in the aftermath of the disaster was common; the subtext apparently being that such differences are matters of the surface, cast aside when real issues must be faced. These arguments seem clearly designed to challenge socialist and trades-union insistence on the fundamental nature of class division. We must remember that the *Titanic* was nearly prevented from sailing by a coal strike in Britain which involved more than a million miners. The Everett memorial volume cites the following from Frederick E. Hopkins, pastor of Park Manor Congregational Church:

> Among the many lessons that we could learn from such a terrible calamity, one of the most important would seem to be this: That it ought to be for a long time more difficult than ever to arouse class prejudice, when this catastrophe has so clearly shown that the first and last thought the first cabin passenger had about the poorest woman in the steerage was that she should be given the first chance for her life no matter what happened to the man or woman of millions and of fame. (1912, p151)

As indignation grew over the disparity in the number of first, second, and steerage class passengers saved, such confidence tended to wane somewhat. It became apparent that many of the poorest women in steerage had been locked below and were thus unable to reach any lifeboat.

By the time that the reader gets to the tenth chapter, he or she may be forgiven for feeling that someone is protesting too much. It is entitled 'Sorrow and Honor and Memory Equal', and precedes a subhead which states that 'Heroism was Uniform and Universal and No Distinction Need be Drawn'. This, however, seems to have been forgotten by the twenty-first chapter, in which the surviving chairman of the White Star Line is pilloried:

> Men like J. Bruce Ismay may write voluminous statements and bring many witnesses to excuse their conduct, but the more they excuse, the more they accuse themselves. They can never answer the indictment of the men who die for the weak. Their clamor for exculpation is drowned by the deep silence of men like [George D.] Widener [who was not saved]. (1912, pp188–9)

The abiding interest in the ship and its fate is doubtless related to the way that both function as a sort of time-capsule, revealing aspects of the Edwardian age[23] much as an archaeological dig does. For a modern reader, the information that the crew's wages were stopped from the moment that the ship went down, and that they received no compensation for lost kit, is a reminder that however much Margaret Thatcher wanted to create a Britain based upon a return to Victorian (or similar) values, there is still some way to go in that direction. Perhaps even more difficult for a modern reader to believe is the story that when the parents of one of the lost

---

[23] Along with others I extend the Edwardian age to the outbreak of the First World War – some time after Edward VII's death.

bandsmen wrote to his employer asking for compensation for his death, they were sent a bill for his uniform – which he managed to lose by wearing it when the ship sank and he perished.

But even at the time many observers were able to see the ship in symbolic terms, as a microcosm of contemporary society. Geoffrey Marcus quotes the following passage from Filson Young's 1913 book *Titanic*:

> If, thinking of the *Titanic* . . . you could imagine her to be split in half from bow to stern so that you could look, as one looks at the section of a hive, upon all her manifold life thus suddenly laid bare, you would find in her a microcosm of civilised society. Upon the top are the rulers, surrounded by the rich and the luxurious, enjoying the best of everything; a little way below them their servants and parasites, ministering not so much to their necessities as to their luxuries; lower down still, at the base and foundation of all, the fierce and terrible labour of the stokeholds, where the black slaves are shovelling as though for dear life, endlessly pouring coal into furnaces that devoured it and yet ever demanded a new supply – horrible labour, joyless life; and yet the labour that gives life and movement to the whole ship. Up above are all the beautiful things, the pleasant things. Up above are the people who rest and enjoy; down below the people who sweat and suffer. (Marcus 1969, p94)

If such a parallel between the *Titanic* and 'civilized society' sprang naturally to mind in 1913, it is easy to understand that discussions about what happened to the ship, how its different classes of passengers were treated, and how their interests diverged, all became ideologically charged issues. I find especially interesting the comparison of the stokers and trimmers to 'black slaves'; there were in fact no 'black' passengers or members of crew on the ship.[24] Nonetheless, the fact that coal-powered ships required what was colloquially known as a 'black gang' allows Young to reveal a fascinating sense of the dependence of White European privilege on the slaves of colonialism and imperialism, along with a recognition that the lot of British workers was not so far removed from that of colonial slaves. It should be clear from comments I have already quoted that, like soccer players facing a penalty shot, those attempting to draw lessons from the disaster reached semi-instinctively for sensitive and vulnerable areas: class, gender, religion (why had God allowed this to happen?), commercial ethics and a modern desire for speed and luxury.

---

[24] Although, as Walter Lord points out, when American newspapers repeated the story about a stoker who had attempted to steal radio operator Phillips's lifejacket, many of them described the stoker (incorrectly) as 'a Negro'. There was a lot of righteous indignation directed against the stoker, although no one saw fit to explain why he had not been provided with his own lifejacket. Lord further adds that 'in a story headlined, "Desirable Immigrants Lost", the New York *Sun* pointed out that, along with the others, 78 Finns were lost who might do the country some good' (1955, p113). As Lord implies, it was clear that the newspaper did not see the country benefiting much from the others – Chinese, Irish, Hungarian, etc.

Wade quotes from the sermon of the Rev. Dr Leighton Parks, of St Bartholomew's Church in New York, who struck the same note as that sounded in the previously quoted comments of the Rev. Samuel H. Greene. Parks focused upon the fact that 'the men on the *Titanic* sacrificed themselves for the women and children'. He went on: 'The women did not ask for the sacrifice, but it was made. Those women who go about shrieking for their "rights" want something very different' (Wade 1979, p67). There were suffragette responses to such comments; in England, Mrs Cecil Chapman

> stated that any suffragette would have preferred to meet her fate alongside her husband. 'I would a thousand times rather go down with the ship under such circumstances,' she said. (The *New York Times* snarled at the 'jangling note' Mrs Chapman had added to the noble picture of male self-sacrifice.) Undoubtedly, Harriet Stanton Blatch, president of the American Political Women's Union, had the best rejoinder. Ms. Blatch stated that since men had drafted the laws that governed the ship, they should have been the ones to go down with it. Asked what her position would be should women receive the vote, she replied, 'Then we would have laws requiring plenty of lifeboats.' (1979, p67)

But as Wade points out, in general this debate caused damage to the suffrage movement which split on whether to endorse the 'women and children first' policy on the grounds that equal suffrage had nothing to do with the best methods to ensure safety in times of panic or the 'immemorial usage of seeking to protect the weak and helpless ahead of the strong', or, rather, to reject this policy in favour of a policy which was gender-neutral (1979, pp314–15). While all this was going on, Wade reports, a rally by anti-suffragettes resulted in a campaign for a monument to be built to 'the everlasting memory of male chivalry', to be paid for exclusively by one-dollar contributions from women. Two weeks after the disaster the wife of the President contributed the first dollar, and over 25,000 other women sent in their contributions:

> The resulting monument, sculpted by Gertrude Vanderbilt Whitney, was unveiled in Washington, D. C. and can still be seen across from East Potomac Park. It consists of an eighteen-foot classic statue of a half-clad male, his arms outstretched in the form of a cross. This stunning figure is posed on a thirty-foot pedestal on which is engraved homage 'to the brave men' of the *Titanic* 'who gave their lives that women and children might be saved.' (1979, p315)

A suffragette demonstration held on Fifth Avenue in New York on 4 May 1912 attracted far fewer participants than expected, and it was widely believed that Annie Nathan Meyer, founder of Barnard College, was correct in her view that after 'the superb unselfishness and heroism of the men on the *Titanic*', the march was 'untimely and pathetically unwise' (1979, p315).

A perhaps more surprising reaction to the disaster came from African-Americans. Surprising, because segregationist laws and customs meant that there were no Black passengers or crew on board the ship. But this, paradoxically, made the disaster more telling a blow for White supremacists, and Wade reports that while it was ignored by the Black intelligentsia,

> In the ghettoes, however, black response to the disaster was one of enthusiasm – cautious enthusiasm, certainly, but as heartfelt as the burden of their oppression. Just as black heavyweight Jack Johnson had recently trounced the 'Great White Hope' in the person of Jim Jeffries, so had inexorable fate sent the white man's 'practically unsinkable' ship to the bottom of the sea. (1979, p317)

While the authorized view of the tragedy was presented in ballads such as one by Mark Beam and Harold Jones entitled 'The Band Played "Nearer, My God, to Thee" as the Ship Went Down' (Wade 1979, p61), North American Black popular culture produced a succession of oral recitations known as 'toasts' on the subject of the loss of the *Titanic*, all of which celebrate the escape of a mythical Black stoker named 'Shine' who rejects the sexual and other blandishments of White passengers and rescues himself by swimming to shore. (Hans Magnus Enzensberger incorporates one of these versions in his poem 'The Sinking of the Titanic'.)

Bruce Jackson includes ten versions of the *Titanic* toast in his evocatively entitled book *'Get Your Ass in the Water and Swim Like Me': Narrative Poetry from Black Oral Tradition* (1974). All of these versions were transcribed during the 1960s, and Jackson gives no indication of when the earliest-known variant dates from. The versions provided by Jackson follow a common narrative line, and are clearly built on some knowledge of the disaster. Jackson's version 52A has 'a thousand millionaires' looking at the hero Shine when he jumps in the ocean and begins to swim – a figure which rises to four thousand millionaires in version 52C. The same version (52C) also builds one of the better-known facts or myths from the sinking into the narrative:

> Folks on the land were singin' 'Nearer My God to Thee,'
> The sharks in the ocean were singin', 'Bring your ass to me.'
> (Jackson 1974, p188)

Factual details are here treated as familiar landmarks which can be twisted creatively by the reciter: it was of course those on the ship who were reputed to have sung 'Nearer, My God, to Thee' (and while the Atlantic is not shark-free, there is no evidence that sharks attacked anyone from the *Titanic*). Moreover, while some of the versions date the disaster accurately, others move it to various dates in May – and one to 3 May 1812! It is clear that what is important to the narratives is the standard situation in which White society is humbled, a situation into which a triumphant Black hero can be introduced. All other facts are of lesser importance and can be changed or adapted to suit the needs of the recitation. Wyn Craig Wade argues that the '*Titanic* toasts' mark 'a seminal stage in black pride', when the African-American sees self-realization to be achieved not through emulation of White values but in their rejection (1979, p318).

Wade also quotes from what he claims is, musically speaking, the best song inspired by the disaster, written by Leadbelly, which contains the lines: 'Black man oughta shout for joy, / Never lost a girl or either a boy, / Cryin', 'Fare thee, *Titanic*, fare thee well!' (1979, p317).

According to an exhibit in the *Titanic* exhibition in the Ulster Folk and Transport Museum in Belfast, in 1911 the White Star Line claimed that

> The *Olympic* and the *Titanic* are not only the largest vessels in the world, they represent the highest achievements in Naval Architecture and Marine Engineering; they stand for the pre-eminence of the Anglo-Saxon race on the Ocean.

The Anglo-Saxon race could hardly object if non-Anglo-Saxons remembered such statements after the *Titanic* foundered, and drew some conclusions from them.

The authorized version, then, ran something like this in the weeks that followed the disaster. The loss of the ship was a terrible accident, one for which no one can really be blamed. But it brought out the best in those involved. The captain went down bravely with his ship; men sacrificed themselves that women and children might live, and although there were examples of bad behaviour, these were generally associated with foreigners; White Anglo-Saxons showed what sterling stuff they were made of, and forgot differences of class and wealth. The main lesson of the disaster, then, was that basically everything should remain as it was, as the disaster revealed the true strength of Anglo-Saxon culture.

But in the face of many subsequently revealed awkward details, claims that the disaster was an act of God looked suspiciously like refusals to face up to the fact that various acts of specific men left much to be desired. This at least formed the substance of a long attack by George Bernard Shaw on the English newspapers and their reporting of the disaster. The polemic was published in the *Daily News and Leader* on 14 May, just a month after the ship went down, under the title 'Some Unmentioned Morals'. Shaw suggested that the effect of a 'sensational catastrophe' on a modern nation was that of a wild defiance of inexorable fate and undeniable fact 'by an explosion of outrageous romantic lying'. He isolated what he described as four 'romantic demands' made when a ship was wrecked: that women and children should be saved first; that all the men should be heroes (except the foreigners 'who must all be shot by stern British officers in attempting to rush the boats over the bodies of the women and children'), and the captain a super-hero; that 'The officers must be calm, proud, steady, unmoved in the intervals of shooting the terrified foreigners'; and that 'Everybody must face death without a tremor; and the band . . . must play "Nearer, my God, to Thee" as an accompaniment to Mr Ismay to go to hell'. (The whole article, along with a reply from Sir Arthur Conan Doyle, a rejoinder from Shaw, and a final comment from Doyle, is quoted in Pearson, [1977, pp140–42].)

Shaw argued, with vitriolic sarcasm, that although all the evidence suggested that none of these romantic requirements were met during the final hours of the *Titanic*, press reports suggested that they were, even to the extent of lying about what actually happened. Although Shaw does not (of course) use the word 'ideology', his concept of the 'romantic demand' makes it quite clear that he had a sophisticated understanding of the concept and a detailed knowledge of the ideological moves being played in the aftermath of the disaster.

Joseph Conrad wrote two essays on the loss of the *Titanic* – one of them only days after the disaster. Both were published in *The English Review*. Conrad's own targets are prophetic of the significance that the *Titanic* disaster was to assume in popular myth: Britain – and especially her outdated and Dickensian institutions such as the Board of Trade (although it is the American inquiry into the disaster which Conrad mocks in terms of 'Bumble-like proceedings' [1921a, p289], while he has nothing but praise for the subsequent British inquiry, the impartiality of which later commentators have questioned); commerce; a blind confidence in technological advance; and a craving for size and luxury. For Conrad,

> [f]rom a certain point of view the sight of the august senators of a great Power rushing to New York and beginning to bully and badger the luckless 'Yamsi'[25] – on the very quay-side so to speak – seems to furnish the Shakespearian touch of the comic to the real tragedy of the fatuous drowning of all these people who to the last moment put their trust in mere bigness, in the reckless affirmations of commercial men and mere technicians and in the irresponsible paragraphs of the newspapers booming these ships! (1921a, p288)

There is much of the subsequent, mythic history of the disaster encapsulated in these words, although one aspect – the inescapable association of the ship and its loss with Britain – is missing, as one might expect from the naturalized Pole whose pro-British sentiments made him, at least in his non-fictional writings, 'more Catholic than the Pope'. Conrad's reference to 'mere technicians' chimes in with his subsequent expression of regret for 'the modern blind trust in mere material and appliances' (1921a, p294) and for his withering and contemptuous dismissal in his second *Titanic* essay of the expert witnesses at the British inquiry:

> It is amusing, if anything connected with this stupid catastrophe can be amusing, to see the secretly crestfallen attitude of technicians. They are the high priests of the modern cult of perfected material and of mechanical appliances, and would fain forbid the profane from inquiring into its mysteries. We are the masters of progress, they say, and you should remain respectfully silent. (1921b, pp310–11)

---

[25] 'Yamsi' was the codename Bruce Ismay used in radioed messages from the *Carpathia* (it is Ismay spelled backwards). Ismay faced great public criticism for having occupied a place in a lifeboat, although both he and Sir Cosmo Duff Gordon were formally exonerated from blame in the report of the British inquiry into the disaster.

The graffitist of the contraceptive dispenser may have added an element of national scepticism to the mix, but his sentiments are in direct line of descent from those of Joseph Conrad.

Throughout his two essays on the disaster, Conrad insistently returns his readers to the contrast between a perceived set of fundamental realities: the sufferings of those who died or faced death, and accounts (or, as Hayden White might have it, emplotments) of the events which gave rise to these experiences:

> I am not a soft-headed, humanitarian faddist. I have been ordered in my time to do dangerous work; I have ordered others to do dangerous work; I have never ordered a man to do any work I was not prepared to do myself. I attach no exaggerated value to human life. But I know it has a value for which the most generous contributions to the Mansion House and 'Heroes' funds cannot pay. And they cannot pay for it, because people, even of the third class (excuse my plain speaking), are not cattle. Death has its sting. If Yamsi's manager's head were forcibly held under the water of his bath for some little time, he would soon discover that it has. Some people can only learn from that sort of experience which comes home to their own dear selves. (1921b, p333)

Like Shaw, then, I would argue that Conrad generally recognizes and rejects the defensive movements of ideology in initial press reactions to the disaster, and he counters them by insisting upon the physical and mental sufferings of those who perished. His humanism is not the prisoner, but the unmasker of ideology.

As years passed – and, in particular, as the years of the First World War passed – the loss of the *Titanic* came increasingly to symbolize the end of an era that, like the ship, seemed to epitomize overconfidence, the immoral enjoyment of an indefensible level of luxury by a small minority who lived off the backs of a downtrodden majority, and a corrupt reliance on institutions that had lost any moral energy they might once have enjoyed.

I said earlier that I would explain what, for me, differentiates myth from ideology. In his *Mythologies*, Roland Barthes states that for him the notion of myth explains a particular process whereby historically determined circumstances were presented as somehow 'natural', and that it allowed for the uncovering of 'the ideological abuse' hidden 'in the display of *what goes without saying*' (1973, p11). He further defines it as 'depoliticized speech' (1973, p142). I have myself suggested that, in recent usage, the concepts of myth and of ideology are interlinked: myths perform an ideological function while ideologies function by means of myths (Hawthorn 1994a, p186). The concepts are clearly related, even interdependent, and are not neatly to be separated. Nevertheless, we may say that whereas ideology is typically overtly combative, and the presence of ideology normally invokes a sense that *debates and disputes connected to power* are being energized, the element of controversy and power manipulation in myth is generally more concealed, such that, as Barthes says, a myth is taken to represent 'what goes without saying' and appears to be (but maybe is not) depoliticized.

Thus if the graffitist's 'So was the *Titanic*' has a clearly ideological force (it explicitly sets itself in opposition to an authority that invites us to reside our trust in it, and draws attention to this opposition), the view that the *Titanic* and its loss somehow symbolize 'the end of an era' assumes more the character of a myth.

There is a case to be made that in a certain sense the myth was there already in 1912, waiting for the *Titanic* to sink. In his *The Wreck of the 'Titanic' Foretold?* (1986), Martin Gardner discusses the many claims that the disaster was prophesied and predicted not only in the forebodings of a number of individual passengers and their friends and families, but also in print. Gardner has much good sense to say about the fact that on any major journey many passengers will have fears and will be nervous – something which they forget once they arrive safely. But he pays more detailed attention to a number of literary works which, published before the disaster, have subsequently been said to have predicted it. Of these the most striking example is perhaps that of Morgan Robertson's novel *Futility*, which was first published in 1898. Robertson's novel involved a collision between a giant steamship and an iceberg, and the steamship was named the *Titan*. This is only the first of many seemingly uncanny parallels between Robertson's fiction and the actual disaster. Martin Gardner draws attention to a number of these. Both the fictional and the real ship were called the largest passenger ship ever built; the *Titanic* was 882.5 feet long and the *Titan* was 800 feet long. Both ships were all steel, with three propellers and two masts. Both were considered unsinkable because of their many watertight compartments. Each could carry about 3000 people, but whereas the *Titan* was filled to capacity the *Titanic* carried only 2235. Both ships had about the same horsepower and a similar displacement, and both had too few lifeboats (twenty on the real ship, twenty-four on the fictional one). The *Titanic* was travelling at 22.5 knots when it collided with an iceberg, while the *Titan* was going 25 knots. Both ships began their fatal voyage in April, both struck an iceberg at near midnight, grazing it on the starboard side. But there were differences. The *Titan* was not on her maiden voyage, was travelling from New York to England, and only thirteen of her passengers survived. (See Gardner 1986, pp31–4 for his discussion of these parallels, from which I have abstracted much of the above.)

It should surprise no one that Robertson's novel was reissued in 1912 with the expanded title of *The Wreck of the Titan; or Futility*. Gardner's commentary on these parallels is worth quoting. He argues that once Robertson had decided to write a novel about the greatest sea disaster imaginable, much of the subsequent detail would follow by natural inference. The size of the *Titan* was greater than that of any existing ship, but passenger liners were getting larger all the time and a ship 800 feet long was clearly within the reach of existing technology. Given such a size, the name *Titan* would certainly not be inappropriate. The use of watertight doors and compartments would lead to a belief in such a ship's unsinkability, and a grazing blow from an iceberg would be the most likely way for such a ship to be sunk (Gardner points out that collisions between ships and icebergs in the North Atlantic were not uncommon at this time).

It seems to me that the real relevance of such 'predictions' is that they bear witness to the fact that before the *Titanic* went down there existed a nervousness that much-vaunted advances in technology might still be insufficient to cope with the unpredictability of the elements, a nervousness that the scene was perhaps being set for a humbling of such technocratic pretensions.

Another striking literary foreshadowing of the event – one to which I have seen no allusion in print – can be seen in Herman Melville's poem 'The Berg', subtitled 'A Dream' (reprinted in Chase 1950, pp399–400).[26] The poem recounts the persona's vision of a 'martial ship':

> I saw a ship of martial build
> (Her standards set, her brave apparel on)
> Directed as by madness mere
> Against a stolid iceberg steer,
> Nor budge it, though the infatuate ship went down.

The poem concentrates on the contrast between the disastrous effect of the collision on the ship and its crew on the one hand, and the complete *lack* of effect it has on the berg. Even the gulls wheeling round the berg 'felt no jar after 'the stunned ship went down'. Most striking are the final lines of the poem which, addressed to the berg, seem more to anticipate Thomas Hardy's 'The Convergence of the Twain' than the disaster itself:

> Though lumpish thou, a lumbering one –
> A lumbering lubbard loitering slow,
> Impingers rue thee and go down,
> Sounding thy precipice below,
> Nor stir the slimy slug that sprawls
> Along thy dead indifference of walls.

The contrast between a human hubris which is, finally, outlasted by a lazily triumphant and slimy slug, along with Melville's use of the words 'infatuate' and 'indifferent', call to mind Hardy's much better-known poem. Melville, like Hardy, uses the convention that ships are referred to as female to make the collision and loss of the ship representative of a more sinister humbling of specifically *female* pride.

Wyn Craig Wade also refers to the experience of Senator William Alden Smith, who was to lead the American inquiry into the disaster. When poring over newspaper reports of the sinking, Smith was struck by a curious coincidence and extracted from his billfold a 'piece of yellowed newsprint he had clipped in 1902'. It was a poem about a shipwreck:

---

[26] I am indebted to my colleague Domhnall Mitchell for bringing Melville's poem to my attention.

Then she, the stricken hull,
The doomed, the beautiful,
Proudly to fate abased
    Her brow, Titanic.

According to Wade, Smith 'had been strangely moved by the poem ten years earlier and had all but forgotten that he still carried it around with him' (1979, p96). It is tempting to speculate on why Smith found such a brief extract so strangely moving, although such speculation is probably pointless so far as Smith's own reactions are concerned. More generally, though, it is interesting once again to note the same pattern of *female* pride being abased. There seems to be a clear element of male wish-fulfilment in such depictions of shipwrecks, one which seems to arise from a male desire to punish women for being sexually attractive but sexually unavailable.

Tim Armstrong adds another contender to the list of poetic prophecies: he refers to a letter to *The Spectator* for the week ending 20 April 1912, in which B. Paul Newman draws the attention of readers to a poem published thirty years previously by the American poet Celia Thaxter, entitled 'A Tryst'. The tryst in question is that between an iceberg and a ship, and Armstrong conjectures that Hardy may have read Thaxter's poem, as both it and his own 'The Convergence of the Twain' depict ship and iceberg as thesis and antithesis, both alternate between descriptions of each, and both picture a version of Fate watching the scene (1992, p31).

Martin Gardner's book attempts to debunk such claims for prophecy (the reader should note the question mark in its title, *The Wreck of the 'Titanic' Foretold?*). He attempts to deflect such essentially superstitious responses into a more scholarly direction, pointing out that concern about a collision between a passenger ship and an iceberg was a quite rational fear in the years before the *Titanic* disaster. Reading newspapers published at or around the time of the disaster one is reminded that other ships besides the *Titanic* were posted missing at this time: generally speaking, the loss of a ship was no more astonishing then than is a fatal automobile accident today. One can add that disasters of this sort, coming at a time of increased religious scepticism and unbelief, quite naturally led to questions about how a belief in a loving and all-seeing God could be reconciled with human tragedies of this order.

Gardner also includes the text of another 'prophetic' work in his book: Mayn Clew Garnett's 'The White Ghost of Disaster', which was published in May 1912 but apparently written before the loss of the *Titanic*. This also involves an account of a disastrous shipwreck, one passage from which I find interesting:

Brownson gazed back over the decks. He watched the crowd impersonally, and it seemed strange to him that so much valuable fabric should go to the bottom so quickly. The paint was so clean and bright, the brass was so shiny. The whole structure was so thoroughly clean, neat, and in proper order. It was absurd. There he was standing upon that bridge where he

had stood so often, and here below him were hundreds of dying people –
people like rats in a trap. (Gardner 1986, p134)

The passage is interesting, I feel, inasmuch as it testifies to a shared
perception of the hidden limits of an apparently unassailable technology
which was current before the *Titanic* went down. That word 'absurd'
exposes what, after Alan Sinfield, we can dub an ideological faultline,
ideological because it is palpable that the seemingly perfect technology,
clean paint, shiny brass and all, has a *meaning*: it represents a society that
has placed much of its social confidence in the safe-keeping of its leading
technology. It does not require any forced reading to see a picture of a
whole society in this description, one in which external cleanliness,
neatness and order are not able to help people who are dying like rats in
a trap. Filson Young's description of the *Titanic* as model of Edwardian
culture has many points of contact with the reverberations of this passage.

In her *Shifting Gears: Technology, Literature, Culture in Modernist America*,
Cecelia Tichi has suggested that by the end of the nineteenth century this
opposition between what she terms a 'gear and girder technology' that can
achieve anything, and a more threatening, repressed, ugly and uncontrolled
natural reality is general; she argues that Willa Cather's novel, *Alexander's
Bridge*, traces this opposition very clearly (Tichi 1987, p41).

Wyn Craig Wade quotes from John B. Thayer's book *The Sinking of the
S. S. Titanic*, which was first published in 1940 – a time when people were
very much conscious of the difference between their own time and that of
the Edwardians:

> There was peace, and the world had an even tenor to its ways. True
> enough, from time to time there were events – catastrophes – like the
> Johnstown flood, the San Francisco earthquake, or floods in China – which
> stirred the sleeping world, but not enough to keep it from resuming its
> slumber. It seems to me that the disaster about to occur was the event,
> which not only made the world rub its eyes and awake, but woke it with
> a start, keeping it moving at a rapidly accelerating pace ever since, with
> less and less peace, satisfaction and happiness. . . . To my mind the world
> of today awoke April 15, 1912. (Wade 1979, p7)

For Wade, the *Titanic*, 'had taken more than human lives; in her plunge to
the deepest abyss of the North Atlantic, she had also taken the self-
confidence and complacency of the English-speaking world' (1979, p33).
Thayer's opinions are confirmed by other writers. The third volume of
Leonard Woolf's autobiography, *Beginning Again*, contains a similarly nostalgic view of the Edwardian era. For Woolf the watershed was the
outbreak of war in 1914: the shooting of Archduke Francis Ferdinand of
Austria, according to him, 'destroyed the civilization of Europe'. Writing
in 1964, Woolf claims that since that shooting we all live against a background of battle, murder and sudden death, and that when the BBC news-
reader starts the news we know that it will be 99 per cent political and will
tell us of some new acts of organized communal violence, while the doom

in the announcer's voice threatens our country, our allies and ourselves – 'helpless individuals, in our personal lives with every kind of disaster and horror'. He concludes: 'But it was not really like that before 1914. . . . I think the main difference in the world before 1914 from the world after 1914 was in the sense of security and the growing belief that it was a supremely good thing for people to be communally and individually happy' (1964, p43). (The use of words such as 'we' and 'us' is worth analysing.)

I have to say that Thayer's and Woolf's opinions seem to me to be pure nostalgia. One has only to read the London *Times* in the days surrounding the disaster to find that the even tenor of British life at that time included fierce debate about the Home Rule Bill and about Welsh Church disestablishment; large advertisements attacking the government for its treatment of suffragette prisoners; reports on the miners' strike and a strike by tailors; and news that the trades unionist Tom Mann had been sentenced to six months in prison. Robert Tressell's account of the lives of working housepainters in the first decade of this century in his novel *The Ragged Trousered Philanthropists* hardly suggests that they would have agreed that they felt either a sense of security or 'communally and individually happy' (the front page of the London *Daily Express* for Tuesday, 16 April 1912 includes in 'To-Day's Diary' six London meetings of the Anti-Socialist Union; presumably those at whom these meetings were aimed were to be dissuaded from finding the wrong way to communal and individual happiness). Nor was the news from abroad so very much more peaceful and even-tenored. It may well be the case that the disaster damaged British self-confidence and complacency, but it did not strike a ship steaming from one earthly paradise to another.

More recently, the *Titanic* has symbolized the hubris of the Edwardian educated social stratum, and nemesis for its smugness, reliance on technology, worship of bigness and luxury and general British complacency. Such symbolic meanings have typically been given a decidedly *nostalgic* flavour from the 1940s onwards. Thus a cultural materialist account of the following comments in Walter Lord's 1955 book *A Night to Remember* might well wonder whether they told us more about 1912 or about 1955:

> Overriding everything else, the *Titanic* also marked the end of a general feeling of confidence. Until then men felt they had found the answer to a steady, orderly, civilized life. For 100 years technology had steadily improved. For 100 years the Western world had been at peace. For 100 years the benefits of peace and industry seemed to be filtering satisfactorily through society. In retrospect, there may seem less grounds for confidence, but at the time most articulate people felt life was all right.
>
> The *Titanic* woke them up. Never again would they be quite so sure of themselves. In technology especially, the disaster was a terrible blow. Here was the 'unsinkable ship' – perhaps man's greatest engineering achievement – going down the first time it sailed.
>
> But it went beyond that. If this supreme achievement was so terribly fragile, what about everything else? If wealth meant so little on this cold

April night, did it mean so much the rest of the year? Scores of ministers preached that the *Titanic* was a heaven-sent lesson to awaken people from their complacency, to punish them for top-heavy faith in material progress. If it was a lesson, it worked – people have never been sure of anything since.

The unending sequence of disillusionment that has followed can't be blamed on the *Titanic*, but she was the first jar. Before the *Titanic*, all was quiet. Afterward, all was tumult. That is why, to anybody who lived at the time, the *Titanic* more than any other single event marks the end of the old days, and the beginning of a new, uneasy era. (1955, pp114–15)

Lord's book deserves better than a stupidly literal reading, but even the least sophisticated of readers must be struck by the exaggerations and evasions here – the wars that have disappeared, the doubts that have evaporated. (Did Tennyson write 'In Memoriam' in vain?) The title of Richard O'Connor's study *Down to Eternity. How the Proper Edwardian and His World Died with the 'Titanic'* (1956) sums up much of what our own age makes of the disaster. Whereas in 1912 anti-suffragists were seeing the disaster as incontrovertible evidence of the strength of traditional rôles and institutions, our own age has interpreted it more as a symbol of their death.

Stephen Kern's *The Culture of Time and Space 1880–1918* (1983) draws a parallel between the disaster and the outbreak of the First World War:

The arrogance, the lack of safety precautions, the reliance on technology, the simultaneity of events, the worldwide attention, the loss of life all evoke the sinking of the *Titanic* as a simile for the outbreak of the war. The lookouts on the *Titanic* were blinded by fog, as the political leaders and diplomats and military men were blinded by historical shortsightedness, convinced that even if war came it would not last long. On the eve of disaster they shared a confidence that the basic structure of European states was sound, able to weather any storm. Europe, they were certain, was unsinkable. The concentration of wireless messages from the sinking ship, the rescue ships, and the coastal stations suggests the flurry of telegraph messages and telephone conversations exchanged during the July crisis. Even the icebergs floating in the path of the liner had an analog in the eight assassins who lay in wait for Francis Ferdinand at various points on his parade route the day he was murdered. He had ignored warnings about the danger from terrorists in the streets of Sarajevo, as the captain of the *Titanic* had ignored wireless messages about the dangerous waters ahead. The captain raced against time for the fastest Atlantic crossing. Another race took place between the armies of the great powers, which rushed to mobilize toward the end of July as the diplomacy began to founder. (1983, p268)

There is something about this particular disaster which encourages such searches for minutely differentiated symbolic clues, as if the *Titanic*'s loss were a highly coded Renaissance painting or piece of medieval church architecture.

Geoffrey Marcus opens his book *The Maiden Voyage* with a declared determination to get back to the 'true facts', but after chronicling these facts he cannot resist the temptation to end his book back with, if not myth and legend, certainly symbolic meaning:

> The loss of the *Titanic* was, surely, a classic case of that overweening pride and arrogance which provokes the wrath of the gods, known to the Greeks of old as *hubris*. (1969, p298)

If Thomas Hardy is sitting with the President of the Immortals, he must be allowing himself a wry smile of agreement. At any rate, Hardy allowed himself a wry poem in the immediate wake of the disaster.

II
Thomas Hardy, 'The Convergence of the Twain'

The Convergence of the Twain

(*Lines on the Loss of the 'Titanic'*)

I

In a solitude of the sea
Deep from human vanity,
And the Pride of Life that planned her, stilly couches she.

II

Steel Chambers, late the pyres
Of her salamandrine fires,
Cold currents thrid, and turn to rhythmic tidal lyres.

III

Over the mirrors meant
To glass the opulent
The sea-worm crawls – grotesque, slimed, dumb, indifferent.

IV

Jewels in joy designed
To ravish the sensuous mind
Lie lightless, all their sparkles bleared and black and blind.

V

Dim moon-eyed fishes near
Gaze at the gilded gear
And query: 'What does this vaingloriousness down here?' . . .

VI

Well: while was fashioning
This creature of cleaving wing,
The Immanent Will that stirs and urges everything

VII

Prepared a sinister mate
For her – so gaily great –
A Shape of Ice, for the time far and dissociate.

VIII

And as the smart ship grew
In stature, grace, and hue,
In shadowy silent distance grew the Iceberg too.

IX

Alien they seemed to be:
No mortal eye could see
The intimate welding of their later history,

X

Or sign that they were bent
By paths coincident
On being anon twin halves of one august event,

XI

Till the Spinner of the Years
Said 'Now!' And each one hears,
And consummation comes, and jars two hemispheres.

To move from contemporary sermons, speeches, newspaper polemics and journal articles on the *Titanic* disaster to Hardy's poem is to become aware of an apparent change of perspective and of tone. Hardy's poem contains no overt acknowledgement of any public debate over the disaster; it gives no indication that it is directed at a reader or listener who needs to be argued with; it presents itself as distant from – or above – polemic. It enters into no specific or particularized recriminations over the event, contenting itself with more generalized and distanced mention of such abstractions as 'human vanity'. Nor – strikingly, given that it was written for a 'Dramatic and Operatic Matinée in aid of the "Titanic" Disaster Fund' and that Hardy lost two friends in the disaster[27] – is there any expression of grief for those who perished. Indeed, such references as those to 'the opulent', 'the sensuous mind', and 'vaingloriousness' could well be read so as to attach part of the blame for the ship's loss to the ship's wealthier passengers – a point to which I will return.

Thus although it is possible to find elements in Hardy's poem which are shared with other, non-literary, responses to the tragedy, the poem's treatment of the event is recognizably distinct; it is unmistakably *literary*. The poem has a highly ordered and ceremonial structure: on a formal level its measured and regular stanzas merge with the repeated use of statement to suggest disinterestedness and profundity. Each stanza seems self-sufficient, enclosed, definitive. And the successive closure of each stanza culminates in a terminal closure in which the finality of the ship's fate is appropriated to seal the poem itself from query or polemic. (Tim Armstrong [1992, p39] suggests that even the shape of the stanzas suggests a ship low in the water – or, one might add, resting on the seabed.) The poem's opening stanza does more than remind the reader of the physical inaccessibility of the wreck; it surely attempts to situate the poetic discourse beyond human debate, beyond the range of human intervention. Just as the ship is now beyond human control – or even (in 1912), human sight – so too the poem stockades its arguments in a space that is clearly labelled 'beyond dispute' (or, to quote from Hardy's own appropriation from Thomas Gray, 'Far from the madding crowd').

We start then with a number of paradoxes. This is an occasional poem, associated with a ceremony the ostensible purpose of which was to raise money for the very recently bereaved, but a poem which has nothing to say about those mourning the death of loved ones or (except extremely indirectly, and negatively) about those who were lost. The poem repeats some themes from more polemical discussions which followed the ship's loss (attributing blame to a love of luxury, for example), but in a manner which invites neither discussion nor debate. Most strikingly, perhaps, the poem invites not so much action or recrimination, as a fatalistic acceptance founded in the belief that the disaster can be attributed either to unchangeable human weaknesses or to malevolent or indifferent suprahuman powers. It is worth considering, for example, the force of that 'human vanity' in the poem's initial stanza, which exploits the double meaning of 'vain': 'selfishly proud' and 'useless, unavailing'. At the same time as the stanza paints humanity as subject to selfish and pathetic pride, then, it also invokes a sense that it is vain for human beings to try to control their destiny – *Vanitas vanitatum*.

---

[27] See his letter to Florence Henniker, dated Sunday 21 April 1912 (Purdy and Millgate 1978, p211).

Even the poem's belittling of the human love of luxury is non-specific in its force (although, as I will argue later, the reader may be encouraged to associate this particular failing more with women than with men). As we have seen, many immediate responses to the disaster pinpointed particular weaknesses which were, it was argued, especially associated with the modern age: a love of luxury, a craving for speed, a worship of size and a blind belief in technology. But the poem's attack on the love of luxury is far less specific than this. Joseph E. Grennen has pointed out that the poem's contempt for human arrogance and love of luxury does not portray these as specifically modern failings, but associates them more with the human race in general. 'Terms like "human vanity," "pride of life," and "vaingloriousness," uttered within a context of frustrated aims and thwarted powers, of human presence represented only by the devalorized tokens of affluence (men as such not once being mentioned), cannot help but evoke powerful overtones of the cynical stance of the author of *Ecclesiastes* and its reverberations down the years' (1988, p197). More specifically, Grennen instances Hardy's use and transformation of 'a medieval alliterating idiom' to widen the scope of the attack on luxury:

> Hardy's description of the fish gazing at the 'gilded gear' lying on the ocean floor finds medieval precedent in a poem like the alliterative *Alexander and Dindimus*, where in a similar context the author refers to the 'guldene ger' of aristocratic victims (*Alexander*, v. 522), or *The Siege of Jerusalem*, in which the 'pride of life' theme is underscored by reference to the 'gilden ger' of the doomed denizens of the city (*Siege*, v. 546). (1988, p198)

In like manner, Grennen argues that Hardy's phrase 'gaily great' echoes the medieval idiom 'gayly great' which occurs, for example, a number of times in the alliterative poem *William of Palerne* (or *William and the Werwolf*) (1988, p199). Such echoes and allusions encourage the reader to associate the disaster more with universal human weakness than with a particular contemporary failing – especially as the only *active* rôle in the history recounted by the poem is played by such non-human abstractions as 'The Immanent Will' and the 'Spinner of the Years'.

As I have already suggested, however, the poem's criticisms are not so generalized as to be entirely lacking in focus. While 'the Pride of Life that planned her' is suggestive of masculine pride, the mention of 'mirrors' and 'jewels' invokes a conventional association of adornment and glass-gazing with women – one which is picked up and set into relief through the similarly conventional association of ships with the female sex (which allows Hardy to use the words 'she' and 'her' in the first stanza and to repeat 'her' in the second). Given that the disaster spawned a vitriolic debate between suffragists and anti-suffragists about what nowadays we would call gender rôles, such a focusing is probably not entirely innocent. In reality the rich people who demanded the level of luxury provided by the *Titanic* were predominantly male and American; Hardy's poem deflects the luxury argument by invoking a traditional view of women which associates them with vanity and a love of jewellery.

To this can be added the point that the whole poem is dominated by the parallel it implies between the ship–iceberg encounter on the one hand, and a particular sort of male–female relationship on the other. Ian Ousby has suggested that although a superficial reading might conclude that in 'The Convergence of the Twain' the 'sinking of the *Titanic* is simply one of those cosmic rebukes to human ambition that Hardy always records with a mixture of wistful regret and grim satisfaction' (1982, p780),

> this level of meaning is both expanded and complicated by the richly sexual connotations of the poem's language: ship and iceberg are lovers, destined at once to meet and be fatal to one another. The archaic 'twain' in the title does not just mean 'two' but carries the suggestion of a pair of lovers; Hardy himself often uses the word this way. Exploiting the convention that applies the feminine pronoun to ships, he describes the *Titanic* in obviously sensual terms: 'stilly couches she'. The iceberg is its 'mate', while their collision is an 'intimate welding' (with its echo of 'wedding') and a 'consummation'. (1982, p780)

For Hardy, Ousby suggests, the meeting of iceberg and ship is representative of the same sort of doomed encounter that is represented by that which brings Alec and Tess, or Jude and Sue together, and he quotes the following striking account of the first meeting between Alec and Tess in Hardy's *Tess of the D'Urbervilles*:

> Enough that in the present case, as in millions, it was not the two halves of a perfect whole that confronted each other at the perfect moment; a missing counterpart wandered independently about the earth waiting in crass obtuseness till the late time came. Out of which maladroit delay sprang anxieties, disappointments, shocks, catastrophes, and passing-strange destinies. (1975, pp67–8)

In all of these meetings, and others, Ousby argues, Hardy draws on a series of connected fables and traditions about human sexuality, the most important of which is Plato's *Symposium*. Hardy, Ousby argues, draws particularly on Aristophenes's bawdy and moving fable about the origins of human sexuality, which posits that originally there were three sexes – men, women and hermaphrodites. According to this account, the original men became homosexuals and the original women lesbians. Zeus cut the hermaphrodites in two, and the halved hermaphrodites 'became heterosexual lovers trying to recover their primordial wholeness' (1982, p780). (Thus the mention in the poem's final line of the 'two hemispheres' which are jarred, points both to the shock caused by the accident in the two halves of the world, but also to ship and iceberg as two halves of a split unity which reunite destructively.) Such a myth gives Hardy a model for a particular type of doomed heterosexual relationship – one in which a man and a woman feel a powerful affinity with each other and are drawn together into an alliance which is mutually destructive. Ousby suggests that behind this model is a perception that such relationships are doomed because the affinity felt by the two participants for each other casts the shadow of incest and the incest prohibition over their union.

Certainly the hinted parallel between the collision and the sex act – most clearly in Hardy's use of the word 'consummation' – leads to a view of sexuality as mutually destructive, and the last stanza of Hardy's poem seems to draw on a traditional association between sexual orgasm and death. At the same time, 'consummation' also recalls Christ's last words on the cross, an echo which Hardy apparently took care to underline. Emerson Brown Jr. has pointed out that by adding an extra stanza (lines 13–15) to the poem as first published, Hardy ensured that the word 'consummation' occurred in the thirty-third line of the poem, thus ensuring a numerological match with Christ's age at the time of his crucifixion (1994, p238).

Two comments seem to me to be permitted at this stage. First, that if interpretative comments such as these are accepted then one of the things which distinguishes this literary treatment of (or response to) the disaster from the non-literary ones considered earlier is that Hardy's poem is far more complex and multilayered in its meaning – to the extent that one might be tempted to refer to its meanings, or reverberations, rather than just to its meaning. But second, that if the debates which followed the disaster involved individuals with preformed agendas seeking to appropriate the disaster to their own ends, there is a sense in which the same is true of Hardy's poem. Once one sees the parallels between the collision as seen in Hardy's poem, and the other human 'collisions' in his fiction mentioned by Ousby, then 'The Convergence of the Twain' becomes almost a finished poem that was waiting for the accident about which it was ostensibly written. It would, too, be wrong to view Hardy's pessimistic view of the chances of a happy and fulfilling heterosexual relationship as a purely personal matter. Hardy lived at a time when gender rôles were changing, and that change was being both championed and resisted. Even a superficial reading of novels such as *Tess of the D'Urbervilles* and *Jude the Obscure* serves to indicate how much the problems of Hardy's lovers are tied in to very specific historical circumstances.

Does the poem's avoidance of the more heated debates which followed the foundering entitle us to see it as somehow beyond ideology? It has, palpably, a different relation to ideology from that which can be traced in the sermons, speeches and polemics from which I have quoted excerpts. However, a studied movement beyond the fierce particularities of the debates which followed the disaster may well itself be ideological, and we should be suspicious of any discursive intervention which claims to assert truths which are general and beyond dispute. To suggest that a general human weakness or love of luxury, or a suprahuman 'Spinner of the Years', is responsible for the loss of the *Titanic*, is in effect to absolve Captain Smith, Harland and Wolff, and the White Star Line from immediate blame.

Moreover, however much 'The Convergence of the Twain' seems to rise above contemporary debate, Tim Armstrong has argued that it does in fact seek an answer to the question that preoccupied those faced with making sense of the disaster:

> The most important question raised by 'The Convergence of the Twain' is what, ultimately, caused the *Titanic* disaster? Or perhaps (a more abstract question): what is the status of our explanation of the disaster. How do the human explanations which we call 'history' relate to the flux of events which brings together a ship and an iceberg? (1992, p33)

Armstrong suggests that the poem contains two separate, and irreconcilable, answers to this question, which Armstrong names the 'Theistic' and the 'Fetishistic'. The theistic answer draws on an abstracted 'Immanent Will' which watches and prepares events, and, Armstrong suggests, is complicit with the sort of moralizing that followed the disaster. This view implies that, along with what in 1 John 2:16 is called 'the lust of the eyes', 'the excessively worldly extravagance of the ship produce[s] a chastisement, a moral lesson imposed from without' (1992, p34).

The fetishistic view Armstrong so terms after Auguste Comte's view of a 'fetishistic' universe of self-motivated objects. Armstrong points out that Hardy had read a great deal on the philosophy of history, including material from Comte, Leslie Stephen, John Stuart Mill, Von Hartman, Macaulay, Froude, and others (1992, p33), and he argues very convincingly both that *agency* is a major problem in Hardy's poem and that doubts about agency can be traced in the history of the poem's successive versions. Armstrong seizes on Hardy's unusual formulation in the poem's sixth stanza, and he suggests that the 'unusual participle' implies an absent subject ('[the Immanent Will] was fashioning'), 'but then withdraws it; it is not the Immanent Will that fashions the ship, not even mankind or the White Star Line seemingly, but just a process of "being fashioned"' (1992, p35). Moreover, he adds:

> Hardy first wrote:
>
>> And so coincident
>> In course as to be meant
> To form anon twin halves of one august event,

where 'meant' seems to be the imposition of Fate. But the poem as revised for the *Fortnightly Review* and in its final version was more ambiguous, saying 'or sign that they were bent / By paths coincident / On being anon.' 'Bent' can be either active or passive here: it seems at first to suggest an outside force that they were 'bent / By.' But then, in the third line of the stanza, the arrival of the adverbial preposition 'on' seems to alter that, indicating that the ships themselves have an embodied will, being 'bent on' collision – an interpretation which suggests Comte's 'Fetishistic' universe of self-motivated objects. Was the collision willed by or somehow built into the *Titanic* itself? Or was it simply Fate? There is a systematic uncertainty at work within these lines, what we could call a 'bent by / bent on' principle which permeates them. (1992, pp35–6)

According to Armstrong, Hardy could not decide between these two very different philosophies of history. On the one hand he wanted to believe that there was an agent behind historical events, while on the other hand – Hayden White *avant la lettre* – he recognized 'the fact that the idea of agency as an imposed direction . . . is bound up with human hopes, expectations, and recognitions, always belated and subject to accident' (1992, p39). While the poem starts by implying a theistic view of the disaster, it moves to admit the possibility that the pattern of luxurious indulgence followed by stern punishment is a pattern imposed by the historian – Hardy himself. As Armstrong concludes:

> In this view, history is always the product of the interaction of human efforts and designs, and ultimately of the act of interpretation itself and the tropes used to describe it (a trope being itself a kind of 'bending' or 'welding' of words). (1992, p39)

It seems to me that this tension at the heart of the poem (Armstrong's argument convinces me in the main) goes a long way towards explaining what I have always found as an effect of mixed bemusement and acceptance that is the product of reading the poem. This dissatisfaction is concealed from the reader because the poem has such a strong closure: the bringing together of the shock of iceberg and ship with sexual climax and the death of Christ on the cross creates such a sense of unanswerability and finality that the poem's earlier contradictions get lost in the force of the climactic conclusion.

But the fact that the poem distracts the reader from a direct consideration of its own contradictions underlines not its absence from ideology but rather the fact that it is ideological and that it operates as ideology classically does: by holding contradictions in suspension and denying that they exist. In the final resort, I am tempted to say, the poem closes off specific criticism of those shortcomings and moral failings which led to the disaster, and encourages rather passivity and fatalism.

I am tempted to say this, but I do not think that it is the whole truth. This is partly because the words you are reading now – along with the articles to which I have referred – are themselves responses to the poem, so that passivity and fatalism are not the poem's inevitable achieved effect. But it is also because the poem's attempt to stifle the clash between theistic and fetishistic explanations seems to me to be not entirely wholehearted. Even those careful attempts to avoid attributing agency are self-advertising; the reader cannot but be made aware of his or her oscillation between different readings of 'bent', or of the avoidance of questions relating to agency in phrases such as 'was fashioning', and thus to be sensitized to the central issue of whether history is, *pace* Hayden White, a chaos of unrelated events (unrelated, that is, until they are 'related' in a narrative), or whether there are such things as cause and effect, moral duty, responsibility and culpability, and so on.

'The Convergence of the Twain' certainly selects from the innumerable chains of cause-and-effect which have been proposed to explain the sinking of the *Titanic* in such a way as to suggest a particular *plot*. What is interesting about this is that if we take two linked concepts from modern narrative theory: story and plot (or to use the terms developed by the Russian formalists, *fabula* and *sjužet*), we can witness an interesting tension between the poem's structure and the suggested underlying structure of actual events upon which it is based.

The poem's account does not follow a strict chronological progression, but it does allow for the reconstruction of a hypothesized 'real' sequence of causally linked events – the story or *fabula* – which has a clear beginning and a clear ending. The beginning is that of the planning of the ship by 'the Pride of Life', a planning which is rapidly followed by parallel events: the 'fashioning' of this 'creature of cleaving wing' on the one hand, and the preparation by the Immanent Will of the ship's 'sinister mate' – the iceberg. Next comes the hemisphere-jarring consummation of their collision. And finally, we have the conclusion given to us in the opening stanzas of the poem: the humbled ship, reclining on the ocean bed, her luxurious trappings degraded by the traffic of the lowest forms of marine life.

The plot of the poem clearly shuffles this sequence around. We start with the chronologically final stage – the ship in its underwater grave. We pan back to the planning of the ship, its subsequent 'fashioning' parallel to the preparation of its sinister mate, and we conclude with the shock of their collision – both literal shock and also metaphorical one.

It is important to note that what we have here is, in Hayden White's terms, a process of double construction. This is because even the hypothesized 'real' sequence of events – the story or *fabula* – itself builds a 'story' from separate 'events'. Even were we able to agree that everything in Hardy's story actually happened, the presentation of these events as story implies *processes of causation* (and, at the same time, excludes other, possible candidates for blame or responsibility).

It is obvious, for example, that although the poem suggests a parallel between the fashioning of the ship and the preparation of the iceberg – even to the extent that it suggests that these two processes were contemporaneous – in reality the iceberg started being made millions of years before construction of the *Titanic* commenced. (For those interested, Richard Brown's book *Voyage of the Iceberg: The Story of the Iceberg That Sank the Titanic* [1983] attempts to chart the time-scale of the iceberg's formation and voyage.) Moreover, the collision did not destroy the iceberg, although it would probably only have survived its encounter with the ship by a few months before melting and disappearing, but so far as the poem is concerned the iceberg ceases to be of any interest after the collision.

If this first-level construction starts to take liberties with 'what actually happened', to organize *events* into a *story*, the second level, when story or *fabula* is transformed into plot or *sjužet*, while it does not actually alter anything in the first level, does adapt chronology in such a way as to suggest a particular meaning or set of meanings not implicit at the first level. (And, of course, the excisions and organizations involved in the first level are retained and not challenged in the second.) On the level of the poem's plot what we are presented with is a progression from humbled pride, through pride, to a climactic process of actual humbling. The word 'consummation' clearly indicates the closure of a finite sequence of events, events which have a beginning and an end, and which are linked by some logic. (You cannot end a purely random and unconnected chaos of events with a consummation. Such a series – like Hayden White's 'chronicle' – is not consummated, it just comes to a halt.) 'Consummation', moreover, echoes Christ's dying utterance, a dying utterance conventionally inter-preted to mean that a particular plot involving disobedience, damnation, sacrifice and, finally, redemption, has been concluded. Christ's 'consum-mation' makes sense of what has gone before (and 'what has gone before' includes too the sins committed after His sacrifice, sins which are symbolically included amongst those paid for by Christ's death.) There is, therefore, a strong case for reading Hardy's poem as a tracing of a similar process of redemption through sacrifice – although it seems likely that this proposed sequence is proffered ironically. As we will see when we turn to Geoffrey Hill's 'Ode on the Loss of the "Titanic"', a view of the disaster as a form of sacrifice is not limited to Hardy – although in Hill's poem the sacrifice is an attempt to appease the 'terse gods' rather than an attempt by God to redeem human sin.

The effect of this process of double organization or construction is, surely, further to insist upon the non-human origin of significant agency. Things are caused to happen by forces apart from humanity and human understanding. Human beings have only a junior rôle in the initiation and control of causation: what they cause is swallowed up (in this case, literally) by what non-human agencies cause or 'prepare'. It is only with an effort of mind that one recalls, after reading Hardy's poem, that so far as the loss of the *Titanic* is concerned, it is neither here nor there whether the formation of the iceberg and the processes which led to it were known. What *is* important is that message after message about ice hazards was sent to the *Titanic* and received by its radio operators. Whether or not the Immanent Will prepared the iceberg, a large number of human wills observed it or its fellows and informed the speeding *Titanic* of the hazard. Hardy's emplotment obliterates such issues from the record, and this obliteration has a specifically ideological thrust. Readers of Hardy's poem are encouraged not to seek for explanations of the disaster that can result in the avoidance of further tragedies, but are in effect counselled to see such humblings of human pride as the inevitable result of a vainglorious concern for luxury. Ironically, of course, there may be some truth in such a conclusion: had the ship's designers and operators had more concern for the safety of all their passengers than for the spectacular luxury of first-class accommodations, then the disaster might have been avoided or at least mitigated in its effects. But this is a conclusion which points to a particular course of action, whereas Hardy's poem implicitly seems to countenance an acceptance of humanity's powerlessness in the face of the Immanent Will. And in this its entrapment by ideological forces is most clear: the typical lesson of the ideological is that things cannot be changed, that they should be left as they are and endured in that form. So that although the opening of 'The Convergence of the Twain' might seem to call for a change in human behaviour (avoid pride, cultivate humility), the dominating tenor of the poem's design on the reader is one which encourages passivity and acceptance of 'what is'. Indeed, the fact that the reader is left with the feeling that Hardy's poetic persona observes the blind and futile activities of doomed humans with a sort of ironic detachment leads to the conclusion that attempts to try to prevent such disasters are laughable.

As I have referred a number of times now to Hayden White, I should perhaps make one thing clear. It is possible to accept White's contention that the gathering together of a number of events to make a story does just that – it *makes* a story – without further accepting White's belief that there are no stories 'in reality', only those made by storytellers, after the event. I do believe that some stories are true, and that some are not. Put another way: I believe that there are processes of cause and effect in the world which can be utilized to construct stories about that world. (As Hardy's poem responds to an actual event we can for the time being postpone consideration of the complex issues raised by a consideration of fictional stories.) Let me give a relatively trivial example. Immediately after the *Titanic* sank there were conflicting accounts as to whether the ship broke in two before going under. A number of witnesses claimed that, at the very end, the ship broke into two pieces and that both were floating independently for a short while before disappearing. The British Board of Trade inquiry rejected such accounts, claiming rather that the crashing noise heard by survivors was that of boilers breaking free, and that the ship went down in one piece. Such an account conformed to the reports of other witnesses. When the sunken ship was eventually located, however, it was found to be in two pieces which were located so far apart that experts have reckoned that the ship must have broken in two at or near the surface. It now seems likely that the Board of Trade inquiry chose to believe accounts which would better testify to the strength of a British ship than those which might not: the inquiry could, after all, have concluded that there were conflicting reports and that it was impossible to decide between them. Whatever the case, since the discovery of the broken wreck we are in a stronger position to decide between the truth of such differing accounts. Unless we deem the reports of those who have actually gone down in pressurized containers to look at the wreck, and photographs of it, as 'texts', we can say that these varying stories are no longer to be treated as texts which can be distinguished only on aesthetic grounds. Some conform to non-textual facts better than others.

Marshall Everett's *Wreck and Sinking of the Titanic: The Ocean's Greatest Disaster* contains a chapter entitled 'The Two Titans' written by Fred S. Miller, which includes the following passage:

Against her had been set in motion a mass for a long time mounting, a century's stored-up aggregation of force, greater than any man-made thing as is infinity to one. It had expanded in the patience of great solitudes. On a Greenland summit, ages ago, avalanches of ice and snow collided, welded and then moved, inches in a year, an evolution that had naught to do with time. It was the true inevitable, gouging out a valley for its course, shouldering the precipices from its path. Finally the glacier reached the open Arctic, when a mile-in-width of it broke off and floated swinging free at last.

Does Providence directly govern everything that is? And did the Power who preordained the utmost second of each planet's journey, rouse up the mountain from its sleep of snow and send it down to drift, deliberately direct, into the exact moment in the sea of time, into the exact station in the sea of waters, where danced a gleaming speck – the tiny *Titanic* – to be touched and overborne? (Everett 1912, p14)

The final question is, like Hardy's poem, possessed of considerable subversive potential; the whole passage indicates that perhaps Hardy's response to the disaster was by no means unique, but rather that it fed off more than his own personal worries. Hardy's obsession with chance and accident is striking but it is not merely idiosyncratic: it is a natural concern in an age in which a belief that God foresees and ordains everything comes into conflict with a widespread secularism which assumes that certain events are purely fortuitous and can neither be predicted nor prevented. We can hazard that while the public debate which followed the loss of the *Titanic* was concerned on the surface to ask 'Who is responsible?', behind this question lay a more profound question: 'What does "responsibility" mean in an age of advanced technology and a less confident and all-embracing belief in God?' While Fred S. Miller stumbles around in the space opened up by such questions, Hardy's poem forces the reader through their complexities and their implications in a more uncompromising manner.

The question has been raised, however, whether Hardy's apparently uncompromising manner is not in fact morally compromised. Jerome J. McGann has, as we saw earlier, insisted on the importance of tracing the documentary history of a poem. Such a task clearly involves what we can call 'thick readings' of documentary evidence – that is, readings which remind us of the contexts which gave these documents their significance. 'The Convergence of the Twain' is not just a poem which Hardy happened to have written which was then published in the programme for the 'Dramatic and Operatic Matinée' held in aid of the Titanic Disaster Fund. A letter to written by Hardy to Florence Henniker and dated 22 May 1912 makes this quite clear:

If you should see the Fortnightly for June, which comes out next week, you will find some lines in it by me on the loss of the Titanic. I wrote them for the matinée in aid of the bereaved ones, & the editor asked me to let him have them. (Purdy and Millgate 1978, p216)

Hardy knew, then, that the first readers of his poem would be those who were present at the 'Dramatic and Operatic Matinée' held in aid of the

Titanic Disaster Fund on Tuesday 14 May 1912 – a month to the day after the *Titanic* struck the iceberg. Hardy's poem was not actually read aloud at the matinée – it forms part of the printed material in the booklet distributed at the matinée which is called a programme and which contains as its central section what we can term the literal programme (the list of actual events and performances). But it *is* the first item that would be encountered once the booklet was opened.

Emerson Brown Jr. draws particular attention to this fact, and comments that the bereaved who attended that matinée or otherwise obtained the programme could read of how opulence, vanity, and Pride of Life made the *Titanic* deserve the fate that befell her. They could also, he continues, read of the sea-worm crawling over the mirrors that once glassed their loved ones' opulence, and they could infer that their loved ones drowned as a result of their sinful attachment to the things of this world (1994, p239). Brown accordingly finds Hardy guilty of a self-indulgent pride in his 'detached and wickedly playful humor' (1994, p240), and he contrasts Hardy's alleged lack of compassion with the much greater respect accorded the dead and the bereaved in Joseph Conrad's two essays on the disaster. It is, Brown suggests, as if Browning had expressed his threnodic compassion for the Duchess of Ferrara by writing 'My Last Duchess' to be read at her memorial service, in the presence of her family, a month after her death (1994, p240), and he concludes with a comment on the relation between what Jerome J. McGann calls the *documentary* history of literary works and the reader's moral responsibility. 'If we are to be not only clever readers but morally responsible ones as well, on occasion we may have to inquire into the motives of writers and even to concern ourselves with the potential reactions of vulnerable members of their original or potential audience. Perhaps that is what good and wise readers have always done – and always will do' (1994, p243).

From this perspective a literary work carries with it a contextualizing relationship with the conditions of its first dissemination which is not just explanatory or illuminating, but also moral.

Brown's confrontation of the moral implications of Hardy's writing of 'The Convergence of the Twain' is a serious one, and needs to be considered carefully. As a first stage in such a consideration we should perhaps remember that the 'Dramatic and Operatic Matinée' was not so much a memorial event as a fund-raising event. Doubtless some of the bereaved did attend it, but even the items of performance were by no means exclusively solemn or sombre. *Ave Maria* was sung, but among the short performances given were some from *King Richard II*, *The Second Mrs Tanqueray*, *The Sunshine Girl*, and *Tosca*. So far as the printed but non-performed material in the programme is concerned, there were suitably solemn pieces such as 'The Heroic Dead' by Alfred Noyes and 'In Memoriam' by Stephen Phillips, but there are also lighter items, including a prose piece entitled 'The French Ideal of Love', by Mrs Belloc Lowndes. The general impression given is that while the poems were specially written for the event, the prose compositions were not. Moreover, Hardy's poem is not the only one which implies criticism of the impulses behind the building and launching of the *Titanic*; Stephen Phillips's 'In Memoriam' begins:

> Man said unto himself: 'Lo! I will build
> A stately palace to defy the deep,
> Vaster of any yet of man conceived.
> And I will furnish it with pomp of gold,
> Splendour of steel, and armoury of iron,
> With gardens, and with purple pleasure-domes,
> Arbours of bloom, and terraces, and streets;
> A city to outride the wildest storm,
> To whisper without wire o'er all the waves,
> And murmur messages from central seas,
> Making the foam her tame interpreter.
> Let Nature strike her, howso'er she will,
> With lightning, or with thunder, or with ice,
> I send her seaward, unassailable.'

It is true that the poem later praises the sterling behaviour of those who were lost, including the less than fully informative claim that 'The man of millions and the man of pence / Went down unmurmuring to an equal tomb'. But it also describes the ship's being launched by Man 'in his pride of heart' – not so very different from the 'Pride of Life' that planned Hardy's ship. Moreover, the echoes of Coleridge's 'Kubla Khan' certainly imply criticism of the despotic ambition which lay behind the ship's construction.

The *Times* report of the matinée (published the following day – 15 May) certainly does not in any way suggest that Hardy's poem was at all inappropriate to the occasion; indeed, Hardy's is the only one of the printed contributions from which the newspaper report includes a quotation – stanzas one and three of the poem. And these two stanzas are precisely those which contain the material to which Emerson Brown takes moral exception. Moreover, although the 'Dramatic and Operatic Matinée' at which Hardy's poem made its first public appearance was the most important event of this sort (it was attended by the king and queen), it was by no means the only one. Many West End plays were presented in special matinées for the purpose of raising money for the disaster fund, and many of these were 'light' rather than 'serious'. It is clear that such fund-raising events were by no means aimed specifically at the bereaved.

Brown's argument is a serious one and demands careful consideration. But the evidence suggests that 'The Convergence of the Twain' was not generally understood to have offended or dismayed those who attended the memorial matinée. Brown seems to have underestimated the extent to which denouncements of the trappings of luxury and opulence were accepted as conventional in funereal or obituary circumstances in Edwardian England. Even Hardy's mention of 'the sea-worm crawling over the mirrors that once glassed their loved ones' opulence' (Brown 1994, p239) may have been taken as an appropriately marine adaptation of those standard graveyard references to the decay of the body which in the Christian tradition were frequently linked to hopes for the survival of the soul.

I think, however, that there may be more complex processes going on here. There is always a morbid aspect to the human fascination with disasters. Robert Ballard, leader of the expedition which located the sunken wreck of the ship, reported that the question most frequently asked him after the ship had been found was whether human remains had been seen in the wreck (they had not). It is as if a blow to the pride of humanity (nature humbles us and deposits the wreck where we cannot even see it) has to be erased by a demonstration of our ability to conquer nature and, by observing their remains, to demonstrate our superiority to those who perished. The obsession with 'raising the *Titanic*' started soon after its loss, culminated with the film *Raise the Titanic!*, and – once it was clear that the shattered wreck could not be salvaged – was then transformed into alternative forms of mastery: filming it, building replicas of it, and so on.

Those critics who have commented on the fact that in Hardy's poem the encounter between iceberg and ship is, among other things, a sexual one, need to add to this the perception that the woman is now a corpse voyeuristically observed by poet and reader. 'The Convergence of the Twain' and *Tess of the D'Urbervilles* have, then, this in common: both culminate in woman suffering the punishment of death. Thus although some of Emerson Brown's criticisms of Hardy and his poem seem to me to miss the mark, I would want to add that Hardy's description of the 'stilly couched' ship/woman, and the mirrors which, instead of glassing the opulent are covered by crawling sea worms, 'grotesque, slimed, dumb, indifferent' (a line crying out for Freudian response, surely), both seem to involve masculine attempts to regain a psychological mastery through a symbolic soiling and humiliation of the female.

In this context it is important to remember that the ship was on its *maiden* voyage, a voyage which was never completed. Hardy's stilly couching wreck, then, is both the product of a consummated but lethal sexual encounter, and also dead virgin, displaying the fate of the female who prefers to have her sensual mind ravished by jewels instead of her body enjoyed by man. The dead ship is punished for her virginity much as Tess is punished for her loss of it: the two cases may seem different, but both ship and woman are seen to merit the punishment they receive because both deny man complete sexual ownership of the desired female. Rape is often accompanied by deliberate extra humiliation and soiling of the victim, both of which appear to add to the perpetrator's sense of possession and power. And the male reader, too, when he reads Hardy's poem is invited to *enjoy*: the ship/woman *deserved it*; look at her now.

These are strategic moves that relate to deeper ideological fissures than those which arise from the faultlines of late Edwardian society. While Hardy's poem engages with such faultlines through deflection (if the disaster is a result of a general Pride of Life then it cannot be blamed on the Edwardian rich in particular), it engages with more long-lasting, permanently self-transforming rifts relating to gender divisions in a concealed but nonetheless traceable manner. The ills that flow from sexual desire have to be revenged through humiliation of the female. Tess has to die, the *Titanic* has to be destroyed and ravaged by the phallic sea worm. 'The Convergence of the Twain' is more than just an occasional poem because although it engages with the ideological stress-points of its time it also takes sides in a much longer-lived struggle to punish women for the pains that men believe are brought to them by sexuality itself. Eve is still guilty and has to be expelled from Paradise and sentenced to death.

Before leaving Hardy it is instructive to look briefly at some lines from a much lesser poem about the *Titanic*. 'Titanic's Knell', by Henry Brenner (1932), is a long narrative poem which recounts the persona's imagined return to the wreck of the ship in the company of Columbus. Brenner's poem is not at all good, but in it we can see more clearly than in 'The Convergence of the Twain' the way in which the disaster continued to be used as an occasion for attacking and punishing women. Brenner's wrecked *Titanic* is described as a 'mangled mistress', clutched in the icy arms of another Titan – the sea. Before her voyage the ship is pictured again as a mistress, 'In all her pride / And self-complacency'. And when the narrator reaches her wreck he observes with Columbus a sight which makes the latter exclaim:

> 'Man hugs the very things
>   That strangle him.'
> For there a woman,
>   With her costly clothes
>   Half rotting on her bones,
>   Lay on the floor.
> Around her were her jewels;
>   In her hand
>   She clasped a diamond Brooch,
> While on her wrists
>   Were studded bands
>   That might have long ago
>   Paid off the debts of poor men!

> (1932, p44)

Bad though this is, it bears witness to that same complex of meanings which can be exposed in Hardy's poem: female pride and love of luxury bring a deserved death and disfigurement to woman. Punishment for the pride that sinks the *Titanic* is displaced on to the female. And although the overt meaning of the couplet attributed to Columbus is that human beings are destroyed by their love of wealth, the use of 'Man' opens up the suggestion that it is men who are strangled by the succubus-like woman they are driven to embrace. We can note that it is the debts of poor *men* which could be paid off by women's finery.

Hardy's poem is immeasurably more sophisticated than this; its contra-dictory impulses are held in a productive tension which never degenerates to the crude assertions of Brenner's poem. Nevertheless, as an emplotment of the disaster – which it undoubtedly is – 'The Convergence of the Twain' allows for readings which slide into accusations of a female guilt which is punished by female destruction. That this emplotment is not, as it is in Brenner's poem, overt, makes it more rather than less effective.

III
Sinking with England
Noël Coward's Cavalcade

Cavalcade was first performed in London immediately after the Stock Market crash and at a time of great national and international turmoil and uncertainty, and it was a smash hit. Clive Fisher's biography of Coward notes that it 'kept nearly four thousand people employed in the dark days of 1931, and over a year took £300,000 at the box-office' (1992, p107). Coward's use of the doomed *Titanic* as one of the play's settings shows clearly how much the ship and its fate had become associated with a particular complex of ideological meanings, but it also demonstrates how the disaster continued to be used to bolster particular ideological forces. It still constituted a potent pool of ideological capital in 1931.

Cavalcade traces a process of decline from order to chaos, peace to unrest, social stability to cultural disequilibrium, national purpose to national *anomie* and loss of bearings. Its characters appear in scenes which stretch from New Year's Eve 1899 to an unspecified evening in 1930, and it follows their fates through the thirty years that the play covers. While at the start of the play we find a united household composed of a happy family and servants who know and accept their place, the final scene of the play takes place in a nightclub in which one of the characters – the daughter of the servants introduced at the opening of the play, who has become a successful entertainer and has thus risen socially – sings a bitter song entitled 'Twentieth Century Blues'. The decline and fragmentation which are traced are associated with social change and class mobility, although the play leaves its audience to decide whether these are the causes or just the products of decline. Also associated with the general process of fragmentation and loss of purpose is war: the middle-class family introduced at the start of the play consists of two parents and two sons; by the end of the play both sons are dead – one killed in the war and one a victim of the *Titanic* disaster. The loss of the *Titanic* is thus clearly identified as a staging-post in the social and cultural decline of England (so-named: the national history depicted is narrower than that which would have been obtained by substituting Britain for England).

It is noteworthy that a sense of loss is expressed by characters from both sides of the social divide in the play; in the first scene of Part II of the play, in which the bourgeois wife is visiting her ex-servants the Bridges – now married and operating a pub – the two wives from different social strata express their shared sense that the world has altered in such a way as to make it clear that, for them, the change has been for the worse rather than for the better. By Part II, scene 10, which is set at the end of the First World War, the same two characters meet and express the same feeling rather more overtly. The ex-servant Ellen's daughter Fanny – the entertainer – is now having an affair with her ex-employer's son:

> ELLEN: I suppose you imagine my daughter isn't good enough to marry your son; if that's the case I can assure you you're very much mistaken. Fanny's received everywhere; she knows all the best people.
> JANE: How nice for her; I wish I did.
> ELLEN: Things aren't what they used to be, you know – it's all changing.
> JANE: Yes, I see it is.
> ELLEN: Fanny's at the top of the tree now; she's having the most wonderful offers.
> JANE: Oh, Ellen!
> ELLEN: What is it?
> JANE: I'm so very, very sorry.
> ELLEN: I don't know what you mean.
> JANE: Yes, you do – inside, you must. Something seems to have gone out of all of us, and I'm not sure I like what's left. Good-bye, Ellen.
> (Coward 1933, p121)

The scene ends with the news that the errant son has been killed in the war.

The nostalgia is one-sided and ideologically charged. The history of the first thirty years of the present century is presented in such a manner as to suggest that it has involved changes which have been uniformly for the worse: even the lower orders have experienced significant losses without appreciable gains. The close of the play attempts unambiguously to enlist a dormant nationalism to reverse the processes which have led to this sorry state of affairs. The audience is presented with a series of 'visions': of the nightclub singer Fanny, of dancers dancing 'without any apparent enjoyment', of six '"incurables" in blue hospital uniform', of Jane and Robert standing with glasses of champagne held aloft (representing the older generation tenaciously hanging on to outmoded values), of Ellen sitting in front of a radio loudspeaker, and of another character – Margaret – dancing with an ominously young man. The final stage directions end as follows:

> *The visions are repeated quicker and quicker, while across the darkness runs a Riley light sign spelling out news. Noise grows louder and louder. Steam rivets, loud speakers, jazz bands, aeroplane propellers, etc., until the general effect is complete chaos.*
> *Suddenly it all fades into darkness and silence and away at the back a Union Jack glows through the blackness.*
> *The lights slowly come up and the whole stage is composed of massive tiers, upon which stand the entire Company. The Union Jack flies over their heads as they sing 'God Save the King.'* (1933, pp138–9)

The list of elements which comprise the 'complete chaos' is interesting: 'steam rivets, loud speakers, jazz bands, aeroplane propellers, etc.'. Industrialism and technological advance are associated with an alien music form (the jazz bands are doubtless linked to the use of a blues song in the final scene) which has replaced English music hall songs such as, no doubt, 'The Girls of the C. I. V.' – sung in an earlier scene set in 1900.

The *Titanic* disaster fits perfectly into such a polemic: Coward is able to plug in to the ship's accumulated symbolic status as a doomed time-capsule, a microcosm of that ordered world that was heading for disaster and disintegration. At the same time, in contrast to other mythic versions, the ship is not seen to be a culpable part of the cause of the process of disintegration which is being traced. Whereas in some versions the *Titanic* represents technology, size and unfounded complacency, in *Cavalcade* it represents Eden before the serpents of war and class mobility had slithered over the wall. And I think that in the case of *Cavalcade* we have a clear example of the transformation of the disaster into myth (a myth which complements rather than replaces the ideological use made of the event). It will be recalled that earlier I referred to Barthes's suggestion that the notion of myth allowed for the uncovering of 'the ideological abuse' hidden 'in the display of *what goes without saying*' (1973, p11). In *Cavalcade*, as we will see, there is no sense that the *Titanic* represents anything controversial: the controversy centres upon England's decline subsequent to its loss. Coward appeals to an apparently shared understanding of what the *Titanic* disaster represented – what it *means*. Within these meanings it is clear that ideology is at work, but it is at work in a concealed way, through an appeal to a presumed common knowledge. The fact that at no point in the '*Titanic* scene' of *Cavalcade* is any statement made of what the ship and its fate represent is important: the audience is led to feel that what it already *knows* is being brought into play. As we will see later on, this is by no means true of all literary uses of the disaster.

The audience is not made immediately aware that Part II, scene 5 is taking place on the *Titanic*, although the setting on 'the deck of an Atlantic liner' and the time: 'About 7 p.m. Sunday, April 14th, 1912' may well have given the game away to many. This information is conveyed dramatically at the end of the scene, when a cloak covering a lifeboat is withdrawn to reveal the inscription 'S. S. Titanic'. The shock effect is fixed and magnified by a fade-out of the lights, which leaves the inscription glowing while the orchestra plays 'very softly and tragically', 'Nearer, My God, to Thee'. (By 1930 it was by no means universally accepted that the ship's orchestra had been playing this hymn at the end: presumably either Coward did not know this, or he could not resist the tug at the heart-strings afforded him by an appropriation of the established mythic version. Most commentators now believe that the final tune played was 'Autumn', although survivor Eva Hart, whose credibility is buttressed by the fact that for many years she also claimed to have witnessed the ship break in half, in a recent television interview was still maintaining that it *was* 'Nearer, My God, to Thee'.)

The only characters present are the newly married Edward Marryot (son of Jane and Robert Marryot) and Edith *née* Harris (daughter of the Margaret who ends the play dancing with the suspiciously young man). For those who have guessed what the setting is, their conversation is suitably infused with dramatic irony:

> EDITH: Wouldn't it be awful if a magician came to us and said: 'Unless you count accurately every single fish in the Atlantic you die to-night?'
> EDWARD: We should die to-night.
> EDITH: How much would you mind – dying, I mean?
> EDWARD: I don't know really – a good deal, I expect.
> EDITH: I don't believe I should mind so very much now. You see, we could never in our whole lives be happier than we are now, could we?
> (1933, p93)

Given the representative nature of the characters in *Cavalcade*, such an exchange has a rather chilling subtext which it is not too hard to isolate: it would have been better had England disappeared in 1912, as it will never again be as happy as it was then. The point is repeated a few lines later (the entire scene comprises only forty-five lines of dialogue), when Edith predicts that their love will wear off with time and Edward will tire of her. When he denies that this will happen she insists, 'Yes, you will one day. You're bound to; people always do. This complete loveliness that we feel together now will fade, so many years and the gilt wears off the ginger-bread, and just the same as the stewards, we shall have forgotten what it was like'. Edward counters that his father and mother are perfectly happy and contented, and always have been – but Edith has her explanation for this. 'They had a better chance at the beginning. Things weren't changing so swiftly; life wasn't so restless.'

There is a curious sense in which Coward's use of the *Titanic* in *Cavalcade* matches with Hardy's in 'The Convergence of the Twain'. If Hardy's poem associates the welding/wedding of iceberg and ship with (among other things) the sexual act, Coward's scene leads us to see the passengers on the doomed ship as about to die at a moment of un-repeatable bliss. The audience is invited to wonder whether perhaps the lucky ones were those that did not get into the lifeboats and who in true Keatsian fashion ceased upon the midnight (or 2 a.m.) with only about thirty minutes of pain as they froze to death.

The reactionary nature of such morbid nostalgia is not significantly qualified by the implied criticisms of war in *Cavalcade*. And the nostalgia performs the function of inverting certain facts about the *Titanic*, which is now seen as a sort of pinnacle of national perfection threatened by external forces, rather than as a tragic disaster which exposed the cultural and national weaknesses which it encapsulated and which brought it about. The disaster thus falls into a long catalogue of British ideological recuperations: disasters are somehow turned on their heads and made into evidence of the sterling stuff of which the English or the British are composed.

For a person of my nationality and generation it is extremely hard to experience Coward other than through the lens of a couple of decades of parody. Growing up in England in the 1950s and 1960s I must have heard innumerable parodies of Coward on such radio programmes as *The Goon Show* and *Beyond Our Ken* (later *Round the Horne*) before I was really aware what they were actually parodying. (Tony Hancock also has a wonderful short parody in a TV *Hancock's Half Hour* in the 1960s.) By the 1950s there was I think a genuine popular understanding of the reactionary ideology underlying such scenes that fed this desire to parody. And it is precisely that sort of stiff upper lip, clipped and hopelessly theatrical dialogue between man and woman such as we meet with in this scene that formed the standard basis for such institutionalized parodies. If a play such as *Cavalcade* seeks to condemn the march of history, history by the time of my own childhood had got its own back. And much the same is true of the *Titanic*. Precisely because of the appropriation of the disaster by a sort of reactionary-nostalgic romanticism, by the 1950s one is certainly able to witness a use of reference to the disaster to mock. Such conscriptions of the myth to a debunking impulse were able to build naturally on many of those original associations which the disaster had but which are ignored by Coward: pride and complacency, inexcusable and rigid class distinction, a greater concern for profit than for the lives of passengers, a wallowing in excessive luxury, and a blindness in the face of a well-advertised approaching danger.

It is just possible, however, that it is Coward who has the last laugh. In his biography of Coward, Clive Fisher notes that 'many of the friends [Coward] had known before fame were convinced that he had written *Cavalcade* as a joke, to mock British patriotism and the Empire spirit' (1992, p110). Fisher notes that Coward inscribed the copy of *Cavalcade* which he sent to Esme Wynne-Tyson after the play's success was assured, 'With love from a National Hero', which, Fisher remarks, 'has a facetious ring to it'. And he further cites a remark by Lyndon Wynne-Tyson to his son: 'Noël wrote *Cavalcade* with his tongue in his cheek as a send-up of the British Empire. He was as surprised as anyone when the public, perhaps influenced by the General Strike atmosphere, took it literally' (1992, p267, n9). Fisher also discusses the fact that *Cavalcade*'s celebration of the Empire has been found by some to stand in sharp contrast to the overt pacifism of a near-contemporary play of Coward's – *Post-Mortem*. Such commentators have suggested that Coward's real views were represented by *Post-Mortem*, while *Cavalcade* was a tongue-in-cheek performance which Coward pretended to take seriously once he saw how seriously it was taken by (such large) audiences.

Given what I have said about the vein of anti-militarism running through *Cavalcade* it will be understood that I find such arguments less than fully convincing. But I do think that Coward was a person who distanced himself from most things, and that while celebrating an imagined Edwardian or late-Victorian golden age he was also, and at the same time, capable of maintaining an attitude of detached semi-mockery towards that which he was celebrating. *The Goon Show*'s parodies of Coward may indeed have been building on Coward's habit of mixing a dash of arch scorn into even the most ostensibly reverently treated subjects. Clive Fisher has much of interest to say about the domination of Coward's life by dissembling and adopted personae: he never admitted his own homosexuality publicly until very late in his life, and disguised it behind an assumed rôle of caddish womanizer. Given that homosexuality was illegal in Britain during most of his life he can hardly be blamed for this, but being forced to maintain such a distance from the values of 'society', it is quite possible too that he found a ludicrous element in the way in which the *Titanic* disaster was turned into an enormous celebration of British national pride. Those conversations *The Goon Show* loved to parody and of which the *Titanic* scene in *Cavalcade* is an epitome may be as much tart commentaries on heterosexual romance as they are celebrations of it.

The sinking of the *Titanic* is now firmly established as one of a number of national disasters by means of which the English (or apologists for the English ruling class) have attempted to define their nationhood. The *Beyond the Fringe* parody of stiff-upper-lip Britishness has a wonderful line in which a real Second World War BBC announcer is mimicked with the words, 'This is the BBC Home Service and here is Alvar Liddell bringing you news of fresh disasters'. The Charge of the Light Brigade, Scott's expedition, the *Titanic*, the Dunkirk evacuation – all have been recruited to testify to and inculcate the ability to lose well. Losing well was clearly something which was increasingly at a premium for a ruling class facing class division at home, competition abroad from Europe and America, and growing national liberation movements in the Empire. Wynne-Tyson's mention of the General Strike is apposite – and as I have already mentioned, *Cavalcade* was first produced in 1931, very soon after the Stock Market crash of 1929. In an important sense, Coward's own views and attitudes are of secondary importance. He may indeed have had an at least partly parodic and debunking aim in writing the play. But if that is the case, the play was soon co-opted and appropriated by a dominant ideology that needed a celebration of the Empire, of Englishness, and of the message that being able to fail greatly and gloriously testified to national character, national unity and an underlying national strength. A man with Coward's perceptive detachment – which allowed him to isolate the components of the national myth – and chameleon-like ability to adopt the rôles which the dominant ideology needed was just what a battered British ruling class required in 1931.

If we think back to Shaw and Conrad we may perhaps appreciate how important their non-English origins are to a full understanding of their response to the *Titanic* disaster. Take just one sentence from the second of Conrad's essays on the disaster: 'But I, who am not a sentimentalist, think it would have been finer if the band of the *Titanic* had been quietly saved, instead of being drowned while playing – whatever tune they were playing, the poor devils' (1921b, p334). This is a statement that certainly does not play the accepted ideological game. There is a humanism here that could never be appropriated the way *Cavalcade* was appropriated in the interests of a dominant ideology. And that tells us something of the moral worth of, respectively, Conrad's essay and Coward's play. It also adds weight to my argument that humanism is not necessarily a disguised version of the dominant ideology, but may indeed represent powerful impulses that are deeply threatening to ruling-class ideas.

However distanced Coward was from the celebratory aspects of his play, two facts are crystal clear. First, that he offered no objection to the way in which the play was used to buttress an uncritically laudatory view of a constructed 'Victorianism', and second, that his play – unlike Conrad's essay – *could* be co-opted to the service of such an ideological construction. Fisher reports that shortly after its opening night, the entire British royal family attended a performance of *Cavalcade* and, as he notes, 'in so doing appeared to sanction the play's conservatism' (1992, p109). Given that so far as the royal family of 1931 was concerned, no distinction was allowed to be drawn between appearance and reality (unlike the home life of our own dear royals), we can say that their attendance at the performance did not just *appear* to sanction the play's conservatism – it *did* sanction it. We need to remember that Hardy's poem was first published in a programme for an event at which the then king and queen were in attendance.

Having said all this I am still left with the nagging feeling that *Cavalcade* does contain a subversive potential within its text. If so, of course it is a potential that was not at all realized in its early performances. Much as Coward and his work were appropriated by the British ruling class, his inability honestly to express and bear witness to his own sexuality seems to have made it impossible for him wholeheartedly to embrace the ideology for which he became a salesman. And this element of reservation, I suspect, explains that theatricality and artificiality that carries with it a less than complete identification with the message that *Cavalcade* was used to endorse – a distance that has subversive potential. I am thus left with a strong suspicion that the Noël Coward who survived in the parodies of the 1950s may already have been there in embryo in the 1930s.

IV
The Voyage Continues

As the *Titanic*'s physical voyage came to an end on the bottom of the Atlantic, its cultural and literary voyage – one that would last much longer, but which would also reach no final port – was only just beginning. Bruce Jackson's account of the African-American '*Titanic* toasts' includes the claim that the sinking of the *Titanic* on 14 April 1912, produced several million words of prose, several motion pictures, a few songs – and one poem (1974, p35). In fact, in addition to the films and songs, it produced several poems, several novels,[28] at least one full-length play and an extended scene in Noël Coward's review *Cavalcade*.

Many of these works are of limited interest. Robert Prechtl's *Titanic: A Novel* (1938) is constructed around an ingenious plot twist which has John Jacob Astor attempting to gain financial control of the White Star Line during the voyage. To resist this Bruce Ismay forces the captain to increase the ship's speed, believing that if it wins the Blue Riband for the fastest transatlantic crossing then White Star shares will rise and the takeover will be prevented.[29] As a number of commentators have noted, Prechtl's national origins are displayed in a scene at which a White Star director declares that the Germans must be destroyed just as the British destroyed the Spanish Armada and the Dutch and French fleets – 'Otherwise the Germans will beat us all along the line' (1938, p176). And when it seems possible that the first ship to reach the sinking *Titanic* will be the *Frankfurt*, the unlikely response is: 'Damn it, it is too bad that a German ship should have to rescue the *Titanic*' (1938, p271). Bearing this in mind along with the fact that the novel was first published as *Titanensturz* in 1937 in Vienna and Leipzig, it is surprising that the novel's preface refers to the way in which the Dreyfus case 'stirred the minds of all civilized people in a manner far exceeding its seeming importance' (1938, p9), and that the novel includes a non-partisan discussion of Zionism and a very sympathetic portrayal of the Strauses, who are portrayed waiting for death reciting from the Old Testament. (The author's real name was Robert Friedländer – Prechtl was a pseudonym – and it seems possible that he was himself Jewish and needed the protection of a pseudonym after the rise to power of Hitler.)

I suppose that if we had to explain why Hardy's 'The Convergence of the Twain' continues to live while Prechtl's novel enjoys only a curiosity interest today, we would have to begin by noting that the complex tensions in Hardy's poem go on challenging readers both morally and intellectually, while Prechtl's novel contains nothing to force the reader to confront his or her preconceptions. Although it has its defenders, especially in his native Canada, I feel that a similar objection can be made to E. J. Pratt's epic poem 'The Titanic', which Pratt finished in 1935. Like Hardy's poem, Pratt's traces the birth and voyage of both ship and iceberg up to their fatal collision, but unlike Hardy their convergence does not lead to any

---

[28] There is an interesting Norwegian novel: *Salme ved Reisens Slutt* (*The Hymn at the End of the Journey*) by Erik Fosnes Hansen (1990). Hansen's novel traces the lives of the *Titanic*'s (fictional) musicians, and seems to present them as representatives of a doomed culture or set of cultures. The American Harry Chapin's song 'Dance Band on the Titanic' (included on the 1977 Elektra album of the same name) also adopts the perspective of one of the musicians, and includes a number of standard mythic elements: 'Even God couldn't sink this ship', 'Nearer, my God, to Thee', and so on. The song strongly suggests that many in 1977 are also, metaphorically, members of the dance band on the *Titanic*. The *Titanic* today is a myth which, like a cup, can be filled with almost anything which the mythologizer wishes to suggest is doomed.

[29] Robert Serling's *Something's Alive on the Titanic* also has Ismay responsible for persuading the captain to attempt to set a new transatlantic speed record (1993, p306).

profound inquiry into the meaning of a historical event as spectacular as the sinking of the *Titanic*. Pratt's lines attempt to involve the reader in the complacency behind the ship's vulnerability, but the effect is curiously flat:

> No wave could sweep those upper decks – unthinkable!
> No storm could hurt that hull – the papers said so.
> The perfect ship at last – the first unsinkable,
> Proved in advance – had not the folders read so?
>
> (Djwa and Moyles 1989, p303)

While the thrust of such lines is clearly intended to inculpate Edwardian complacency, there is an important sense in which they rather incriminate a complacency on the part of the poet himself. As with much popular realism the reader is left uninvolved, a detached observer enjoying the obscurity of the auditorium while the players are subjected to all sorts of moral inquisitions. This aspect of Pratt's poem seems to me to stand in very sharp contrast to the probing self-scrutiny that we find in a work such as Hans Magnus Enzensberger's 'The Sinking of the Titanic', about which I will have much more to say below.

Pratt's use of dialogue also leaves much to be desired, especially when the constraints of his chosen verse-form create more bathos than pathos:

> 'Twas a lucky streak
> That at Southampton dock he didn't lose her,
> And the *Olympic* had a narrow squeak
> Some months before rammed by the British Cruiser,
> The *Hawke*.
>
> (1989, p312)

Like Jean-Pierre Ronfard's much later play *Le Titanic*, Pratt's poem attempts to make pointed use of a game of chance on the ship. According to Heinz Tschachler, Pratt's aim here is to equate the motives behind the building of the ship with those of the gambler (1989, p97). Of this we can perhaps remark that, like Ronfard's use of a game resembling roulette, which is won by Adolf Hitler, the point seems forced and mechanical – and perhaps a little unconvincing. Of all the many things that the *Titanic* and its loss have been taken to symbolize, gambling seems one of the less illuminating.

Most of all, however, I have the feeling that Pratt's poem exposes the limits of a particular sort of realism – of a belief that a coherent linear narrative (an emplotment of a classic sort) can help us to display the significance that the disaster had, has, and can have. It also suggests that the epic is not the most appropriate genre through which to explore the reverberations of the disaster. The example of our next text may perhaps offer some confirmation of both of these hypotheses.

V
Geoffrey Hill, 'Ode on the Loss of the "Titanic"'

Geoffrey Hill's 'Ode on the Loss of the "Titanic"' is the fifth poem in the sequence of six which together make up 'Of Commerce and Society', a sequence subtitled 'Variations on a Theme'. 'Of Commerce and Society' is one of Hill's earlier works, published in his first book-length collection, *For the Unfallen: Poems*. The ode's place in this sequence has a clear defining force: the loss of the *Titanic*, the reader can expect, will be set in the context of a culture in which commercial considerations leach into other parts of the body politic. As Vincent Sherry has expressed it, in 'Of Commerce and Society' 'Hill traces the consequences, in history as well as in art, of the view of society as an outgrowth of commerce'. 'View' is perhaps a little timid: Hill's sequence traces the actual insinuation of the commercial into the lifeblood of society and its manifestations in a range of events and institutions. For Sherry, the whole sequence is a sustained attack on the 'middle-class faith in material progress, and the whole romantic-humanist creed of material perfectibilism', a myth towards which, according to Sherry, Hill had already shown his antipathy (1987, p64). As Sherry's comments suggest, and as study of the 'Ode on the Loss of the "Titanic"' will, I think, demonstrate, the context of 'Of Commerce and Society' liberates some of the traditional meanings of the *Titanic* disaster from their safe confinement within the Edwardian era and allows them to prowl around European history in a more threatening and challenging manner. There is a sense in which there is a cultural materialist dimension to Hill's poem, inasmuch as it utilizes the way in which the disaster reflects upon Edwardian society to offer an indirect comment on the poet's time.

I hope that it is not just my own interests that lead me to see the Hill that Sherry's comments present us with as a very Conradian figure: one deeply sceptical of the belief that the free play of 'material interests' will lead to a better life for those with whom these interests play. Such a free play, along with a belief in its power to enrich human life, the ode suggests, corrupts as absolutely as does the silver in *Nostromo*. In Conrad's novel, material interests interpose themselves between human plans and their fulfilment, acting like a prism to deflect and distort the trajectory of human designs and conceptions so that what people get is very different from what they have schemed to achieve.

'Commerce', we need to remember, can have a more general meaning than 'trade'; it can be used to denote a range of processes of exchange and interaction – including those in which the poet deals. *For the Unfallen* manifests a comparable concern with chains of mediation, and especially with the unpredictability of their results; like *Nostromo* it contains much deliberation on the sometimes seemingly random nature of causes and effects, results and retribution. Many of the poems in the collection are concerned with how those spared by fate respond to the sufferings of those not so lucky: 'The Distant Fury of Battle' – one of the most powerful poems in the collection – sums up in its title this representative modern experience, that of being made aware of extreme suffering taking place at a distance from the (so far) safe observer. In such circumstances pity or charity can easily merge into voyeurism or *Schadenfreude*, and 'Of Commerce and Society' circles around the problems which attend the observation and the depiction of a suffering which is not one's own – the poet's own trading in suffering.

> *Ode on the Loss of the 'Titanic'*
>
> Thriving against façades the ignorant sea
> Souses our public baths, statues, waste ground:
> Archaic earth-shaker, fresh enemy
> ('The tables of exchange being overturned');
>
> Drowns Babel in upheaval and display;
> Unswerving, as were the admired multitudes
> Silenced from time to time under its sway.
> By all means let us appease the terse gods.

(I quote the text as published in Hill [1985]; in the earlier version in Hill [1959] the third line ends with a colon.) According to Henry Hart,

> In 'Of Commerce and Society', the sea of turbid words and drowned bodies is Conrad's 'destructive element', into which Hill's poet, like Marlow, must dive. Hill also associates the sea with Hardy's 'Immanent Will', as depicted in 'Lines on the Loss of the Titanic.' (1986, p78)

It seems, however, hard to equate Hill's *'ignorant* sea' with Hardy's 'Immanent Will'; despite its allusion to various deities, Hill's poem offers a more uncompromisingly secular view of natural forces than does 'The Convergence of the Twain': the variety of absolute powers invoked has a similar effect to that obtained by Hardy's catholic yoking together in one poem of Immanent Will, Pride of Life, Spinner of Years, and (by implication) Christ. Rather than underwriting a particular religious or secular interpretation of the disaster's significance, the ode presents its trinity of supreme powers as representative of the need for a regular appeasement of the terse gods – by whatever name. Hart's invocation of Conrad seems more to the point here, although in the passage in *Lord Jim* to which Hart is alluding the trader Stein countenances *submission* to that destructive element into which man falls at his birth: diving is hardly an option. Stein's destructive element, moreover, is used as a metaphor for life in general; when Conrad wanted to refer to the physical sea he referred in terms that certainly do have something in common with Hill's 'ignorant sea'.

The 'façades' against which Hill's ignorant sea thrives are, we presume, both material and metaphorical, both the thin bulkheads of the *Titanic* and also the fragile conventions by which a society conceals from itself its dependence upon the good will of the elements. When the *Titanic* went down, both were breached. Vincent Sherry sees Hill's *Titanic* as 'an emblem of a shapeless, haute-bourgeois culture' (1987, p67), but it should be noted that the poem refers to 'our' and 'us'; while it draws on many of the conventional associations of the *Titanic* – including those of Edwardian self-complacency and class division – it also depicts the ship as a representative of the human willingness to shelter behind inadequate façades of many different sorts. Indeed, the poem's reference is both of a specific and a more generalized nature: the *Titanic* had a swimming pool and was furnished with statues, but the sudden shift to 'waste ground' broadens the scope of the opening lines. 'Babel' doubtless takes in both those problems caused during the sinking when many non-English-speaking passengers, particularly in steerage, were unable to understand what was going on. But on another level it gestures towards the sin of pride of those who thought that, like the constructors of the tower of Babel, they could build a ship which, in the words of the myth, God himself could not sink. And thus the reference beams out to illuminate and condemn all who believe that technology can offer them a total protection against the ignorant sea or the terse gods – blind natural forces or chance and accident. The *Titanic* suffers a literal 'upheaval', its stern raised high in the air before the final plunge, but the upheaval which drowns Babel is also a more generic one; the upheaval which awaits, eventually, all attempts to use commerce and technology to deny the power of the elements.

'Babel' has other associations. A comment in an essay by Hill on the poetry of Allen Tate suggests that he associated the *Titanic* with a particular sort of linguistic misuse. According to Henry Hart,

> The sinking of the *Titanic* in 1912 fits into the poet's scheme not simply because it involves a misuse of language, but because it provides an adequate symbol for the relations between Europe and America during the modernist era. The *Titanic* is Hill's symbolic boat that ferries the political and poetic spirit across the Atlantic. He reveals some of its significance in his essay on Allen Tate when he discusses a century in which
>
> > reality becomes the incestuous possession of a dedicated few; while millions are deployed for war or profit by the crassest of political jargonings. Was not the 'Titanic' disaster partly the result of rhetoric? A sinkable ship was called 'Unsinkable'; and the realists and practical men, who are always the blindest dreamers of this world, were swamped by a slogan. And the innocent, as always, died too. No poet would dream of booking a passage on an unsinkable ship!
>
> Hill's poem records not the arduous redemption of 'fatted marble' by poets but the holocaust of both language and bodies by political demagogues. Babel is toppled and the politicians' babbling tongues are let loose over the world. Hill takes arms against a sea of rhetoric in a magnificent rhetorical display of his own . . . (1986, p77; the quotation is from Hill 1958, pp8–9)

Whereas Hardy's 'The Convergence of the Twain' ends with a sense of closure underlined by the potent word 'consummation', Hill's ode ends with a hesitation between sacrificial eagerness and indifference: 'By all means' straddles both 'by every means possible' and an unenthusiastic 'if you wish'. The ambiguity acknowledges both the indifference of the terse gods and also the fact that sacrifices such as that of the *Titanic* do at least have the effect of reminding us how thin and insubstantial are our façades.

As Hart points out, the ode makes reference to 'Poseidon, the earth shaker, Christ, the cleanser of temples, and Jehovah, the destroyer of linguistic towers' (1986, pp77–8). As the *Titanic* sank tables were, literally, overturned (although it appears that the pursers were able to return valuables to many passengers before this happened). But the loss of the ship overturned metaphorical as well as literal tables: it plunged the stock market into gloom and struck a blow at the White Star Line from which it never recovered. And as it led to the iceberg patrol and revision of Board of Trade safety regulations, it was perhaps an appeasement of the terse gods which – whether the gods responded or not – was of some effect.

Written and published in the Britain of the 1950s, Hill's 'Ode on the Loss of the "Titanic"' shows a major poet defamiliarizing an event which has attained a mythical status: taking it out of its cosy sequestration in a mythical past and opening up its significance for the present, for perhaps all presents. It achieves this not through an ideological sleight-of-hand which, by generalizing the causes of the disaster releases those responsible for it from blame, but by showing how the responsibility in question was not merely that of a set of individuals but also of a set of values, the values of a commerce-corrupted society able so effectively to lie to itself that it needed the 'appeasement' of the disaster to be brought to some limited awareness of what lay beyond its own façades. And to the extent that there is an ethical continuity from that society to our own, the poem regretfully indicates the continued need for such periodic appeasements. When British Prime Minister Harold Macmillan told his electorate, 'You've never had it so good', he was uttering a sentiment that would have been recognized by the Britain that launched the *Titanic*. In the 1950s the sea was still a 'fresh enemy' that demanded a respect which could still only be guaranteed by periodic drownings. The tower that Macmillan was confidently building towards the sky has long since tumbled, but new ones are always under construction.

VI
A Modernist *Titanic*

While Geoffrey Hill's 'Ode on the Loss of the "Titanic"' consists of two four-line stanzas, Hans Magnus Enzensberger's 'The Sinking of the Titanic' contains thirty-three cantos,[30] and makes up a book of about a hundred pages in its English translation. (The translation is by the poet himself.) The poem is a remarkable meditation on a series of themes which arise out of – or are linked to – the *Titanic* disaster. Enzensberger's poem is a triumph of late modernism, a work which, like all great modernist literature, confronts fragmentation, disintegration and suffering with a committed humanism. The discontinuities and meanderings of the poem seem to imply that the significance of the disaster cannot be captured through the sort of linear narrative to which E. J. Pratt commits his 1930s epic about the foundering, but must rather be suggested through multiple perspectives and fragmentary accounts. What unifies Enzensberger's poem is not its narrative continuity – it has little[31] – but (as with the best modernist work) the coherence of its moral concerns. Throughout the work Enzensberger plays, overtly and implicitly, with the trite phrase, 'we are all in the same boat', but giving it importantly varying reverberations by means of contextual shifts. Thus in the first poem in the twenty-second canto we can read the sharp remark that 'We are all in the same boat, all of us. / But he who is poor is the first to drown'. But in the thirty-first canto, which sets a scene strongly suggestive of a post-nuclear catastrophe, the last line gives the cliché without comment: 'We were all in the same boat'.

Additionally, and also in common with the modernist tradition, the poem contemplates itself and the relationship of its discourse to the values which it maintains and espouses. In one sense both the poem and its maker are like the ship: as Enzensberger explains in the poem, he first wrote a poem entitled 'The Sinking of the Titanic' in Havana and mailed it to Europe without taking a copy (there was no carbon paper in revolutionary Cuba). Like the ship, the poem disappeared without trace. The poem we have, then, is an attempt to raise two lost vessels: the historical *Titanic* and Enzensberger's missing poem. The problematic issue of how texts capture lost realities is thus both discussed and enacted by the rewritten poem.

The sequence includes many relatively 'straight' accounts of the disaster amongst the various separate poems which make up the work. The opening poems are concerned with the impact of ship and iceberg, and they clearly draw on eyewitness accounts. (John Jacob Astor ripping open

---

[30] For Philip Brady, a 'work subtitled *Eine Komödie*, comprising thirty-three cantos and opening in three-line stanzas, declares its debts to Dante and acquires a literary-historical context' (1989, p9). Enzensberger's own English translation is subtitled 'A poem'.

[31] Although it is possible to trace in the poem a progression from the initial impact with the iceberg through the successive stages of the ship's sinking.

a lifesaver to show his wife what it contained, in the second canto, for example. Unlike the stoker who tried to steal the radio-operator's lifesaver, first-class passengers clearly experienced no shortage of such equipment.) There are other poems which are directly concerned with the *Titanic* and its fate. The seventh canto takes the form of a guided tour around the ship, and reprints the first-class dinner menu from 14 April 1912. The twelfth canto describes the situation of the ship once its fate had become clear; the first poem in the seventeenth canto describes the actual sinking; the first poem in the eighteenth canto describes the situation immediately after the sinking, from the perspective of lifeboat passengers listening to the cries of the dying. The first poem in the nineteenth canto recounts the well-attested story of the saving of a Japanese passenger who had lashed himself to a wooden door; the twenty-first canto opens with an account of all the premonitions of disaster many claimed to have had subsequent to the foundering; the twenty-fifth canto gives us the strange story of the five Chinese stowaways found on collapsible C lifeboat.

But intermixed with such accounts – which themselves involve various disorienting digressions and shifts of perspective – are poems concerned with quite other matters. The second poem of the second canto is entitled 'Apocalypse. Umbrian Master, About 1490', and details the businesslike manner in which the master approaches the fulfilment of his commission. Elsewhere in the sequence we find other accounts of the artistic rendering of earth-shattering events: the second poem in the seventh canto, for example, is entitled 'Last Supper. Venetian. Sixteenth Century'. The single poem in the twenty-sixth canto gives us the script of the closing sequence of a film on the *Titanic* disaster itself. Other poems in the sequence suggest different forms of apocalypse: the eleventh canto consists of a single poem which recounts the suffering of those dying crushed together in various situations including that of a stockcar (cattle truck), thus suggesting some horror from the Nazi holocaust; the thirtieth and thirty-first cantos seem to be set in some post-nuclear holocaust of the future.

Such cutting together of different sorts of apocalyptic disaster makes of the sinking of the *Titanic* a model for all such disasters in which the innocent suffer – and indeed the thirteenth canto consists of a montage of two hymns associated with the *Titanic* disaster ('Nearer, My God, To Thee' and 'Autumn', and two songs by Bruno Balz ('Das kann doch einen Seemann nicht erschüttern' and 'Davon geht die Welt nicht unter'). The montage has, paradoxically, a unifying effect: it undercuts any idea that the *Titanic* disaster was something unique, and sets it in a context of regular blows to human complacency – much as does Geoffrey Hill's invocation of the tower of Babel.

But Enzensberger also attempts more tendentiously to link the ship and the Cuba of the 1970s – the home, as he sees it, of idealist dreams as doomed as those dreams represented by the *Titanic* in 1912. His *Titanic* thus comes to represent if not human folly in general, then certainly illusion, complacency, or any misplaced confidence in the power of human institutions. Such more generalized scepticism does not however prevent

Enzensberger from sharp commentary on the asymmetricalities such illusion or complacencies visit upon the human race. The poem's second canto ends as follows:

> Those down below are always the first
> to understand danger. Hastily they collect
> their bundles, babies and ruby-red feather beds.
> The steerage may not be fluent in English or German,
> but it does not need an interpreter to find out
> that the First Class is always first served
> and that there are never enough milk bottles,
> shoes, or lifeboats for all of us.

The observation is representative of the way in which a fierce sense of social injustice is blended throughout 'The Sinking of the Titanic' with a bleak and pessimistic determinism. The Cuba of 1960s and 1970s idealism is seen to sink as surely as the *Titanic* of the complacent and materialistic optimism of 1912. And in all this the poor go on being without milk, shoes and lifeboats. In the poem's third canto, Enzensberger's persona recalls working at the original poem in Havana, remembering from his present vantage point ten years after in Berlin 'the rare light days of euphoria':

> Nobody ever gave a thought to Doom then,
> not even in Berlin, which had outlived
> its own end long ago. The island of Cuba
> did not reel beneath our feet. It seemed to us
> as if something were close at hand,
> something for us to invent. We did not know
> that the party had finished long ago,
> and that all that was left was a matter
> to be dealt with by the man from the World Bank
> and the comrade from State Security,
> exactly like back home and in any other place.

Such comments invite speculation about the poem's own genetic context, and a number of commentators have pointed out that Enzensberger's poem partakes of a more general pessimism, one associated both more generally with the Western European Left of the 1970s and also with the West German intelligentsia of the same period. The fifth canto of the poem portrays a generally passive and quietist steerage on the *Titanic* refusing to be incited to throw the privileged overboard and to save themselves and their own children – a clear expression, surely, of that pessimistic leftist Western European intellectual despair in the face of a domestic working class which refused to join students and intellectuals at the barricades in the late 1960s. A comparable pessimism comes through in the first of the two poems which constitute the tenth canto, in which a violent political disagreement between a Russian exile B. and the owner of a Manchester mill ends with both in one of the lifeboats, never to be heard of again, and survived by the table at which they argued:

> Only their table is still around,
> a bare table afloat in mid Atlantic.

Given that Friedrich Engels, Marx's collaborator, at one time owned a Manchester mill, and that Leon Trotsky's real name was Bronstein, the suspicion arises that what we have here is a parodic version of the fierce battles between sectarian sections of the Left, battles which will leave nothing substantial behind them as their participants disappear from the general wreck of their hopes.[32] (The mill owner's commitment to 'the advantages of iron discipline / and the blessings of strict authority' are thus to be taken more as parodic versions of an implied Stalinism than as imputed beliefs of a representative Victorian/Edwardian mill owner.)

The second poem in the twenty-first canto, entitled 'Keeping Cool', also seems to present an ironic view of the apocalyptic beliefs of the Western European Left of the 1960s and 1970s, presenting the reader with

> a small flock of people dressed in black coats,
> led by a prophet with steel-rimmed spectacles
> and flared nostrils, motionless, silent, waiting
> for Doom to come.

The wistful backwards glance at earlier certainties recurs in the first poem in the twenty-ninth canto, in which the persona looks back to a time when 'the end' was still believed in:

> We believed in some sort of end then
> (What do you mean by 'then'? 1912? 1917? '45? '68?)
> and hence in some sort of beginning.
> By now we have come to realize
> that the dinner is going on.

The poem then cuts to what the reader by now recognizes as the menu for the last dinner ever eaten on the *Titanic*. What such poetic manoeuvres suggest is that really significant changes do not occur when people plan for or expect them: the prophets waiting for Armageddon on the mountain top have to crawl back disappointed – as the Western European Left of the 1960s and 1970s is seen doing in the second poem in the twenty-first canto. But when we least expect it, when we are feeling secure, eating our fine dinner, calamitous change will come – not, as T. S. Eliot warned us, with a bang, but with a whimper, or – as Enzensberger reminds us – with a scraping sound, a sound as of linen or canvas being torn. (This is how eyewitnesses described the sound of the impact between iceberg and the *Titanic*.) I will return to this issue later on.

On one level, then, the poem reasserts a traditional Romantic view of the poet's responsibility to go on shouting in the dark in spite of his or her

---

[32] Engels is mentioned by name in the twenty-second canto; the ninth canto makes reference to 'a few forlorn old Trotskyites'.

conviction that nobody – or few – will listen. The poem's closing lines portray the poet, swimming in the sea after the foundering, surrounded by thousands and thousands of utterly empty, sodden trunks:

> I wail and swim.
> Business, I wail, as usual, everything lurching, everything
> under control, everything O. K., my fellow beings probably drowned
> in the drizzle, a pity, never mind, I bewail them, so what?
> Dimly, hard to say why, I continue to wail, and to swim.

Enzensberger's swimming poet is not the self-confident Shine of the *Titanic* toasts, swimming to land and rejecting the blandishments of those marooned on the sinking ship. The poem reproduces an adapted version of one of the toasts as its twentieth canto, and the simple macho individualism of Shine's presumably contented and passive drunkenness at the end of the toast contrasts with the wailing and swimming of Enzensberger's persona at the close of his own poem, a sombre determination reminiscent of Gramsci's 'pessimism of the intellect, optimism of the will' except that the poem's 'will' is rather less ambitious than is Gramsci's. In the second poem of the tenth canto, the poet approvingly recalls seeing on TV the inhabitants of Heimaey in Iceland who, faced with a volcanic eruption and encouraged by the example of 'an elderly man in braces', sprayed the advancing lava with garden hoses

> and thus postponing
> not forever perhaps, but for the time being at least,
> the Decline of Western Civilization, which is why
> the people of Heimaey, unless they have died since,
> continue to dwell unmolested by cameras
> in their dapper white wooden houses,
> calmly watering in the afternoon
> the lettuce in their gardens, which, thanks to the blackened soil,
> has grown simply enormous, and for the time being at least,
> fails to show any signs of impending disaster.

This is how one cultivates one's garden in 1970. From the pessimistic perspective of Enzensberger's poet it is better to water the lava than to argue politics or to try to incite the steerage to revolt – even though such watering will at best postpone the eventual catastrophe and produce bigger lettuces, while the poor will continue to lack milk, shoes and lifeboats.

If this were the only conclusion reached by the poem it would hardly escape banality (or ideological complicity with some rather reactionary forces), or merit extended study. Fortunately, although the poem's view of the present and the future is haunted by the sort of pessimistic and at times self-indulgent determinism which I have discussed, its view of the past, and of the past's accessibility to the present, raises troubling and challenging questions for the reader. Indeed, one of the crucial questions raised by recent theorists and presented in the opening sections of this book – do we regain the past through our emplotments or do we recreate or invent it? – is central too to 'The Sinking of the Titanic'. The sixth canto of the poem asks such questions directly:

> Unmoved, I look at this bare room in Germany,
> at the high ceiling, which used to be white some years ago,
> at the soot coming down in tiny flakes,
> and while the city around me is darkening rapidly,
> it is my pleasure to recover a text
> that probably never existed. I fake my own work,
> I restore my images. And I ask myself what the smoking lounge
> looked like on board the *Titanic*, and whether the gaming tables
> were checkered or covered with baize. What was it like in actual fact?
>   And in my poem? Was it in my poem
> at all? And what about that thin,
> absent-minded, excited man roaming Havana, involved
> in disputes, metaphors, endless love affairs – was that me?
> I'm not prepared to take an oath on it. And in ten years from now
> I shall not be sure that these very words are my own,
> written down where Europa is at its darkest, in Berlin,
> ten years ago, that is, today, in order to take my mind
> off the evening news and the endless succession of endless minutes
> that sprawl before us the closer some sort of end seems to be.
> Two degrees below zero, everything outside is black now,
> even the snow. I am overcome by an enormous calm. I don't know why.
> I gaze outside like a god. There is no iceberg in sight.

The canto homes in on that paradoxical sense that our culture has of the past: irretrievably lost, yet somehow visible and full of emotional significance; unfamiliar and yet not quite alien.

Recapturing the past is, for Enzensberger, rather like raising the *Titanic*: a task whose difficulty seems vitiated by its pointlessness, and yet a task which we are impelled to undertake. When the past does emerge above the surface of the water it seems no longer what it was, repelling as much because it is (or was) *ours* as because it is changed. In spite of this, of course, the whole of 'The Sinking of the Titanic' *is* committed to raising what has remained sunk in the past for many years: the poem explores the way in which stories about the past constitute a large part of the means whereby we structure ourselves and our present – while itself continuing this very process by setting a range of experiences against patterns extracted from the disaster.

The passage of time is often as imperceptible as the alteration of the colour of the ceiling in the poet's room in Berlin; we need cataclysmic changes to signpost time, and we need reconstructions of the past to give us a sense of our own present. Faced with a set of historical changes which are almost inconceivable in their range and complexity, we need events such as the sinking of the *Titanic* to frame and set limits, to define periods of time, to put boundaries around changes in consciousness and experience which are far more imperceptible than the fading of a ceiling. If we cannot even be sure that our recollections of ourselves are accurate, cannot even be sure that self-consciousness maintains a consistent identity over time ('was that me?'), then what sort of truth can be found in our reconstructions or emplotments of events which took place before our birth?

Later on in the poem, such questions are approached from different perspectives. In the sixteenth canto the poet sarcastically lists a series of what we may term emplotments of the *Titanic* disaster. The canto begins:

> The sinking of the *Titanic* proceeds according to plan.
> It is copyrighted.
> It is 100% tax-deductible.
> It is a lucky bag for poets.
> It is further proof that the teachings of Vladimir I. Lenin are correct.
> It will run next Sunday on Channel One as a spectator sport.

The final line of the canto is: 'It isn't anymore what it used to be'.

Such grim playfulness raises starkly the issue of whether the past is, *pace* Hayden White, merely a receptacle into which we bundle our present concerns, just a screen on to which we project our own neuroses. *Can* the past ever be 'what it used to be'? *Can* we ever recapture the past in a way that does no violence to its integrity, that is more (or at least as much) *it* as it is *us*? At times 'The Sinking of the Titanic' seems to suggest that our relationship to our own past is doomed by a primordial split between experience and knowledge. The second poem in the eighteenth canto is entitled 'Further Reasons Why Poets do not Tell the Truth', and it opens

> Because the moment
> when the word *happy*
> is pronounced
> never is the moment of happiness.
> Because the thirsty man
> does not give mouth to his thirst.
> Because *proletariat* is a word
> which will not pass the lips of the proletariat.

This gap between concrete experience and rationalization or abstraction is, the poem suggests, perhaps the ur-division, the postlapsarian curse of knowledge that forever separates us from knowledge of ourselves. The canto ends with the final explanation:

> Because it is someone else,
> always someone else,
> who does the talking,
> and because he
> who is being talked about,
> keeps his silence.

This is true, the poem suggests, even when we are talking about ourselves. If Edward Said's discussion of Orientalism has reminded us that this discourse is fundamentally premised upon one set of talking, writing, observing people imposing their views *of* another set of people *on* these other people, then we might say that Enzensberger's poem sees rationality itself as a sort of Orientalism. (What Said says about the Western emplotments of a silenced Orient can be compared to what Tillie Olsen says of more domestic deprivations of voice in her 1978 study *Silences*.)

The subjects of experience are emplotted by the subjects of the intellect: they are not allowed to speak for themselves, cannot utter their own emplotments. What we write and think about the *Titanic* can never *be*, or even recapture, the experience of those on the ship. Whereas early generations were, as we have seen, confidently prepared to explain what the disaster signified, what it represented or stood for, Enzensberger's persona reminds us that talk about the disaster is like talk about a dream: it can never fully recreate the dream experience. Our next-day retelling omits what made the dream memorable: our domination by the rule-framework of the dream; that which is lost when we tell rather than live through it.

It is, as we saw earlier on in the theoretical section of this book, only one short step from such a perception to believing that if the full richness of the past cannot be recaptured then it does not, or did not, exist. Enzensberger opens the first of the two poems which make up the twenty-seventh canto as follows:

> 'In actual fact nothing has happened.'
> There was no such thing as the sinking of the *Titanic*.
> It was just a movie, an omen, a hallucination.

The whole tone of this particular poem is, however, bitterly ironic, and the thrust of its critique is against what we can term a postmodernist denial of the past rather than against any belief that we do have some grasp of the sufferings of the dead. At the same time, the poem asserts in the face of those who believe that the sinking of the *Titanic* actually changed things, that in *that* sense nothing *did* happen: that belief that 'the sinking of the *Titanic*' changed the world is false. As the poem goes on sarcastically to remind us,

> the rich have remained rich, and the Commandantes
> Commandantes; in the Turkish bath Mrs Maud Slocombe,
> the world's first ship's masseuse, is doing her duty,
> still going strong.

The poem does not, however, remain at the level of this simple sarcasm. From a shift into the fantasy that the Cuba of revolutionary idealism is also the *Titanic*, it moves against itself to underline its attack on the pseudo-intellectualism of those who deny the ur-reality of those who experience and suffer the events of history:

> The only one to have second thoughts is a judicious whore
> who thinks: 'This is the way the world will end,

to the cheers of witty men who think it is all a joke.'
The poets, too, are still hanging around
at the café Astor, helping themselves
to Cuba libres from plastic cups.
They look slightly seasick and remember dutifully
the steerage passengers, the Chicanos, Eskimos
and Palestinians. The phony poet nods
to the middling poet; the middling poet
winks at the real thing; then each of them
retreats to his own cabin, leaning back in his dry easy chair
and writing, as if nothing had happened, on the dry sheet:
'In actual fact nothing has happened.'

Such reflexive self-knowledge acts as a guard against the danger that the poem might, from satisfaction at its rejection of one sort of pseudo-intellectual denial of actuality, fall into a smug self-congratulation. Even when the poet does remember 'the Chicanos, Eskimos and Palestinians', he or she should vigilantly guard against any belief that the past and its sufferings have been fully recovered.

'The Sinking of the Titanic' is, then, a poem which includes itself in its attack on those related intellectual propensities: denial of the past and the belief that the past can be recaptured in its experienced fullness. But it does not countenance a fashionable modern despair which asserts that as the past can never be fully recovered, no such recovery should be attempted. In spite of that deterministic pessimism that does run through its lines, the poem comes back time and again to the moral responsibility of the poet to engage in such attempts at salvage. And indeed its renewed attempts to 'get at' the sinking of the *Titanic* are themselves emblematic of the ways in which we must attempt what we know can never fully be achieved. There is, for example, a curious foreshadowing of the techniques of the New Historicists – of, especially, Stephen J. Greenblatt – in the second poem in Enzensberger's nineteenth canto. The poem is entitled 'News Wires of April 15, 1912', and it consists of just that: juxtaposed reports current on the day the first reports of the sinking were released to the reading public. The poem opens:

> The Tripoli War. Conflicts in German Social democracy. Seventh
> International Congress on Tuberculosis. Outrageous Behavior of
> Dortmund Workers on Strike.
> New York 24-hour lending rate 3⅜. New York sight bills on
> Berlin 95⅛. London light crude 39/3 cash.

The poem gathers momentum after this, moving through a montage of newspaper small advertisements, shipping news, court news, stock-exchange reports, advertisements, and so on. Sandwiched amongst this succession of items is brief, potent comment:

> Tucked in our warm beds we hardly notice when our earthbound

fellow creatures are shivering outside, when vicious April frosts kill
without mercy the delicate tissue of prematurely flowing buds.

The rapid transition from the wired newspaper items to the human
comment mirrors at one level the world's ignorance of the disaster at the
moment when these messages were sent and published, but at another
level it serves to remind the reader of the gap there always is between such
official reports and announcements and the sufferings of those whose pains
are not deemed to be newsworthy. To this extent the comparison I drew
earlier with the technique of juxtaposition favoured by Stephen J. Greenblatt is perhaps unfair: Greenblatt's non-literary texts are generally more
concerned with experienced realities than with objectified facts, although
of course the dividing line between these two categories is by no means
always crystal clear.

The poem ends, powerfully, with a paragraph which includes the first
(incorrect) report of the disaster to the *Titanic*:

> Frankfurt. The German Trade Counselor in Calcutta draws attention
> to the excellent export opportunities for motorcars in British India.
> New York. Today's early Reuter cables confirm the fact that all pas-
> sengers of the *Titanic* have boarded the lifeboats safely and in calm
> waters.

The misleadingly optimistic report throws a strong shadow of doubt over
all the preceding reports, while its confinement to a brief mention at the
end of the poem gives some sense of the *smallness* of the disaster as initially
experienced in April 1912, and of its relatively minor place in a universe of
other events. For us, 15 April 1912 may mean but one thing, but this
meaning relies upon an emplotment which selects and deletes from a
teeming world full of complex and interconnected processes, not all of
which were such as to be chosen for report.

But 'The Sinking of the Titanic' does not deny that the past leaves its
traces – although, unlike some of the theorists at whose work we looked
earlier, it seems to recognize that many of these traces are not textual. The
first poem in the twenty-ninth canto starts with a wistful look back at the
time when 'we' still believed in 'the end',

> as if anything
> ever were to founder for good, to vanish
> without a shadow,
> to be abolished once and for all,
> without leaving the usual traces,
> the famous Relics from the Past

In a sense, of course, the whole poem is itself one of those relics, on a par
with the *Titanic*'s last dinner menu and the eight hundred crates of shelled
walnuts 'last seen at 42 degrees 3 minutes North / and 49 degrees 9
minutes West'.

> Something always remains –
> bottles, planks, deck chairs, crutches,
> splintered mastheads –
> debris left behind,
> a vortex of words,
> cantos, lies, relics –
> breakage, all of it,
> dancing and tumbling
> after us on the water.

From this perspective the poem (along with the reports of inquiries, plastic models of the *Titanic*, and plans to lift the wreck) is but another piece of debris.

I said earlier that the poem recognized that much of this debris is not textual, and yet in the first poem in the twenty-ninth canto the speaker admits that

> But the dinner is going on regardless,
> the text is going on, the sea gulls
> follow the ship to the very end.

Even if historical objects and events exist in non-textualized forms, we may have access to them only by textualizing them. The debris which the *Titanic* leaves behind on the sea surface as it plunges to the ocean bottom is not just physical: the ship also bequeaths an unending stream of textual relics to posterity, one which seagull-critics such as myself pursue and pick at.

I said earlier that I would return to the issue of how the start of momentous change is experienced by human beings. One perception which 'The Sinking of the Titanic' shares with Joseph Conrad's novel *Nostromo* is that human beings seemed doomed to misrecognize portents: the dawning apocalypse is taken for the merely quotidian; the announced catastrophe turns out to be nothing out of the ordinary. And it is when an individual feels that never again 'is it going to be as quiet / as dry and warm as it is now' (first canto) that he or she may be on the edge of painful extinction. The same sense of irony is played with, in a more crude and exploitative manner, in the *Titanic* scene in Coward's *Cavalcade*, but whereas Enzensberger's use of the first person involves the reader in the irony, Coward's scene allows the audience to enjoy their safely spectatorial position and their superiority to the doomed couple. In all of this there is in 'The Sinking of the Titanic' a certain contradiction: on the one hand we never notice when momentous change takes place; on the other, momentous change does not take place, and things stay the same when we are convinced that a revolution has occurred. But such hesitation is also apparent in *Nostromo*, in which novel Conrad suggests that human beings regularly fail to notice when real change occurs, but believe that it has actually taken place when what they are experiencing is actually a new version of something old. Both writers recognize that very often *'plus ça change, plus c'est la même chose'*, while fundamental change sneaks up unnoticed like the iceberg on the *Titanic*. The collision thus becomes a token of the separation of ordinary people in the present century from a perception of the forces causing and governing real change – a matter which is also of some concern to W. H. Auden in his poem 'Spain', about which I will have more to say in my next chapter.

The first canto of Enzensberger's work focuses in on the seemingly trivial nature of the collision between iceberg and ship as experienced by many of the *Titanic*'s passengers – the sound of an endless length of canvas or a snow-white strip of linen being torn, which is actually how a number of passengers described the sound of the collision:

> This is the beginning.
> Listen! Don't you hear it?

Many do not hear it. (One crew member in the *Titanic* actually rang through to report that he had seen lifeboats in the sea, having managed to remain oblivious of the fact that the ship had struck an iceberg and was sinking.) In contrast, of course, there are the prophets of doom in the poem 'Keeping Cool' (twenty-first canto) who announce and await the day of reckoning, but have eventually to admit that it is not coming and to 'slowly come down / and join us in the nether regions of routine'. A more immediate juxtaposition occurs in the first of the so-called 'interludes' in 'The Sinking of the Titanic': the second poem in the second canto: 'Apocalypse. Umbrian Master, About 1490'. The poem takes us into the tired preparations made by the painter for his work, until he is ready, dips his brush in burnt umber and starts painting:

> destroying the world is a difficult exercise.
> Hardest to paint are the sounds – for example
> the temple being rent asunder, the beasts
> roaring, and the thunderclaps. Everything, you see,
> is to be rent asunder and torn to pieces,
> except the canvas.

In the real disaster, doom's opening shot is just that – the sound of canvas being torn. In the artistic rendering of apocalypse canvas is the only thing that is not torn, and everything else is to be rent asunder. Real disasters, genuine apocalypse, these are not announced to human beings by the clichés of towers and pinnacles crumbling. It is we in retrospect who project such clear pointers of change on to the banality of history. When we announce Armageddon (or socialist revolution) we find, too soon, Enzensberger suggests, that we have just been playing with matters of the surface. After a while we will have to come down from the mountain, and the man from the World Bank will take over.

The painter of the Last Supper in the seventh canto's second poem is, we are given to understand, more knowledgeable about such things. (The poem immediately follows the poem which enacts a guided tour of the *Titanic* and reproduces what was that ship's last supper: the menu of the final dinner consumed on the ship.) The painter has had to field questions concerning his picture:

> Do you think it is normal
> to depict Saint Luke
> with a toothpick in his hand?
> Who put the idea into your head
> to sit Moors, drunkards and clowns
> at Our Lord's table?
> Do we have to put up with a dog
> sniffing around, a dwarf, a parrot
> and a Mameluke bleeding from the nose?

Throughout the poem what the painter prizes in his picture is precisely this sort of trivial, naturalistic detail – as if he realizes that events of great magnitude such as the Last Supper or the sinking of the *Titanic* are not heralded by striking portents but are accompanied and ushered in by the familiar and the everyday – an insight which, incidentally, lies at the heart of W. H. Auden's 'Musée des Beaux Arts'. Indeed, in the first of the two poems which together constitute the twenty-first canto, those who – after the event – claimed to have witnessed potents and premonitions are ridiculed. As the close of the poem indicates: if there were such warnings, none of the dead seem to have heard or heeded them. What runs through 'The Sinking of the Titanic' is a thorough pessimism concerning our ability to recognize change when it starts. As the first poem in the twenty-second canto tells us,

> In the beginning there was only a small sound,
> a scraping sound easy enough to describe.
> But where it would lead to I did not know.

We are back, full circle, to that pessimistic element of defeatist determinism in 'The Sinking of the Titanic'. As I have suggested, I agree with those critics who associate this element in Enzensberger's work with the situation in West German intellectual circles in the 1960s and 1970s. Is the poem vitiated by it? I think not – mainly because it is in tension with a more vibrant humanism in the work which feels a fierce sense of solidarity with the poor and underprivileged, and which implicitly counsels an active form of resistance on their behalf. In one of the better discussions of Enzensberger's poem, Paul West makes what I think is an important point:

Some poets have an insufficient sense of the world's clutter. They pare down to essentials, as they're supposed to, but leave the sense of chaotic phenomena behind; the poem no longer comes out of the world, but sits on the page pristine, no longer evoking its origin in the mess. The trick, of course, is to create the artifact that's not only self-sufficient but also implies the irrelevances that have acted upon its making, so that it doesn't end up like a piece of heraldry – an amalgam of homogeneous archetypes – but perches elegantly on the brink of untidiness. (1981, p99)

The 'clutter' in Enzensberger's poem reminds us (and him, no doubt) that the world is always more complex than our formulae; at the same time it forces the reader to retain an awareness of the detail of the human suffering that was at the centre of the *Titanic* disaster. Pessimism is neat. It leaves no exceptions, no stubborn or recalcitrant detail. Enzensberger's clutter stands as a barrier in front of easy generalizations or glib retreats into a fashionable despair.

And when the clutter is human, it forces us to reach through the debris and the reality-denying textualizations, the wise-after-the-event smugnesses and the comfortable sinking of the *Titanic* into myth. West recognizes that at the heart of Enzensberger's poem there is a quest for something that is not just textual, something that is real:

> The poignant saliences are there of course: from 'That April night's menu' to the first radiogram '*0015 hours Mayday CQ Position 41° 46´ North 50° 14´ West*' (did they use 'Mayday' for distress even then?), and these take their place in our minds all over again as Enzensberger, with deliberately averted eye, reminds us of *A Night to Remember*,[33] not that bad a movie, and *Titanic* ashtrays, *Titanic* T-shirts, almost as if he comes to his theme backhandedly, through its shoddiest appearances in popular lore, which puts him in the position of searching for the *Real Titanic*, hardly available at all, and raises the question I raised at the beginning of this: How can we know except through empathy? It is typical of Enzensberger that he should feel easiest with the *Titanic*'s myth, where it is most an emblem, and least easy with how the victims' consciousnesses died. (1981, p104)

It is just those bits of uneasiness, of awkward clutter, that are perhaps the work's moral centre – possessed of the same ethical force as is Shaw's and Conrad's contrasting of cynical newspaper romancing and real drowning. And it is perhaps these same awkwardnesses, questions of how real people really died, that keep bringing the poem back to a nodal question which is expressed directly in the sixth canto: 'What was it like in actual fact?' Without empathy, as West suggests, we will have no chance of getting near to an answer to this question. Conrad, who felt that were Yamsi's[34] manager's head to be forcibly held under the water of his bath for some little time then he might soon discover that death has its sting, would probably have seen nothing to disagree with in this. But then, as Conrad added, 'Some people can only learn from that sort of experience which comes home to their own dear selves' (1921b, p333). How history and

---

[33] The film that Enzensberger seems to have in mind, given the mention of Barbara Stanwyck and Clifton Webb in the first poem in the ninth canto, is probably the 1953 film *Titanic* rather than *A Night to Remember*.

[34] Although, as I have already pointed out, 'Yamsi' was how Bruce Ismay, Chairman of the White Star Line, signed his Marconi messages, in the essay in question Conrad claims to be using the name as a generic one for all the *Titanic*'s designers, directors, managers, constructors, and others.

literature could help those not so limited to learn from experience was a topic on which Conrad had his own views – as we will see.

VII
The Irish Connection

As I have already argued, in the public at large the *Titanic* and its loss soon became associated not just with an age or with the human race in general, but with Britain. But the ship's national associations were, and remain, more complex than this. Technically, the ship was built in what was, and formally remains, a part of Britain: the northern-Irish town of Belfast. It was built by Harland and Wolff, a shipyard that had a history of close collaboration with the White Star Line and which, unlike most of the British shipyards around in 1912, still exists today. Belfast was a city as divided along sectarian religious lines in 1912 as it is today, and Harland and Wolff is a yard in which few Catholics have ever worked. Some of those who have tried have lived to regret the attempt. Mary Costello entitles her recent 'Memoirs of a Belfast Girlhood' *Titanic Town*, and recounts early on in its pages the history of her grandfather, Paddy Mohan:

> Paddy Mohan worked on the Titanic, but only briefly. When his co-workers discovered that his name was not truly Victor or George or Robert they threw him into Belfast Lough, and a clatter of spanners after him. But the bold Paddy escaped, lived to fight another day. So they were bound to have no luck of the ship. Ill-fated. Like the city itself. (1993, pp25–6)

Others, according to accounts I have heard from the members of the Belfast Catholic community, have not been so lucky.

In Ireland, then, and more especially in Belfast, the ship symbolized something more than just British achievement when it was launched; by symbolizing British achievement it also registered and underwrote Ireland's position as a part of Britain – a fact that the Home Rule movement had challenged and had raised into a very pressing political issue by 1912. Paradoxically, however, many of the steerage passengers on the ship's maiden voyage were (mainly Catholic) Irish emigrants heading for a new life away from 'British' Ireland to the United States. And by an odd irony it was to Ireland that Bruce Ismay retired, a man broken by the disaster.

When the ship sank, then, this had a powerful symbolic potential in Ireland – and especially in Belfast. Catholic folk-myth suggested that the ship's loss was a divine punishment for discrimination against Catholics by the shipbuilder, and much was made of the myth that if the code used to refer to the ship while it was under construction was held up to a mirror it spelled out 'NO POPE HERE' (a belief to which Mary Costello refers in her *Titanic Town*).

At the same time, as more Catholic than Protestant Irishmen had been the victims of the disaster, it was possible to use the *Titanic*'s building and loss to argue that in Ireland Protestants got the privileges and Catholics suffered the hardships. More generally, however, the loss of the ship was a severe blow to Protestant and Unionist pride in Ireland, and especially in Belfast. And although most Catholics joined in the more general British sense of public grief at the disaster, in popular myth the meaning attributed to the ship and its sinking had something in common with the response of Black Americans, to which I referred earlier. A friend of mine from Belfast gave me a book on the *Titanic* inscribed: 'Built by prods, sunk by Brits'. His allegiances probably do not need spelling out. If the technological jewel of Protestant Belfast could sink, so too could British domination over Ireland. Great technological achievements or disasters are endowed with political meanings of this sort: the *Hindenberg* disaster, the launching of the first *Sputnik*, the *Challenger* catastrophe – all were given a meaning that went far beyond the merely technological. The *Titanic* has always had a set of very special meanings in Belfast. To this day many in the town are proud that the ship was built there, and on the seventy-fifth anniversary of the foundering it seemed natural that the Ulster Folk and Transport Museum in Belfast should organize a special exhibit devoted to the ship.[35]

But if the piece of graffiti to which I have already referred were found in Belfast, it would have a meaning rather different from that which it had for me in England. It would make the implicit threat that continued British control over Northern Ireland is no more assured than was the *Titanic*'s safe arrival in New York. And when we find mention of the ship in a literary work with an Irish writer we will need to be open to a rather different set of meanings from those which we might find in a work by a writer from another nation or culture. As we will see, the posthumous literary life of the *Titanic* in Irish – and especially Northern Irish – literature feeds off a unique complex of meanings and associations that are not shared with other cultures.

Frank McGuinness's play *Observe the Sons of Ulster Marching Towards the Somme* (first performed in Dublin in 1985) provides a good example of the way in which the more local symbolic associations of the ship and its fate could be tapped in a literary work. McGuinness's play focuses upon a group of volunteers in the 36th (Ulster) Division during the First World War. The play opens at the start of the war and culminates at the start of the Battle of the Somme, a battle which opened on the actual anniversary of the Battle of the Boyne in 1690 and in which thousands upon thousands of Ulstermen were killed. The whole play portrays a culture which cannot escape from its own history, a culture represented by men who, as the play

---

[35] Outside Belfast and Ireland the associations are somewhat different. A syndicated piece of satire by Erma Bombeck entitled 'Visit Northern Ireland Before Peace Ruins It', published in the *Austin-American Statesman* 28 February 1995, remarks ironically of Belfast: 'Forget the fact that this is the place that brought you the Titanic and the DeLorean car: there are "Sniper at Work" T-shirts to be bought for the folks back home'.

progresses, find themselves to be part of a historical trajectory that is essentially tragic.

Thus the most colourful and disturbing character in the play – Kenneth Pyper – changes from cocksure and destructive joker at the start of the play, to one who admits that his creativity is blocked and perverted by a lineage which refuses to let him go, refuses him his individuality. Pyper reports how he attempted to do something with 'my heart and my eyes and my hands and my brain' by escaping from a privileged position as a member of the Irish Protestant ascendancy and going to Paris to sculpt:

> PYPER: [. . .] Something I could not do here as the eldest son of a respectable family whose greatest boast is that in their house Sir Edward Carson, saviour of their tribe, danced in the finest gathering Armagh had ever seen. I escaped Carson's dance. While you were running with your precious motors to bring in his guns, I escaped Carson's dance, David. I got out to create, not destroy. But the gods wouldn't allow that. I could not create. That's the real horror of what I found in Paris, not the corpse of a dead whore. I couldn't look at my life's work, for when I saw my hands working they were not mine but the hands of my ancestors, interfering, and I could not be rid of that interference. I could not create. I could only preserve.
> (McGuinness 1986, p56)

This sense of predestined doom, of being locked into a historical process which condemns Ulster to a sterile, uncreative and tragic duplication of the past finds a perfect symbol in the *Titanic* and its fate. Earlier in the play a scene set in Ulster moves from a beating of the lambeg drum (one of the cultural shibboleths of Protestant Ulster) into a discussion of the ship. Nat McIlwaine, who has been beating the drum, suddenly kicks it. When asked why he has done this, he suddenly asks the others if they know what he is thinking of – and tells them:

> MCILWAINE: That boat.
> MOORE: I see nothing before me.
> ANDERSON: The *Titanic*?
> MILLEN: The end's in sight.
> ANDERSON: What brings the *Titanic* into your mind?
> MCILWAINE: The drum. The noise of it. It's like the sound she made hitting the Lagan.
> ANDERSON: We weren't to blame. No matter what they say.
> MCILWAINE: Papists?
> (MCILWAINE *spits*.)
> MOORE: I'm drenched.
> MILLEN: That's with sweat.
> MOORE: I think it's blood. But it's not my own. I never saw that much blood, Johnny.
> MILLEN: It's not ours.
> MOORE: The whole world is bleeding. Nobody can stop it.
> (MOORE *slowly continues his crossing*)

ANDERSON: Every nail they hammered into the *Titanic*, they cursed the
   Pope. That's what they saw.
MCILWAINE: There was a lot of nails in the *Titanic*.
ANDERSON: And he still wasn't cursed enough.
MCILWAINE: Every nail we hammered into the *Titanic*, we'll die in the
   same amount in this cursed war. That's what I say.
ANDERSON: What are you talking about?
MCILWAINE: The war's cursed. It's good for nothing. A waste of time.
   We won't survive. We're all going to die for nothing. Pyper was
   right. I know now. We're on the *Titanic*. We're all going down.
   Women and children first. Women and children. Damn the Pope. Let
   me die damning him. (1986, pp49–50)

The *Titanic* offers itself as a perfect symbol for a doomed generation of
Ulster Protestants, going down in the Battle of the Somme as helplessly as
those passengers and crew in the ship which represented their pride.

Shortly after this exchange one of the participants protests that the
Titanic went down because it hit an iceberg. McIlwaine gloomily retorts:
'The pride of Belfast went with it'. The idea of men constructing their own
obliteration, building something that will destroy them and what they
stand for, transfers effortlessly from a ship produced in a yard operated on
sectarian lines to the divided community of which that yard is a part.

More recently, Derek Mahon and Robert Johnstone have both written
poems related to the disaster. Mahon's short, twenty-one-line poem 'Bruce
Ismay's Soliloquy' offers a more nuanced and detached view of the
foundering and its aftermath. The poem avoids the sectarian associations
of the ship, and presents Ismay as one of the casualties of the disaster. The
poem is cast as a soliloquy delivered by Ismay himself, in his later
retirement in the west of Ireland. (Michael Davie reports [1987, p137] that
Ismay bought a retreat in County Galway without seeing it, while the
British inquiry was still in progress.) In Mahon's poem Ismay is portrayed
as a broken man, sunk like the ship he deserted and doomed periodically
to relive the sufferings of those he abandoned. In contrast to Hans Magnus
Enzensberger's portrayal of Ismay in his 'The Sinking of the Titanic'
('J. B. Ismay, Esq. K.B.E., F.R.G.S., / shipowner of S. S. *Titanic*, / President,
White Star Line / of America, Inc., coward, / eyes like glass marbles, /
pomade-greased hair'), Mahon's depiction is a sympathetic one. Ismay is
seen as more ignorant than wicked or cowardly, and doomed to relive the
destruction of his ship and its passengers.

Central to the poem is a view of Ismay as victim, one underpinned by
a comparison with the ship itself – broken by the collision and lost forever.
And behind *this* conceit lies a view of Ismay as fundamentally ignorant of
the lives of those travelling in his ship, those 'dim / Lost faces' he never
understood. At this distance of time it is easier to see Ismay as product of
a set of circumstances (national, ideological, gender, class), than as self-
originating and responsible for his own actions. Written in Northern
Ireland, the poem bespeaks a living awareness of a modern context in

which physical proximity does not guarantee human sympathy or understanding.

'Bruce Ismay's Soliloquy' appears in an anthology entitled *Poets from the North of Ireland* (Ormsby 1990). In the same collection are two poems by Robert Johnstone which both build on the *Titanic* disaster. 'Robot Camera' associates the poet's reactions to the first underwater shots of the sunken ship with his childhood experience of nearly drowning while swimming, and the nightmare which combines both experiences as he appears to be in the wreck where corpses wait to dance with him in the ballroom. A second poem, 'Undertakers', adds a more specifically Northern Irish emphasis, as the vision of the ship sent out from Halifax to pick up bodies after the disaster merges with scenes of carnage from the 'Troubles' in the six counties. Visions of the dead from the *Titanic* laid out at the Mayflower curling rink are juxtaposed with more recent pictures from divided Belfast such as the mummified remains of one killed in the fireblast of a hotel bombing.

This local emphasis does not, however, call on the specifically sectarian associations of the ship, but rather seeks to broaden out the lesson of the disaster, to see it as a token of all occasions on which the innocent suffer and the uninvolved walk by:

> Walk down any street
> and you could be in a necropolis,
> Warsaw, Leningrad, some maiden city.
>
> The starved or sick lie in their overcoats
> like drunkyards on the pavement. One walks by.

Like Geoffrey Hill's ode, Johnstone's poem moves the reader to interrogate the ways in which we witness the sufferings of others, to ruminate on matters of compassion, voyeurism, and engagement. If we want misery, it is there on the streets: do we prefer to contemplate the *Titanic* and its cargo of human misery because such contemplation makes fewer demands on us? Our concern with the fate of the *Titanic* and its passengers is thus used by Johnstone to explore more worrying issues relating to the bearing of witness.[36]

'Undertakers' feeds off an acquaintance with the sectarian divisions of Northern Ireland without taking up any overtly sectarian position. The

---

[36] A fine recent poem by the English poet Peter Walton (1993) entitled 'Details', explores the premise that in 'vast disasters' it is the 'small identities of halted life' that are most telling for the onlooker. Walton appeals to the evidence of Pompeii, an unspecified plane crash, and the *Titanic* disaster. The poem's concluding lines remind the reader that in the wrecked ship divers found 'The empty shoes of all those people drowned / And eaten away by sea creatures – theirs, / Worn that night, since everywhere they lay in pairs'. The poem allows us to wonder whether our fascination with such details may be neither morbid nor voyeuristic, but attributable to the trans-historical human charge they carry, one which enables us to conceive of halted, individual lives, rather than 'victims' or 'statistics'.

more specifically Irish associations of the *Titanic* – cultural and political –
are passed over in silence by both Johnstone and Mahon; their use of the
ship and its fate is radically different from the use made by Frank
McGuinness in *Observe the Sons of Ulster Marching Towards the Somme*.

What conclusions can we reach from this survey of literary and non-literary
responses to the disaster?

One of the paradoxes with which we are faced with is, I think, this: the
disaster was a gigantic shock to most literate Europeans and Americans –
something unexpected, something for which they were not prepared. And
yet contemporary responses to the disaster, whether literary or not, seem
to form themselves by reference to opinions, attitudes, positions which pre-
date its occurrence. Faced with the unusual, we take refuge in the familiar.
It is only at a later stage, as the event becomes assimilated in our culture,
that its truly *novel* significance can be more fully investigated. Nevertheless,
such use of pre-existing patterns of belief did not necessarily condemn the
writers concerned to complicity with a dominant ideology. Both Shaw and
Conrad were clearly aware of – and hostile to – attempts to use the disaster
to underwrite doctrines of class collaboration, patriarchy and general
conservatism. Hardy's 'The Convergence of the Twain' represents a more
complex case: the poem gestures in the direction of a fatalistic and
conservative attribution of blame to ideologically non-sensitive forces, but
simultaneously opens up a space in which such gestures may be perceived
for what they are. The Hill and Enzensberger poems both resist moves to
limit the implications of the disaster to a safely compartmentalized past;
their involvement of the reader in the moral issues raised by the foundering and its aftermath also have a clearly oppositional force. *Cavalcade*,
although ultimately complicit in the reactionary use and extension of the
disaster's mythic meanings also seems to leave a space for oppositional
reading – although it is a space which is badly signposted in the text and
which is visible to us perhaps only because of the footprints of history.

We can add, too, I think, that the more a work of literature encourages
the reader or audience member to subject his or her own processes of
response and understanding to analysis, the more profound its effect. This
reflexive element is one essential reason why E. J. Pratt's poem on the
Titanic is, I believe, inferior to the poems by Geoffrey Hill and Hans
Magnus Enzensberger. Thomas Hardy's 'The Convergence of the Twain'
does not overtly encourage the reader to partake in such self-analysis, but
the poem's own half-tortured grappling with the forces behind the poet's
interest in the disaster has the effect of leading the reader towards a similar
self-scrutiny.

Finally, I hope that any reader who started this book with the belief that
humanism is always complicit with a dominant ideology may have been
led to reconsider this position. I certainly think that an unqualified
commitment to the value of human life and experience (not, however, a
human life and experience that is outside history) lies at the heart of the
value of the best of the literary works I have so far considered.

5

POETIC ENGAGEMENTS

Struggles and Retrenchments

I
W. H. Auden, 'Spain'
To-day the Struggle

Few literary works written in the present century present us with the complexities of historical engagement more directly than does W. H. Auden's poem 'Spain'. The poem was written in March 1937, and as Auden had returned to England from Republican Spain very early that same month it is safe to assume that its composition was informed by Auden's experiences there, and that it arose both out of these and (perhaps even more) out of a more general public awareness of the significance of the Spanish Civil War – a view of the struggle there as a symbol of the possibility of resisting and even defeating the fascist takeover of Europe.

At the same time, however, the poem was a part of this struggle. When it was published in May 1937 in pamphlet form and sold for the price of a shilling, its dustcover announced that 'All the author's royalties from the sale of this poem go to *Medical Aid for Spain'*. More importantly, the poem was actively used in campaigning for support for the Republican forces and in aid of medical aid for the Republican wounded – Spanish and International. In an essay entitled 'W. H. Auden: Poetry and Politics in the Thirties', Arnold Kettle recalls that the first time he heard the poem read aloud was by Ian Watt at a lunch-time meeting in Cambridge which ended with a collection for Spanish medical relief (1979, p99). Such a mode of transmission was by no means unique: the rise of a new politics of anti-fascist unity subsequent to the development of popular-front policies – especially in France – and in particular the mobilization of solidarity for the

Spanish Republic in Britain, revolutionized what one can inadequately call the sociology of literature at this time. The formation and rapid growth of the Left Book Club nurtured a politically conscious and committed collectivity which, if it would be naïve just to say that it gave readers their own powerful voice, certainly significantly altered the balance of power between publishers, authors and readers. In particular, through the organization of local readers' groups, it revolutionized the nature of the reading process, which hitherto had been almost exclusively individual, private and (relatively) passive, rather than collective, public and active. In their *Britain in the 1930's* Noreen Branson and Margot Heinemann point out that along with those poets who actually fought in Spain for the Republic, writers such as Herbert Read, Stephen Spender, C. Day Lewis, J. Bronowski, A. L. Lloyd and Louis MacNeice all wrote poems in tribute to the Republican forces, and Jack Lindsay produced *On Guard for Spain* specifically for mass declamation at meetings (1971, p278).

Auden's poem, then, was produced during a relatively brief period of time when aspects of what we can term the machinery of literary production and dissemination were being radically altered and expanded as part of a more general popular movement. As we read the poem today, we read a work which has, inevitably, slipped back into a context of more traditional forms of dissemination. It is one of Auden's 'selected poems', or a poem in an anthology of 1930s poems, sitting in a library waiting to be checked out. But for many of those who read it in the middle of 1937 the most important thing about it was not that it was a poem but that it was part of a struggle which was increasingly recognized as a struggle for civilization and against barbarism, and a struggle which could not be postponed. Moreover 'Spain' was itself a part of the movement which led large numbers of people to see the Spanish Civil War in this way. If we are to understand the full force of the poem, then, we must study the political and documentary contexts of its composition and initial dissemination.

The poem still bears some evidence of such contexts. It is certainly ideally suited to declamation: its ordered rhythm permits the reader to develop a momentum which culminates in a conclusion that is not merely aesthetically satisfying but which calls to action as the uniqueness of the historical moment – its dangers and opportunities – is stressed. And even today the poem's declamatory potentialities help the reader to recapture some part of the sense of urgency out of which it emerged and to which it appealed – although to this it should be added that some of Auden's later alterations to the poem reduce this sense of urgency. 'They walked the passes: they came to present their lives', individualizes (and probably romanticizes) the essentially collective and objective moral force of 'They walked the passes. All presented their lives'.

For many years, though, it seemed hard critically to engage with the poem without encountering the roadblock of its author's later hostility to it. Auden tried first to amend the poem, then to reject it, and finally to suppress it. In his foreword to his 1966 *Collected Shorter Poems*, Auden quoted the concluding lines of the poem and insisted: 'To say this is to equate goodness with success. It would have been bad enough if I had ever held this wicked doctrine, but that I should have stated it simply because it sounded to me rhetorically effective is quite inexcusable' (1966, p15).[37] For many years the poem (along with others written during this time) was excluded by Auden from the canon of his work. In a valedictory note for a posthumous collection of tributes to the poet entitled 'Some Memories', Cyril Connolly reports that in his own copy of the poem Auden has crossed out the final two lines of the poem and written 'This is a lie' (1975, p70). When Robin Skelton asked Auden for permission to include various of his poems (in their original form) in his anthology *Poetry of the Thirties* (1964), Auden agreed on the condition that Skelton make it clear that 'Mr W. H. Auden considers these five poems to be trash which he is ashamed to have written'. (The poems involved were 'Sir, No Man's Enemy', 'A Communist to Others', 'To a Writer on his Birthday', 'Spain' and 'September 1, 1939'.) Such authorial disapproval chimed in both with cold-war political attitudes, and New Critical disapproval of (or disbelief in) politically engaged literature, and forced anyone wishing to defend or praise the poem to feel a very distinct sensation of swimming upstream. I have in front of me an (American) library copy of the pamphlet publication of the poem. The old loan slips pasted to the cover tell what is, I suspect, a representative story. In the late 1930s or early 1940s the pamphlet could be loaned for a maximum of three days, while between 1943 and 1968 it was borrowed only ten times. Even as late as November 1995 John Lanchester feels no need to qualify his dismissal of the poem as 'never anything more than a second-rate piece of rabble-rousing' (1995, p5). It seems that encouraging readers to join or support those fighting Franco can now be dismissed as rabble-rousing – and second-rate rabble-rousing at that.

In other words, so far as the poem's emergence, dissemination and life (or death) through the decades since 1937 are concerned, it is clear that both authorial and non-authorial forces have played – and continue to play – their part. One may be forgive the ironic comment that at least so far as 'Spain' is concerned, Roland Barthes got it right: the birth of the reader had to be at the expense of the death of the author. Since Auden's (literal) death it has become considerably easier to confront the poem and its changing interactions with history.

---

[37] In his preface to *W. H. Auden: Selected Poems* (1989), Edward Mendelson accepts Auden's case without question, stating that Auden 'dropped entirely such poems as "Spain" where the "struggle" is more important than its consequences and goodness is equated with victory' (1989, pxix). It seems safe to bet that such interpretations – especially those referring to 'goodness', a concept which is not invoked by the lines in question – would never have gained any currency had they not first been circulated by the author himself. In the immortal words of Mae West, 'Goodness had nothing to do with it'. The whole point of Auden's closing lines is that the secular stars which look down, unlike the Christian God Auden was later to re-embrace, neither see nor are motivated by moral concerns. It is human beings who have to make a world unprotected by a benign God conform to their moral wishes.

This is not to argue that there remains nothing to say about Auden's later rejection of the poem, or of the interpretations upon which this rejection was ostensibly based. Arnold Kettle, reacting to Auden's claim that the poem's closing lines express the wicked doctrine which equates goodness with success, responds that 'Since this is patently *not* what the lines do express, the explanation of his treatment of them can only be, I think, that on some level he remained conscious of their authenticity and feared it' (1979, p99). Frank Kermode has admitted that he finds it hard to believe that Auden could have so badly understood his own poems 'unless it was from a simple desire to escape the memory of what it had been like to write them' (1988, p78), and responding to Auden's reaction to the final stanza of 'Spain' he maintains that to him the stanza seems

> exactly right. Heaven and earth leave us to our moment; choice is necessary, failure irredeemable. When he said this was 'unforgiveable', Auden had changed his mind about history and redemption; but that cannot hurt the poem, which ends with a remark as clear-sighted and as urgent as that which ends Marvell's poem . . . (1988, p79; 'Marvell's poem' is 'An Horatian Ode: Upon Cromwell's Return from Ireland')

Margot Heinemann and Noreen Branson have suggested that many of those writers of the 1930s who were committed to Left political action reacted both to the agony of defeat (of the Spanish Republic) and to a recognition that their own side no longer seemed wholly without guilt (1971, p279). Joseph Conrad's *Nostromo* provides an apposite comment: 'To him, as to all of us, the compromises with his conscience appeared uglier than ever in the light of failure' (1984, p364). In a recent essay, however, John Bridgen stresses more internal than external factors, claiming that after writing the poem, 'Auden was to change so much that he actually forgot what he originally meant in "Spain"' (1990, p131).

It is tempting to follow such speculation further, and yet the temptation needs to be resisted: Auden's poem is more important than Auden's subsequent view of his poem. One point does, however, demand to be made. The life of the writer in history affects the relationship of the writer to his or her work; this relationship is not just an 'internal', personal matter, but one which is affected by a larger set of relationships between the writer and his or her changing world. And what may be a historically volatile relationship between a writer and his or her work is something that generations of readers have, too, to come to terms with when they read the work – even if such coming to terms involves ruling this information out of court in New Critical fashion. The historical life of a literary work is – like the historical life of all texts – not a matter of mechanical repetition, of endless stampings out of its original and 'true' meaning or significance. But neither is it a matter of a succession of complete transformations, of acting as an empty shape which can be reformed such that endlessly new meanings can be poured into it or extracted from it. Auden had no patent on his poem's meaning for others – but others can never completely separate 'Spain' from his subsequent comments on it, as these comments are a part – and a representative part – of its passage through time.

One of the things which Auden changed when he revised the poem was its title. 'Spain' became 'Spain 1937', an amendment which bespeaks, among other things, a loss of confidence in the existence of a wide general readership fully aware of the reference of the earlier title. In 1937 'Spain' is not just the name of a country or political unit but the label of a struggle, an issue, a moral and political crisis and point of decision – like 'Vietnam' in the 1960s. The change of title has a curious effect. In one sense it can be defended in terms of its attempt to point to the expanded meaning that the name had at the time that the poem was written and published, but the alteration also has an oddly limiting effect inasmuch as it makes of the whole work a period piece – one to be looked at almost as a piece of memorabilia, a quaint relic like a valve radio or Oxford bags. 'This is the sort of thing we said in 1937 – funny, isn't it?' The poem is often now published in its original form and with its original title – although editorial custom is still inconsistent here. (Thus Edward Mendelson, in his 1977 edition of *The English Auden*, publishes the poem in its revised form, while offering it in its initial form – apart from three small early changes – in his 1989 edition of Auden's *Selected Poems*.) The original title certainly has a less distancing effect on the reader, who is able more effortlessly imaginatively to project him- or herself into the context from which the poem emerges and to which it appeals. The amended title immediately situates the reader at a distance from the poem, looking at it from the vantage point of his or her present rather than experiencing it from within the 'now' of the poem's genetic and referential contexts.

This is by no means to say that such experiencing involves no element of intellectual distancing. Indeed, it is only on the basis of the reader's imaginative involvement in an understanding of the poem's emergence from and engagement with a specific historical situation that its intellectual challenges and conclusions make sense. Put another way, it is only through a sympathetic understanding of the comprehensive challenge that a particular historical moment presented in 1937 that the reader can deal with the intellectual challenges which survive in the work. Indeed, we should remember the obvious point that it is precisely at those moments when historical events impinge upon individuals' personal lives that they are most likely to ask more general and distanced questions concerning the nature of historical development and change. A study of history is not normally the child of contentment.

John Bridgen provides us with a useful way in to more analytical and interpretative discussion of the poem:

> 'Spain' is an attempt both to celebrate and to plead for a natural order in which the private and the public spheres are in harmony. In 'Spain' Auden attempts to validate the natural law tradition of History in which 'Time' is 'the refreshing river'. The poem suggests that mankind must return to History's natural evolutionary order so that the individual can shape his own life and make his own decisions. The chaos resulting from power

politics and war has caused man to question whether History really is a purposive beneficent force. Auden feared that the choice and the 'proposal' of many at that particular crucial moment of History would be 'the suicide pact, the romantic / Death' rather than 'To build the Just City'. 'Spain' is in this sense a call both to action and to faith. 'To-day the struggle' in order that tomorrow we may readjust to the vital and natural course of historical evolution. By reasserting History in this sense, Auden was resisting Hegel's denial of individual ethical will. He was disillusioned by the conduct of the Spanish Civil War, but he believed, despite Hegel's teaching, that individual choices could return History to the order of natural law. It is probably significant that in 'Spain' the actions of the volunteers are described in terms of natural metaphor. (1990, p131)

Bridgen's understanding of the poem's underlying view of history is, I think, interesting but wrong – although this is not to say that the poem contains nothing to underwrite such an interpretation. But what Bridgen calls 'the natural law tradition of History' seems to involve a view of history's 'naturally' progressing like a train which transports its passengers from one age to another. This process has been interrupted by the 'un-natural' intervention of human beings, who have been forced off the train and must somehow get back on to it so that life can continue as before.

But for me the whole thrust of 'Spain' is one which underwrites a *new* relationship to history, an unprecedented attempt by human beings in the mass to take charge of the passage of history so as to initiate a qualitatively distinct era in which human beings are no longer at the mercy of blind and inhuman forces. (This, I would add, is one reason why it is important to remember that the poem was first read by 'empowered readers': readers who were organized, active and conscious of their collectivity. Their own reading situation offered a perfect platform from which to attempt to reach out to an understanding of the possibility that mankind in general might adopt a similarly active, collective and organized attitude towards contemporary history.) The whole structure of the poem (Yesterday / To-day / Tomorrow) implies not a return to what was, but a change to what has never been. Moreover, 'to-day the struggle' is surely not offered as an alternative to the suicide pact or the romantic death, but as the necessary prelude to achieving the freedom to be able to choose between such alternatives and others such as building the just city. Thus it is important to note that although the poem's picturing of 'yesterday' is of a progression of history based upon human activities rather than natural processes – a history structured by culture and not by nature – it is also a history which has been hidden from those involved in it, for they have been aware only of local events, limited advances. Yesterday may have consisted of the counting frame and the cromlech, the divination of water, the abolition of fairies and giants, or the miraculous cure at the fountain – all the result of purposive human activities – and yet 'the poor in their fireless lodgings' can still declare that 'Our day is our loss, O show us / History the operator, the / Organiser, Time the refreshing river'. Bridgen argues that 'Time the refreshing river' is something to which individual choices could return humanity, implying that 'the chaos resulting from power politics and war' has diverted this river away from human beings. But the structure of the poem implies, rather, that the alienation of the poor from History the operator or Time the refreshing river is not something that has just happened, but something which, up to now, has been a permanent condition, a fact of life. Those generations of cultural changes detailed in the poem's opening stanzas have contributed to – even constituted – 'History the operator', but the logic of this history has been hidden from those fuelling its dynamic. Today's struggle, from such an interpretative perspective, is not a way back to yesterday, but a way forward to a tomorrow in which the poor are, for the first time, made acquainted with – even transformed into – History the operator. The geographical movement towards a central point which is enacted by those 'Many' depicted travelling to Spain mirrors this movement in which the enormous diversity of life shrinks down to the single point of struggle: 'Madrid is the heart'.

The poem's mention of Madrid introduces, however, a complication. As Nicholas Jenkins has pointed out, the Spanish Republican forces were split on certain key political issues which had practical consequences for the conduct of the war:

> [W]hen [Cyril] Connolly got back to England – a month or so before Auden – he too discussed the republican divisions, in the piece 'A Spanish Diary' which he published in the *New Statesman & Nation*. Connolly sets out two opposing positions: 'The Communists and Socialists say "First win the war, then attend to the revolution"'. The poem's main assertion is, of course, a perfect encapsulation of this argument: 'To-morrow . . . / all the fun under Liberty's masterful shadow . . . /To-morrow . . ./ The eager election of chairmen / By the sudden forest of hands. But to-day the struggle.' And, Connolly continued, 'The younger Anarchists and the P. O. U. M. say, "The war and the revolution are indivisible and we must go on with both of them simultaneously."' Sure enough, 'Spain' pointedly counters this revolutionary impulse. . . .
>
> As the war dragged on, the language and structure of 'Spain' became increasingly compromised by their links to a Government which was more and more clearly the tool of a repressive Soviet foreign policy. In the end, having broken down so comprehensively the barriers between public imperatives and the private moral conscience, the poem had no defences against the tide of History, and it was swamped. It was against this wholesale debasement, not against a particular line or phrase, that Auden, later on, took such drastic measures. (1990, pp92–3)

Jenkins's presentation of this issue is a loaded one which sees all revolutionary virtue on the side of the Anarchist/P. O. U. M. faction, but he is correct in saying that the impulse of Auden's poem favours the political position of the Communists and Socialists: the policy of 'first win the war' was linked to a demand to defend Madrid at all costs. However, my suspicion is that this is less a matter of deliberate political choice than an independently reached conclusion on Auden's part that the struggle was so important that all differences on the anti-fascist side must be overlooked in the interests of defeating Franco. And this conclusion, I also suspect, arose less from the particularities of the struggle in Spain and more from a widely felt need to achieve maximum solidarity with the Republican forces. Those in the poem who leave their personal commitments and individual pleasures are not in Spain, but travelling to Spain. Moreover, given that Auden was neither Anarchist not Trotskyist his lack of sympathy with a political line that stressed the need to combine war and revolution is hardly surprising. This is, of course, not to deny that Auden reacted against some of the things that he saw in the ranks of those loyal to the Communists and Socialists, nor to seek to conceal his objections to aspects of the rôle played in the struggle by the Soviet Union. But I do not think that the detail of 'Spain' was determined by Auden's conscious alliance with one political grouping in Republican Spain: it was the product of a clear belief that in the face of the unprecedented threat posed by fascism, those opposing fascism should work for maximum unity. The politics of the popular front have come in for considerable criticism from an unholy alliance of Right and ultra-Left in recent years, and yet it has to be insisted that at no time since the 1930s has the Left gained the mass popular support which it achieved as a result of popular-front policies.

According to John Bridgen, 'the actions of the volunteers are described in terms of natural metaphor' (1990, p131), but this is only partly true. Comparisons between the volunteers and migrating gulls or flower seeds certainly do suggest a natural – and unconscious – process. But the process is initiated because the volunteers in various places *hear* a call and respond to it, and 'All presented their lives' can by no means be read as a purely natural process: it refers to a conscious and deliberate action. Many observers have commented on one particular alteration: in the line 'They clung like birds to the long expresses that lurch' 'birds' was changed to burrs – an alteration which certainly does lessen the implied element of will involved in the action. (It also weakens the simile: it is easier to picture birds than burrs clinging to an express.)

Auden also removed certain stanzas from the poem altogether. Of the three stanzas quoted below, Auden removed the final two and amended the first to accommodate the omission:

> On that arid square, that fragment nipped off from hot
> Africa, soldered so crudely to inventive Europe;
>   On that tableland scored by rivers,
> Our thoughts have bodies; the menacing shapes of our fever
>
> Are precise and alive. For the fears which made us respond
> To the medicine ad. and the brochure of winter cruises
>   Have become invading battalions;
> And our faces, the institute-face, the chain-store, the ruin

> Are projecting their greed as the firing squad and the bomb.
> Madrid is the heart. Our moments of tenderness blossom
> 　　As the ambulance and the sandbag;
> Our hours of friendship into a people's army.

A range of commentators have attempted to fix the precise relationship between the private and the public, the psychological and the political, which is mapped in these lines. Arnold Kettle quotes Samuel Hynes's argument that these lines treat the Spanish Civil War in psychological and not political terms, and as an eruption of the sickness of modern society:

> In Spain, the enemy is *us* – our fears and greeds (as usual Auden invokes himself in the class he condemns), and the people's army is psychological, too, a sort of metaphor for loving feelings. It is more than a metaphor, though; in Spain 'our thoughts have bodies', what was mental has become physical, and therefore mortal. (Hynes 1976, pp253–4)

Kettle disagrees, arguing that the precise relationship between the private and the public is left open in the poem, and denying that it underwrites a view of the mental as more basic than the real. According to Kettle, in this poem Auden 'seems to be saying that the political decisions or choices which have to be made about Spain today are essential because history (a keyword in the poem) is not a force outside men and their dilemmas and neither are men and their dilemmas outside history' (1979, p98).

I think that Kettle is right that the posited relationship between mental events and political actions is far from simple. What the poem certainly does do is reject a view of mental events as self-referring or unattached to the world of – as Forster had it – telegrams and anger. 'Our thoughts have bodies' does not necessarily claim that our thoughts have produced these bodies, but it does make it unambiguously clear that what we do with our thoughts has implications in a world of killing and conflict. It is possible that Auden is drawing a contrast between Spain and (say) England: we should note that the poem tells us that '*On that tableland scored by rivers, /* Our thoughts have bodies' – in other words, that the impulses which in a country such as England may remain as mental events have been granted a physical embodiment in Spain. By implication, then, the moral responsibilities that we associated with the task of categorizing our mental impulses and deciding what to do with them have now been transformed into political responsibilities; at this time, the poem suggests, moral duties present themselves, and have to be responded to, in political terms. Thus 'Madrid is the heart' extends the conceit: Madrid is not just the capital, the political centre, the highest military goal, it represents the highest moral duty, the duty of love traditionally associated with the heart. Those positive moral impulses which would at one time have led to acts of personal tenderness or friendship blossom now into ambulance, sandbag, or the strengthening of a people's army. History at this point has fused with individual consciousness and conscience: 'yesterday' history proceeded apart from the personal; 'to-day' the struggle has fused the two together.

Such an interpretation can be strengthened by reference to the work of another poet. The Scottish poet Sorley Maclean's lyric sequence *Poems to Eimhir* was first published in Gaelic in 1943 and in English translation in 1971. The poems in the sequence were composed in the 1930s by a poet who describes himself as a 'Bolshevik' in the thirtieth poem in the sequence, and their stunning lyric intensity comes from Maclean's placing of his poetic persona's unreciprocated love for the 'Eimhir' of the title in a context of the anti-fascist struggle and, especially, of the moral claims made on the individual by the Spanish Civil War. Two stanzas in the eighteenth poem in the sequence are of particular relevance to an understanding of the context from which Auden's poem sprang – although Maclean's poem clearly dates from a slightly later time, when the Republic had been defeated by Franco's forces:

Today I clearly understand
the gulf that cracks across the mind,
strife on behalf of human-kind,
the choice that catches at our breath,
immortal dying or a living death.

Mine is a hopeless death alive
because I did not force my love
out of my splendid private grove,
because when History strode by
I loved a woman in my secret sky.

(Maclean 1971, p26)

Maclean's poetic sequence serves to remind us that recognizing the moral imperatives of a particular historical moment may well be easier than acting upon these imperatives; it also confirms that for many the stark alternatives presented by the Spanish Civil War had the effect of revolutionizing the way in which 'the personal' and 'the political' were apprehended. The force of Maclean's 'when History strode by' has much in common with Auden's 'History to the defeated'; both personify history as a stern and inflexible force which makes moral demands and can neither wait, nor help or pardon.

What is striking about the final stanza of 'Spain' – those lines to which Auden later took such great exception – is not that they equate goodness with success, but that they confront the battle between goodness and evil from an unflinchingly secular perspective. Indeed, far from equating goodness with success the lines suggest that if evil triumphs then there is no hope for goodness, there is no divinity ready to sympathize or to forgive this failure. It seems likely that it is the uncompromisingly secular vision of these lines, a vision which places all moral responsibility on human beings rather than sharing it between man and God, which Auden (who was to re-enter the Anglican communion a few short years after writing the poem) could no longer countenance. What these lines do, powerfully and magnificently, is to block off excuses and other-worldly hopes; they force the reader to look defeat in the eye and to see what it involves. There is no consolation prize in history.

In the course of time, as I have noted, Auden went on to reject parts – and then all – of this poem. This rejection has become associated with a more general set of positions on his part concerning the ineffectiveness of poetry. In the posthumous tribute volume to Auden edited by Stephen Spender, Anne Freemantle reports Auden's later beliefs as follows:

> I asked him whether he no longer felt himself a political animal and he replied: 'I know that all the verse I wrote, all the positions I took in the thirties, didn't save a single Jew. These attitudes, these writings, only help oneself. They merely make people who think like one, admire and like one – which is rather embarrassing.' Asked whether he ever wrote political – or *engagé*, as he preferred to call it – verse, he replied, 'In 1968 I wrote a poem on the invasion of Czechoslovakia. My spies tell me it is very well known in the USSR.' He did not, however, believe that poets could affect the political climate:
>
>> The social and political history of Europe would be just the same if Shakespeare, Dante and Goethe had never written. The only people who affect the political climate are journalists who try to produce the truth, and writers in countries where there is no freedom – so any statement from any writer carries weight. But the poet is really like Dr Johnson: 'I write a little better to endure the world and a little better to enjoy it.' (Spender 1975, pp89–90)

Commentators have linked such later remarks to the following lines in Auden's 'In Memory of W. B. Yeats':

> For poetry makes nothing happen: it survives
> In the valley of its saying where executives
> Would never want to tamper; it flows south
> From ranches of isolation and the busy griefs,
> Raw towns that we believe and die in; it survives,
> A way of happening, a mouth.

Those I have spoken to who were active in the struggle for support of Republican Spain have disagreed that 'Spain' made nothing happen, and have suggested that it played a significant part in convincing many that a commitment to Republican victory was the overwhelming moral imperative of the time. Moreover, if poetry makes nothing happen then it is hard to see why Auden should have reacted so strongly against what he saw as the wickedness of the poem's closing lines.

Arnold Kettle, in responding to the lines I have quoted from 'In Memory of W. B. Yeats', cites the following comment from Auden's 1935 essay 'Psychology and Art Today':

> You cannot tell people what to do, you can only tell them parables; and that is what art really is, particular stories of particular people and

experience, from which each according to his own immediate and peculiar needs may draw his own conclusions.

Kettle comments: 'The last statement is a rejection of poetry as propaganda; but it is an acceptance of the political rôle of the poet and of the fact that poetry can and does make something happen' (1979, p95).

Auden's own claim that his political poetry 'didn't save a single Jew' is, surely, a piece of Aunt Sallyism. Few have claimed that any engaged writing has such a measurable effect. But those who lived through the anti-fascist struggles of the 1930s have insisted on the importance of the work of writers such as Auden in the building up of resistance to fascism – a resistance which may not have saved Republican Spain but which certainly helped to unite many in struggle during the Second World War.

If we interpret the term 'ideology' in a broad manner as a system of ideas linked to power and power interests, then literature engages in ideological struggles, and ideological beliefs and commitments certainly *do* make things happen – or not happen. Kettle remarks, dryly, of Auden's poems and of his subsequent treatment of them, that 'history and ideology get into them all' (1979, p85). At the same time, I agree with Frank Kermode that '*good* poems about historical crises speak a different language from historical record and historical myth', that they make history strange, and interact with their historical contexts in ways calling for subtlety and caution (see p69). When I quoted Kermode's comments earlier I also referred to Jerome J. McGann's view that our inherited cultural materials represent and enact goals which simultaneously display their own insufficiencies, alienations, self-contradictions, and that only imaginative work does this – *et tout le reste est idéologie* (see p70). The difference is, I think, that Kermode defines ideology in a far narrower sense than does McGann, as something like 'the conscious manipulation of knowledge in the selfish interests of an empowered group'.

Both Kermode and McGann, it will be seen, concentrate upon the way in which major literature is able to present us with the complexities of a particular set of historical experiences in a manner different from that provided by history or myth. Not only did 'Spain' make things happen; it also allows us more insight into the happenings which it initiated, and to which it responded, than we get either from a historical account or from (a narrowly defined) ideology or myth. 'Spain' is *difficult*, and in our grappling with this difficulty we enact some of the historical complexities – or difficulties – from which it arose and which it addressed. It made something happen in the people who read and heard it in 1937 and it makes something happen in us today; and in wrestling with what it makes happen in us we come nearer to the reality (no scare-quotes) of the popular front against fascism than we would were we to restrict our concern to narrowly 'historical accounts'. As we struggle with 'Spain' we encounter what Foucault calls the literary work's 'modifiable heaviness', its refusal to allow us to pour our preconceptions into it without resistance.

II
John Keats, 'To Autumn'
Sowing the Seed of Opposition

I would like, at this point, to go back one hundred and twenty years to another poem which (I think) both arises out of and addresses a concern with historical process – John Keats's poem 'To Autumn'. I will approach this poem through Jerome J. McGann's discussion of it in his 'Keats and the Historical Method in Literary Criticism', – reprinted in *The Beauty of Inflections: Literary Investigations in Historical Method and Theory* (1985) – partly to illustrate the critical procedure of one of the most intelligent and perceptive of historicist critics, but partly to argue that intelligence and perceptiveness do not offer any guarantee against error.

As his starting point McGann takes Geoffrey Hartman's (1975) essay on the poem. His purpose is not to disagree with Hartman's contention that 'To Autumn' is an ideological poem 'whose very form expresses a national idea and a new stage of consciousness' but to take issue with Hartman's view that 'To Autumn' is a poem 'without an explicit social context' – that is, that it does not make the immediate factual context of its composition in *c.* September 1819 an explicit part of the poem (1985, p50).

McGann argues that to understand the explicit social involvement of 'To Autumn' we must 'reconstitute the initial stages of the poem's socialization', which means asking ourselves the question: 'when and where and by whom was the poem originally published?' (1985, pp50–51). 'To Autumn', he reminds us, was first published in the so-called 1820 volume of Keats's poems, which was published by Taylor and Hussey, the same publishers responsible for the publication of *Endymion* in 1818 – a volume which had been the immediate target of very hostile reviews. Consequently, McGann continues, when approached by Keats to publish the 1820 volume, Taylor and Hussey were interested but wary, and the 'key fact in the pre-publication history of the 1820 poems is the insistence by Keats's publishers that the book not contain anything that would provoke the reviewers to attack'. Thus the 1820 volume 'was constructed with a profoundly self-conscious attitude towards that climate of literary opinion which prevailed at the time' (1985, p52). In contrast, then, to other books published around the same time, such as Byron's *Don Juan* volumes and all of Shelley's works published in 1819–20 (including, for example, *Prometheus Unbound* and *Oedipus Tyrannus*), Keats's 1820 poems 'were issued not to provoke but to allay conflict' (1985, p53):

> In sharp contrast to a poem like *Prometheus Unbound*, Keats's mythologi-
> cally oriented works in his new book presented their early readers with
> ideas about art, myth, and imagination which did not open an explicit
> ideological attack upon the book's audience. The *Lamia* volume represented
> Keats's effort to show his readers how they might, by entering his poetic
> space, step aside from the conflicts and tensions which were so marked an

aspect of that period. The whole point of Keats's great and (politically) reactionary book was not to enlist poetry in the service of social and political causes – which is what Byron and Shelley were doing – but to dissolve social and political conflicts in the mediations of art and beauty. (I should note here that although the 1820 poems were politically reactionary at the time of their publication, they were deeply subversive at the time of their rediscovery by the Pre-Raphaelite Circle). (1985, p53)

McGann qualifies these comments with a footnote, part of which reads as follows:

It is, I hope, unnecessary to point out that the 'reactionary' and the 'subversive' character of Keats's poems is, in this context, a function of particular historical circumstances, and that the fundamentally *critical* aspects of the poetry persists through these changes. In both cases we see that Keats's poems refuse to be reconciled with the 'actual world', though in each case the poems pass their critical judgements on the world from different points of vantage. (1985, p53)

(I must note in passing that I have problems with the implication that the possession of 'fundamentally *critical*' aspects can, in the right context, make a poem reactionary.) McGann argues that all of the above matters constitute an 'explicit' part of a poem like 'To Autumn' because they were quite literally *made* explicit in the event of the poem's publication – although the explicit character of these subjects for today's reader reveals itself only through a historical analysis (1985, pp53–4).

McGann goes on to relate these defining contextual matters to such facts as that Keats chooses a slightly yet recognizably archaic style for the poem, and that he reinforces the poem's self-consciously assumed mythic quality by reference to mythic divinities such as Ceres and Bacchus. Furthermore (the argument continues) the second stanza of the poem superimposes images of contemporary peasant labourers on the androgynous figure of the pagan divinity, and all assume highly stylized poses in the poem. This is because they are picturesque figures, entering the poem via Keats's experience of them in the artistically mediated forms of various eighteenth-century paintings and engravings, and the landscapes of Claude and Poussin (1985, p54). This 'Romantic Classicism' has, McGann argues, a specifically ideological significance:

The poem's special effect is to remove the fearful aspects of these themes, to make us receive what might otherwise be threatening ideas in the simpler truth of certain forms which the poet presents as images of The Beautiful. (1985, p56)

McGann proposes that Keats's poem asks us to believe that all autumns are the same, and he half implies that this is because the *actual* autumn of 1819 – although a rich one in terms of the harvest – was also a very troubled one socially and politically. Keats wrote the poem in Winchester, in mid-September. But four days after Keats's arrival in Winchester on 12 August the massacre at St Peter's Fields (Peterloo) had taken place. This event called forth a politically focused and polemical response on the part of Shelley, whereas 'Keats's poem is an attempt to "escape" the period which provides the poem with its context' (1985, p61):

> Keats's autumn is the emblem of a condition freed from all weariness, fever, and fret, and his effort to describe such an autumn 'impersonally' is the sign of his own attempt to achieve such a condition in himself. But these lines remind us that the poem has been born in a desire, and that Keats's ideal autumn is not an impersonal or even an abstract autumn, but the dream of a mind that recalls the lost promise of the spring. (1985, p60)

For McGann,

> 'To Autumn' dramatizes Keats's self-conscious polemic for an art of sensations rather than an art of thought. The poem is not impersonal, it is tendentious and ideological in quite specific ways. Its message is that the fine arts, and by extension imagination generally, are more humanly productive than any of the other more practical sciences of the artificial. More even than this, 'To Autumn' argues for the power of a specific type of imaginative art, that is, for an art that can imagine the sufficiency of the imagination. (1985, p60)

McGann concludes that Hartman's view of the poem as an 'imagined picture . . . self-harvesting like the poet's own thoughts' is both a correct and a traditional view,

> But it is a view which agrees to read the poem simply, that is, wholly in terms of Keats's own artificially constructed fantasy. It takes the poem to be true, exclusively true, when in fact such a work – like all human works – is true only in the context of its field of social relations. The Romantic idea of imagination becomes, in Hartman's essay, a universal rather than an historical phenomenon. (1985, p62)

McGann is only one of a number of recent commentators who have tried to insist on the reactionary and escapist nature of Keats's poetry – a position which is very reminiscent of a much earlier critical commonplace typified by the comment of H. W. Garrod that for 'thinking of the earth Keats had in fact small aptitude; or it was an earth peopled only by flowers and the scent of flowers, or men and women whose nature was that of flowers and scents' (1926, p27). (And to do Garrod justice he goes on, immediately after making this comment, to add that 'And yet, more fully I think than we realize, he shared with the poets his contemporaries the revolutionary conscience; and this is his last word to us, not, I think, his truest word, but his last word, upon the office of the poet' [1926, pp27–8].)

More recently, Marjorie Levinson has picked up and developed a number of McGann's points. Thus Hartman's view of Keats's 'self-harvesting' picture becomes, in Levinson's book *Keats's Life of Allegory*, a social offensiveness which, according to Byron, stemmed from self-reflection, masturbation, and middle-class acquisition and display (1988, p18). For Levinson, the masturbatory element in 'To Autumn' is clear:

> Masturbation, that unnaturally hasty act, dreams of a 'slow time': a duration which neither wastes nor realizes, at once history's negation and its fulfillment. 'Deathwards progressing / To no death was that visage'. (Or, for a categorical association, purposiveness without purpose', Kant's definition of aesthetic experience.) Many of our fondest moments in Keats's poetry describe this condition: 'Their lips touched not, but had not bade adieu.' (The very time signature of 'To Autumn' is a code for this kind of *durée*; it is also the subject and object of this *undying* poem.) (1988, p27)

So: for McGann, 'To Autumn' is reactionary in its retreat from a world of struggle, a retreat from *history*, to an autumn of the imagination, a poetic funk-hole in which all autumns are the same. Levinson supports such a view, and underwrites Byron's sarcastic comments on Keats (Levinson helpfully gathers some of them together: 'a sort of mental masturbation – frigging his *Imagination*'; 'Johnny Keats's *piss a bed* poetry', 'the drivelling idiotism of the Mankin', 'dirty little blackguard Keates'; 'Self-polluter of the human mind' [1988, 18].)

All of this is very different from the received opinions of a decade or so ago, when the Garrod line on the complete alienation from a real world of politics, poverty, sexuality and war enjoyed by Keats's poetry was overturned in favour of a perception of the ways in which Keats's response to such matters informed his poetry through and through. Keats's radicalism was discovered and investigated (a useful brief survey of the evidence is provided by Elizabeth Cook in her introduction to the Oxford Authors *John Keats* [1990]).

I would like to ally myself with this older tradition of Keats criticism, and to do so through a consideration of 'To Autumn'. A good starting point is to be found in Marilyn Butler's *Romantics, Rebels and Reactionaries: English Literature and its Background 1760–1830* (1982). Butler notes that

> Keats's 'Hyperion, and the revised version 'The Fall of Hyperion', as well as 'The Ode to Autumn', are not now read as political or public poems. Yet 'Hyperion' does after all describe a revolution, the overthrow of the Titans by the Olympian gods. Its main literary source, *Paradise Lost*, is about the father of all rebellions, Satan's. There is evidence in the letters that Keats, a great reader of Hazlitt's journalism, had become interested in the French revolution and in the greater revolution that was still accomplishing . . . (1982, p151)

Frustratingly, Butler develops an argument about the two versions of 'Hyperion' as political poems, but does not come back to do the same for 'To Autumn'.[38] But she does go on to quote a long passage from a letter

---

[38] Arnold Davenport has argued that 'the main point of ['To Autumn'] as I see it is, after all, the main subject of *Hyperion* in which the glory of the new Gods shines out to

Keats wrote to his brother George and his wife Georgiana between 17 and 27 September, 1819. 'To Autumn' was written on 19 September or very soon after. The passage deserves to be quoted at some length:

> All civiled countries become gradually more enlighten'd and there should be a continual change for the better. Look at this Country at present and remember it when it was even thought impious to doubt the justice of a trial by Combat – From that time there has been a gradual change – Three great changes have been in progress – First for the better, next for the worse, and a third time for the better once more. The first was the gradual annihilation of the tyranny of the nobles. when kings found it their interest to conciliate common people, elevate them and be just to them. Just when baronial Power ceased and before standing armies were so dangerous, Taxes were few. kings were lifted by the people over the heads of their nobles, and those people held a rod over kings. The change for the worse in Europe was again this. The obligation of kings to the Multitude began to be forgotten – Custom had made noblemen the humble servants of kings – Then kings turned to the Nobles as the adorners of their power, the slaves of it, and from the people as creatures continually endeavouring to check them. Then in every kingdom therre was a long struggle of kings to destroy all popular privileges. The english were the only people in europe who made a grand kick at this. They were slaves to henry 8th but were freemen under willian 3rd at the time the french were abject slaves under Lewis 14th The example of England, and the liberal writers of france and england sowed the seed of opposition to this Tyranny – and it was swelling in the ground till it burst out in the french revolution – That has had an unlucky termination. It put a stop to the rapid progress of free sentiments in England; and gave our Court hopes of turning back to the despotism of the 16 century. They have made a handle of this event in every way to undermine our freedom. They spread a horrid superstition against all innovation and improvement – The present struggle in England of the people is to destroy this superstition. What has rous'd them to do it is their distresses – Perpaps on this account the pres'ent distresses of the nation are a fortunate thing – tho so horrid in their experience. You will see I mean that the french Revolution put a temporry stop to this third change, the change for the better – Now it is in progress again and I thing in an effectual one. This is no contest between whig and tory – but between right and wrong. (Cook 1990, pp506–7)

What is striking if one comes to this passage immediately after reading 'To Autumn' is the way in which historical change is described through metaphors of natural growth: 'The example of England, and the liberal writers of france and england sowed the seed of opposition to this Tyranny – and it was swelling in the ground till it burst out in the french revolution'; 'To swell the gourd, and plump the hazel shells'. Given that the line in the poem and the line in the letter were written at more or less the same

eclipse the Titans, the loss of whose old grandeur is the price that must be paid for the new beauty' (1958, p99).

time there is, surely, a strong case for investigating parallels between poem and letter at a more thematic level. At the same time, although the letter mentions 'the present struggle in England', Keats's poem – unlike Auden's – does not tell its readers: 'To-day the struggle'. Its contribution to the struggle against reaction and obscurantism is clearly *ideological*: 'to destroy' the 'horrid superstition against all innovation and improvement'.

The inevitability of the passing of the seasons is a traditional subject for poets, but it is one which can be used in a number of different ways. As seasonal change takes a cyclical and circular form it can be used to indicate a stability and permanence which underlies all human experience of change. Thomas Hardy's 'In Time of "The Breaking of Nations"', for example, contrasts the volatility and impermanence of political institutions ('Dynasties') with the enduring nature of a life linked to the cultivation of the soil – a life lived in harmony with natural cycles rather than artificial (i.e. political) upheavals and change. (I might also add that it has always seemed to me to be a poem which *because* of its failure to appreciate the far-reaching nature of historical change makes a claim which is simply untrue. The 'man harrowing clods' will *not* 'go onward the same / Though Dynasties pass', and the Hardy who wrote *Tess of the D'Urbervilles* and recognized that the mechanization of farm labour changed the whole relationship of human beings to the land and to one another had already understood this fact.) But seasonal change can also serve as a reminder that change – the decay of the old and the birth of the new – is always with us, and at a time of liberal pessimism such a reminder can be given clear political overtones. 'If Winter comes, can Spring be far behind?': few of Shelley's readers can have thought that he was primarily interested here in just the weather.

Keats's use of the metaphor of organic growth to represent social and political change in his letter to his brother and sister-in-law is important because it associates this metaphor with *linear* rather than with *cyclical* change: the line of development which Keats is plotting in the letter is not one that goes round and round, always returning to its starting point at some time, but one which goes forward – sometimes for the better and sometimes for the worse – but nevertheless forward. The evidence from the two Hyperion poems is also consistent with the view that for Keats historical change might be for better or for worse but it was hardly reversible. The other significant element in Keats's portrayal of historical change in the letter is that for Keats such change is neither wholly automatic nor entirely the result of human effort; the letter underwrites neither a wholly voluntarist conception of historical development nor one which follows a logic which is independent of human understanding or effort. Finally, one should note that this human understanding and effort includes (although it is not limited to) the work of 'the liberal writers of france and england': writers have a rôle to play in this struggle.

Now 'To Autumn' is not 'Spain', and many recent attacks on and dismissals of Keats's poetry seem to be concerned to condemn it for this. Keats was certainly not above writing more overtly propagandist poetry, and in a letter written 22 September 1819 he declared that 'I hope sincerely I shall be able to put a Mite of help to the Liberal side of the Question before I die' (Cook 1990, ppxxii–xxiii). But to condemn 'To Autumn' and other poems as reactionary because they are not 'Spain' is to fall back into a sort of ultra-leftist or Proletcult view of literary value, one which rejects all literary works which fail to address themselves to the immediate task of rousing the masses to revolution. It is worth remembering that Lenin criticized Proletcult positions, and that Engels, writing over half a century after the death of Keats, reminded a writer that 'a socialist-biased novel' aimed at 'bourgeois readers', 'fully achieves its purpose, in my view, if by conscientiously describing the real mutual relations, breaking down conventional illusions about them, it shatters the optimism of the bourgeois world, instils doubt as to the eternal character of the existing order, although the author does not offer any definite solution or does not even line up openly on any particular side' (1956, pp39–40).

'To Autumn' was written at a time of extreme social unrest, but also at a time of disappointed liberal hopes so far as developments in France were concerned. The restoration of the monarchy in France in 1815 led to a situation in which reactionary forces throughout Europe attempted to claim that it was now 'back to normal', that a terrible experiment had been made, had failed, and that things were now able to return to what they had always been. In other words, 'To Autumn' was composed at a time comparable in some ways to the time *after* the defeat of the Spanish Republic in the late 1930s – that time when W. H. Auden was beginning the task of undoing the political implications of his earlier verse. In such a situation any poem which appealed to people's understanding that change was always irreversible, that even defeats and apparent reverses never really took one back to square one, presented a clear ideological challenge to the ruling order. To put it another way, Keats's poem is written after that defeat which, as Auden's poem reminds us, history can neither help nor pardon – and it does rather more than just to say 'alas'.

What seems to me to be absolutely central to this poem is its insistence upon a tension between apparent stasis and actual change. Keats takes that part of the year in England at which time does seem to have slowed down or stopped, and even within this general framework he focuses in upon periods of rest and inactivity: waiting for the fruit to ripen, pausing in the middle of labour, observing the end of the day. But the poem is, at the same time, utterly saturated with change and movement; nothing is still, nothing is uninvolved in process. Most obviously, the three stanzas of the poem register temporal staging-posts: in the first stanza the harvest is still maturing, in the second the work of harvest is under way, and in the third stanza the stubble-plains inform us that the harvest is completed. But this insistence upon an omnipresent movement is observable at the level of local detail. The first stanza is packed with verbs of growth and movement: 'load', 'run', 'bend', 'fill', 'swell', 'plump' – and the *unexpectedness* of change is stressed in 'to set budding more, / And still more, later flowers for the bees', where syntactical closure is twice postponed in such a way as to frustrate our expectation that some sort of stasis will be achieved. Clearly the syntactical postponements, aided by deft use of the line-break, enact a situation in which the desire for and expectation of rest is repeatedly frustrated.

At a simple level this is obviously meant to capture what is presented as a typically autumnal experience: we keep thinking that autumn has reached its peak and that winter will follow, but we keep being surprised by yet more, and more fulfilled, autumnal satiety. But at a deeper level what such lines do is to chip away at confidence (or resignation) concerning any finality, any situation in which change has been arrested. In this quintessentially autumnal world, winter cannot be denied: 'to set budding more, / And still more, later flowers for the bees, / Until they think warm days will never cease' reminds *us*, of course, that warm days will cease and that the bees will die. We are put into a position of superior knowledge, the knowledge that no set of affairs is eternal, that ignorance of change is no defence against change. To this extent 'To Autumn' is as much a political poem as is Shelley's 'Ozymandias', a work which also mocks those who have believed that, in effect, warm days will never cease.

Of course, whereas 'Ozymandias' puts the reader in a position of superiority towards once arrogant power, 'To Autumn' has us enjoying that sense of autumnal stasis. But the point is that it does not *just* do this: at the same time as we are led to share that sense of time having stopped, we are also made continually aware on a more intellectual plane that it has not. In the second stanza, for example, the furrow is 'half-reaped' and a personified autumn's hook 'Spares the next swath' – but the very way in which such apparent stasis is worded makes us aware that the reaping will continue and that the next swath has enjoyed but a temporary reprieve. And by the third stanza that ominous note which has run through the whole poem is more insistent and more overt. The reader is told not to think of the songs of spring – but such advice inevitably encourages such thought, along with thought of winter. The day is 'soft-dying' and the light wind 'lives or dies', the 'stubble-plains' reveal that that swath has now been cut, and the fact that the small gnats 'mourn' is utterly in character with the note of lament struck in this stanza. Appropriately, the poem ends with mention of the red-breast (the bird traditionally associated with winter) and with the 'gathering swallows' – gathering to fly south.

It might be objected that the final stanza of the poem in particular associates change with death, and can thus hardly be said to inspire revolutionary optimism. In like manner, of course, the first Hyperion poem takes the reader through the grief of the challenged old order and seems quickly to run out of steam as it moves over to portray the birth of the new order. But to argue thus would, I think, be to attempt far too mechanical a political reading of the poem. After all, 'To Autumn' is, among other things, about autumn. Its political significance is neither overt nor to be traced in mechanical parallels as if it were a *roman à clef*. It is a poem which reaches out to its readers' common experiences of seasonal change and constructs out of them a more abstract pattern of stasis undermined by mutability, a pattern which could not but have had a political significance in the England of 1819. Whether Keats actually intended that his readers should so respond, or that he was aware of the possibility of such a response once he had written the poem, is neither here nor there. The important point is that at the level of his creative intelligence he recognized a parallel between a common human experience of 'change-in-stasis' and his intellectual understanding of the way in which 'All civiled countries become gradually more enlighten'd and there should be a continual change for the better'.

Thus Jerome J. McGann is, I believe, quite wrong to argue that, to repeat,

> The *Lamia* volume represented Keats's effort to show his readers how they might, by entering his poetic space, step aside from the conflicts and tensions which were so marked an aspect of that period. The whole point of Keats's great and (politically) reactionary book was not to enlist poetry in the service of social and political causes – which is what Byron and Shelley were doing – but to dissolve social and political conflicts in the mediations of art and beauty. (1985, p53)

It is, I believe, precisely 'the conflicts and tensions' of the period through which he is living in 1819 which force a particular view of history on to Keats, a view which informs his whole understanding of change and development in a poem such as 'To Autumn'. 'To Autumn' is not, as McGann implies, an escapist poem, or a poem which recommends or countenances escape. It is a poem which enlists an understanding of social and political causes in the task of investigating the relationship between our experience of the passage of time and time's underlying tensions and dynamics. It is a poem which forces the reader to recognize that any attempt to step aside from larger conflicts and tensions is liable to produce but a brief respite from their pressure. I also believe that McGann is absolutely wrong to talk of the refusal of Keats's 1820 poems to be reconciled with the 'actual world'; in 'To Autumn' we see that the inescapably mutable nature of the actual world is presented in such a way as to demonstrate first that any attempt to leave that world will be doomed to failure, and second that any belief in the permanent nature of the world as it now is, is also illusory.

Finally I think that McGann is also quite wrong to argue that '"To Autumn" dramatizes Keats's self-conscious polemic for an art of sensations rather than an art of thought'. 'To Autumn' is a highly intellectual poem. By this I mean that although its language and images are highly evocative of sensual and emotional experiences, these experiences are seen to be subordinate to processes of change and development which are apprehended not sensually or emotionally but intellectually. In the last resort the structure of 'To Autumn' is one which is based upon intellectual understanding and not sensual experience.

In like manner, I am also quite unable to accept Marjorie Levinson's view of 'To Autumn' as a sort of masturbatory indulgence in 'dreams of a "slow time": a duration which neither wastes nor realizes, at once history's negation and its fulfillment', and as an *'undying* poem' (Levinson is punning on the slang use of 'to die' for 'to achieve orgasm'.) The whole impetus of 'To Autumn' is towards that death which remains unrecognized *within* the poem but which the reader is constantly reminded cannot be avoided. It is not Keats, or 'To Autumn' which is masturbatory, but those experiences of stasis within the poem which lead to a belief that time can be controlled by the individual. And these are exposed by the poem as illusory.

Both 'Spain' and 'To Autumn' were written at a time during which public events forced a consciousness of the relationship between struggle and historical change on to their creators, and although both use metaphors of natural growth to describe processes of historical change both also are very much concerned with the way in which individuals can consciously participate in and aid – or hinder – such processes. Both poems recognize the desire to escape from history which motivates those individuals who live through such periods of struggle, but neither poem underwrites or countenances withdrawal or fatalism. Of course, much of what I have said is present overtly in 'Spain' and only by implication in 'To Autumn'. But readers living through periods of acute social and political crisis become very good at detecting what is implied rather than stated openly (a quick reading of Thomas Love Peacock's fiction written during the early nineteenth century is enough to confirm that readers must have been familiar with the political use of metaphors of organic growth). Reading these poems at other times, in other places, we are presented with insights and truths which are not merely local. We may apply these truths and insights in ways the poets could not have foreseen, but if we read these poems with both eyes open then the dead (and I do not just mean dead poets) can teach us things both about themselves and their time, and about ourselves and our time.

It seems to me, in fact, that McGann's and Levinson's critiques of 'To Autumn' reveal much about their own experiences of history, about their own lack of sympathy for that painstaking work of ideological reconstruction which is absolutely necessary at a time of reactionary advance. What Keats says to his readers – and his rulers – is comparable to what Galileo is reputed to have muttered after his forced recantation to the Inquisition: 'And yet it moves'. Being told that things move is what no reactionary authority wants to hear or to think about. Keats knew that things did move, and he knew that understanding this would weaken reaction and strengthen opposition to it. And no poem insists more effectively upon the fundamental and unstoppable fact of change than does 'To Autumn'. When radical change is impossible, being reminded that other forms of mutation and transformation are taking place has a moral force. 'To Autumn' is not 'England in 1819' or 'The Mask of Anarchy'. But to blame it for this is to display a sort of ultra-leftist impatience with the political constraints of the late twentieth century rather than fully to engage with the complex moral and political possibilities of 1819.

6

THE NOVELIST
AS HISTORIOGRAPHER

Histories about History

The two novels considered in this chapter are both the product of, and about, history (in both senses of the word[39]), simultaneously works which are born of, and engage with the problems of understanding, complex historical forces. They are also both works which address the two meanings of the phrase 'to write history', and which ask whether our skill in writing history[b] is related to our ability to write history[a] – that is, to direct and control the historical process itself. Both Joseph Conrad's *Nostromo* and Virginia Woolf's *Between the Acts* address two interlinked questions: what it is that determines the direction taken by human history, and what status do different attempts to write historical accounts enjoy? My main concern, however, will be with each work's consideration of problems of historiography – of how and why we write history[b], and with the various claims advanced for different historical accounts: truth, predictive power, comprehensiveness.

Such a focus of interest carries us back to many of the theories and debates discussed in the opening chapters of this book. The difference is, of course, that the problems of historiography with which I am now concerned are those isolated and scrutinized in works of fiction. As a result we are, I think, able to look at the same theories and debates considered in my opening chapters from an interestingly altered perspective. As we will see, this is not something of which Conrad and Woolf were unaware.

[39] The distinction between 'history as "what happened"' and 'history as "an attempt to recount what happened"' is particularly important in *Nostromo* and *Between the Acts*. Where this duality threatens to introduce confusion I will refer to these two alternatives as history[a] and history[b].

I
Joseph Conrad, *Nostromo*
History as Speculation

Conrad confronted the respective claims of fiction and history[b] directly, in his essay 'Henry James: An Appreciation', published a year after the publication of *Nostromo*, in 1905. In the essay he refers to James's attempt to claim for the novelist 'the standing of the historian', and agrees that such a claim is 'the only adequate one':

> I think that the claim cannot be contested, and that the position is unassailable. Fiction is history, human history, or it is nothing. But it is also more than that; it stands on firmer ground, being based on the reality of forms and the observation of social phenomena, whereas history is based on documents, and the reading of print and handwriting – on second-hand impression. Thus fiction is nearer truth. But let that pass. A historian may be an artist too, and a novelist is a historian, the preserver, the keeper, the expounder, of human experience. (1921c, pp20–21)

Like so much of Conrad's non-fictional prose, the comments seem at first to be clear and straightforward, but become rather more puzzling the more the reader tries to work out exactly what they mean. The initial contrast between the second-hand nature of history[b] and the (by implication) more first-hand nature of fiction ('fiction is nearer truth' because its sources are nearer reality, are primary rather than second-hand) is clear enough.

What is also apparent is that fiction, for Conrad, involves some combining of the writer's non-textual observation of the specifically *human* ('social phenomena', 'human experience') with something that lies perhaps partly hidden from direct human scrutiny, some underlying *material* reality ('the reality of forms').[40] As we will see, in *Nostromo* Conrad makes it clear

---

[40] 'Forms' can mean a variety of things in Conrad's writing: '(physical) outlines' (often indistinct), 'conventions or manners', and the observable, material manifestations of that which is hidden. Most likely it is the third of these to which Conrad alludes when claiming that fiction is based upon the reality of forms. In *Nostromo*, for example, we are told of Decoud that his individuality 'had merged into the world of cloud and water, of natural forces and forms of nature' (1984, p497). In the later *The Shadow-Line* the narrator tells us that 'nothing in the way of abstraction could have equalled my deep detachment from the forms and colours of this world' (1985, p35). Conrad frequently associates the word with the word 'material'. In *The Secret Agent* we learn that a padlock was the only object in the Professor's room on which the eye could rest 'without becoming afflicted by the miserable unloveliness of forms and the poverty of material' (1990, p225); in 'The Planter of Malata' we have a reference to 'the solid forms of the everyday material world' (1950, p12); in 'The Return' it is 'the protean and enticing forms of the cupidity that rules a material world of foolish joys, of contemptible sorrows' (1947, pp177–8); in *Lord Jim* Marlow talks of 'all forms of matter – which, after all, is our domain' (1983, p246); and in *Victory* we have 'the world of material forms' (1986, p406).

that what human beings *experience* constitutes only a part – and perhaps only a subsidiary part – of the totality of human history.

Conrad's contrasting of fiction and history[b] has, so far as the latter term is concerned, a textualist ring to it; history[b] is a matter of interpreting texts, texts which (as Conrad insisted very frequently) had no guaranteed relationship to extratextual reality. Historians are artists, and novelists are historians: once again, Hayden White (or Louis Montrose) *avant la lettre*. But if Conrad's view of history[b] comes close to that of certain recent post-structuralist or textualist writers here, his conceptualization of fiction does not. Fiction, according to Conrad, is based upon a direct contact with that reality with which documents engage only at second-hand: 'the reality of forms and the observation of social phenomena', 'the preserver, the keeper, the expounder, of human experience'. This essentially realist view of fiction is very much at odds with the formalism of textualists such as White, and with a range of post-structuralist extensions of well-established formalist positions. For Conrad, fiction's claim to present a fuller account of history[a] than that presented by the historians resides in its ability to dramatize and display the ways in which the experienced and the non-experienced constitute separate determining forces which at times interpenetrate and at times diverge from each other. And in *Nostromo* Conrad confronts the issue of the relative power of these two elements – confronts, to use the jargon of Marxism, the issue of the primacy of superstructure or base. His answer is more complex than many of those answers given by others who have attempted to establish such a hierarchy of determining forces – both Marxist and anti-Marxist.

Nostromo is a novel which presents the reader with a familiar complex of political developments – South American revolution, counter-revolution, regional secession and international involvement – along with some of the human aspirations, experiences and actions which both arise out of and contribute to these developments. I say 'some of' because, as Robert Holton has so convincingly pointed out, the subject-positions examined or even recognized in *Nostromo* are, like lifeboat places in the *Titanic*, not allotted to all. As Holton puts it, Conrad 'encourages critical attention to focus . . . on the subjectivity of certain selected figures and their complex networks of relationships – both interpersonal relationships and relationships to the overall movement of history', and he reminds us that '[n]owhere in the novel are the natives given the opportunity – as the Blancos frequently are – to articulate a political position or to narrate a version of historical events' (1994, pp58, 59). These natives represent an absent centre, and Holton argues that while we are given paternalistic depictions of them (from the viewpoint of Emilia Gould) and more racist ones from Captain Mitchell, they are never allowed to articulate their own history by means of their own discourse. Instead, they are either exiled to an anonymous and timeless past, 'as picturesque essentially premodern scenery', or they are seen through European eyes as enjoying a lifestyle essentially either absurd or irrational (1994, p69). Conrad's notable (and morally admirable) anti-imperialism should not blind us to the real possibility that, along with many well-meaning liberal contemporaries, he may well have assumed that many 'natives' were actually without a subjectivity. I have elsewhere pointed out in the course of a study of Conrad's use of Free Indirect Discourse, that in his first novel, *Almayer's Folly*, the slave-girl Taminah's consciousness is never rendered for the reader, and that this may well be related to Conrad's apparent belief that she had no conscious subjectivity (Hawthorn 1990, p5). If this seems far-fetched, consider the following passage describing Taminah:

> In that supple figure straight as an arrow, so graceful and free in its walk, behind those soft eyes that spoke of nothing but unconscious resignation, there slept all feelings and all passions; all hopes and all fears; the curse of life and the consolation of death. And she knew nothing of it all. She lived like the tall palms amongst which she was passing now, seeking the light, desiring the sunshine, fearing the storm, unconscious of either. The slave had no hope and knew of no change. – She knew of no other sky, no other water, no other forest, no other world, no other life. She had no wish, no hope, no love, no fear except of a blow, and no vivid feeling but that of occasional hunger, which was seldom. . . . The absence of pain and hunger was her happiness, and when she felt unhappy she was simply tired, more than usual, after the day's labour. – Then in the hot nights of the S. W. monsoon she slept dreamlessly under the bright stars . . . (1994, p85)

How could such a being have a discourse to write her own history when she lacks even a consciousness to understand her own sensations, which have to be interpreted and reported on by a paternalistic European narrator? Robert Holton refers tellingly to Frantz Fanon's depiction of the colonial world as one in which 'the natives "form an almost inorganic background for the innovating dynamism of colonial mercantilism"' (1994, p90, quoting from Fanon [1963], p41). In the above passage we can note that the palms receive Taminah amongst them as equal: natural, unconscious, ignorant, and inarticulate – needing another's discourse in order to be depicted.[41] She is allowed feeling but not thought – a reminder that the attribution of a 'structure of feeling' may not necessarily confer full personhood on the recipient.

There is, then, an ironic sense in which the thrust of *Nostromo*'s attack on partial histories can be turned against the novel itself. For while the narrative repeatedly exposes the histories and historians it depicts as partial (in both senses of the word), the history told *by* the novel is in certain ways as partial as those it both contains and exposes.

Nostromo, of course, repeatedly contrasts the disparity between the understandings of those non-natives involved in the history of Costaguana

[41] So much so that at some stage in the text's history a typesetter or an editor changed Conrad's manuscript 'amongst which' to 'amongst whom', an error found both in the second English edition and also in the very widely used Dent edition (Conrad 1947). See the textual apparatus in the new Cambridge Edition text (Conrad 1994). The error clearly conformed so well to the perceived tenor of the passage that it remained uncorrected for many years.

– their plans, desires, interpretations, interventions – and what are seen as the 'real' or effective forces which have actually brought about certain states of affairs. This is not to say that the novel denies that human beings contribute to historical change, but it does deny that, in most cases, they so contribute knowingly or effectively. We are told, for example, that 'even the acute agent of the San Tomé mine' is deceived by the stupid and vain Pedrito Montero:

> It could never had entered his head that Pedrito Montero, lackey or inferior scribe, lodged in the garrets of the various Parisian hotels where the Costaguana Legation used to shelter its diplomatic dignity, had been devouring the lighter sort of historical works in the French language, such, for instance as the books of Imbert de Saint Amand upon the Second Empire. But Pedrito had been struck by the splendour of a brilliant court, and had conceived the idea of an existence for himself where, like the Duc de Morny, he would associate the command of every pleasure with the conduct of political affairs and enjoy power supremely in every way. Nobody could have guessed that. And yet this was one of the immediate causes of the Monterist Revolution. This will appear less incredible by the reflection that the fundamental causes were the same as ever, rooted in the political immaturity of the people, in the indolence of the upper classes and the mental darkness of the lower. (1984, p387)

The distinction drawn here between 'immediate causes' and 'fundamental causes', it needs to be stressed, cuts across and is complicated by another distinction: that between a cause of the revolution which 'nobody could have guessed', and others which, by implication, were available to discovery by intelligent investigators. The 'fundamental causes', it is implied, exert a pressure which could be termed *tendential*, one which can be confirmed or frustrated by more accidental or adventitious pressures. It should not escape our attention that one of these more accidental elements results from acts of *reading*. Reading changes people's pictures of the world and of themselves, and it is in part on the basis of such pictures that they may attempt to intervene in the world, may try to alter the passage of events.[42]

I want, shortly, to turn to further examples of a human misperception of the elements involved in determining the path of historical development in the novel. Before I do this I want to propose that what Conrad indicates are 'fundamental causes' of revolution can be contrasted with a very different sort of fundamental cause to which the novel obsessively returns. The fundamental causes mentioned above are, generally, what Marxists would call superstructural ones; they involve mental states rather than material factors. But throughout *Nostromo* a different sort of fundamental

---

[42] The reading of non-literary texts may have a beneficial effect in the world of Conrad's fiction, as it does in *Typhoon*, but the reading of fictional texts seems rarely if ever to do so. The title character of *Lord Jim* is one of very many in Conrad's fiction who is corrupted by a course of 'light holiday reading'. See Hawthorn (1994b) for a discussion of Conrad's theory of reading.

cause is repetitively indicated: 'material interests'. From the start of the novel an opposition is traced between the non-materialistic Mrs Gould, and her husband who pins his hopes to these 'material interests'. Even 'the most legitimate touch of materialism was wanting in Mrs. Gould's character' (1984, p75). When her husband says of the American millionaire Holroyd that

> 'Of course a man that sort can take up a thing or drop it when he likes. He will suffer from no sense of defeat. He may have to give in, or he may have to die to-morrow, but the great silver and iron deposits shall survive, and some day shall get hold of Costaguana along with the rest of the world.' (1984, p82)

she objects that, 'This seems to me most awful materialism'. Her husband interrupts and does not allow her to finish what she has to say.[43] His position is straightforward:

> 'Any one can declaim about these things, but I pin my faith to material interests. Only let the material interests once get a firm footing, and they are bound to impose the conditions on which alone they can continue to exist. That's how your money-making is justified here in the face of lawlessness and disorder. It is justified because the security which it demands must be shared with an oppressed people. A better justice will come afterwards. That's your ray of hope.' (1984, p84)

Throughout the novel Gould repeatedly rejects words and eloquence in favour of what he clearly sees as the real foundation of material interests. And to a considerable extent Gould is proved right. The silver mine – symbol of material interests in the novel – *is* the most important single factor in determining what happens in *Nostromo*. The mine does not directly initiate events, of course; its influence is obtained indirectly and through its conscription of human plans and desires. But without the mine, the foreign involvement in the affairs of Costaguana which underwrites the secession of the new and silver-rich Occidental state, would not take place.

The prophetic nature of Conrad's novel goes a long way towards confirming the accuracy of its analysis of the hierarchy of determining forces which initiate and fix historical change. The twentieth century has seen many revolutions, many examples of foreign intervention, many cases of secession – and more often than not silver mines or their equivalents have played a key rôle in the unfolding of events. Different analyses of the past can, we should remember, be judged in part by reference to the success with which the principles which have guided them can correctly predict the outcome of as-yet unresolved historical processes. There seems little doubt that although – as Conrad shows – silver mines and the reading of historical romances can both contribute to processes of historical change,

[43] For a very stimulating account of the import of (among other things) the act of interrupting another's speech in Conrad, see Fogel (1985).

the permanence of such change is likely to have more to do with silver mines than with reading the books of Imbert de Saint Amand.

But if such a conclusion might seem to buttress traditional Marxist views of the way in which the determinants of historical change can be ranked, it has to be added that Charles Gould – the person who believes in the efficacy of material interests – ends up destroying himself and his marriage. The material interests *do* 'impose the conditions on which alone they can continue to exist', but they are, ironically, conditions which destroy the person who has recognized this fact. It is, additionally, worth noting that the use of a personification at this point ('material interests' rather than 'the actions of the foreigners who own and control the mine') helps to conceal and disguise agency in much the same way as did blaming the loss of the *Titanic* on the actions of a desire for luxury instead of on the White Star Line and its servants.

I will return to this point, but first I want as promised to consider some other examples of human misperceptions of what it is that controls the path or logic of history[a]. The most obvious candidate in the novel for the position of unsuccessful historian is Don José Avellanos, whose *Fifty Years of Misrule* ends up being physically dispersed in the course of the secessionist struggle, its newly printed pages 'littering the Plaza, floating in the gutters, fired out as wads for trabucos loaded with handfuls of type, blown in the wind, trampled in the mud' (1984, p235). The symbolism is unusually crude for Conrad: liberal history[b] is no match for the crudities of a power politics which it treats as aberration and fails to recognize as norm. Faced with the realities of such power politics, liberal history[b] becomes so much waste-paper. Avellanos's 'misrule' is in fact the rule, not the misrule. A few pages after the above comment (made by Martin Decoud in his letter to his sister), the dismissal of liberal illusions is extended to the parliamentary hopes of Avellanos and others. Pamela H. Demory has suggested, convincingly I think, that with the name 'Avellanos' Conrad is punning on that of Avellaneda, 'the writer who usurped Cervantes' characters and published a "false" sequel to *Don Quixote*'. According to her, 'both Avellanos and Avellaneda . . . are bad historians; and both novels demonstrate in various ways that history is a construction, that historical truth is relative' (1994, p2).

Another palpably unsuccessful historian in *Nostromo* is the English Captain Mitchell. Indeed, his candidature for this office is given overt authorial support: 'Captain Mitchell, feeling more and more in the thick of history, found time for an hour or so during an afternoon in the drawing-room of the Casa Gould, where, with a strange ignorance of the real forces at work around him, he professed himself delighted to get away from the strain of affairs' (1984, p136). Much later in the novel we are told of him that he is 'penetrated by the sense of historical importance of men, events, and buildings' (1984, p475), but this sense is clearly uninformed by any penetration *into* 'the real forces at work around him'.

In contrast to Don José Avellanos's and Captain Mitchell's very limited understanding of the forces which determine the course of history[b] are the more penetrating perceptions of Martin Decoud and Mrs Gould. *Nostromo* seems to give far more credence to Decoud's understanding of 'the real forces at work around him' than to that of Captain Mitchell:

> 'No, but just imagine our forefathers in morions and corselets drawn up outside this gate, and a band of adventurers just landed from their ships in the harbour there. Thieves, of course. Speculators, too. Their expeditions, each one, were the speculations of grave and reverend persons in England. That is history, as that absurd sailor Mitchell is always saying.' (1984, p174)

What Decoud understands is the way in which brute force *combines with* material interests and ideas ('speculations' carries both meanings) to determine the direction of historical development. Decoud's 'That is history' carries, one feels, the assent of the narrative.

Of Mrs Gould we are told early in the novel that she knew the latest phase in the history of the mine: 'It was in essence the history of her married life' (1984, p66). What is striking about this comment is that for once we have a welding together of history[a] and history[b]; the history of Mrs Gould's married life is both 'what happened' and also her memorial account of what happened.

What I want to draw attention to is the fact that while *Nostromo* seems to support both Decoud's and Mrs Gould's claims to being better historians than either Don José or Captain Mitchell, it is also clear that neither one of them is without shortcomings, for while Decoud lacks Mrs Gould's ability to combine a lived sense of what happened with an ability to reconstruct this process, Mrs Gould (whose character, we remember, lacks even the most *legitimate* touch of materialism) lacks Decoud's understanding of the historical effectiveness of brute physical force. A real 'history[b]', *Nostromo* implies, must unite the insights of both Decoud and Mrs Gould. And perhaps the nearest we get to such a combination is in Dr Monygham's comment late on in the novel to the disillusioned Mrs Gould:

> 'No!' interrupted the doctor. 'There is no peace and no rest in the development of material interests. They have their law, and their justice. But it is founded on expediency, and is inhuman; it is without rectitude, without the continuity and the force that can be found only in a moral principle. Mrs. Gould, the time approaches when all that the Gould Concession stands for shall weigh as heavily upon the people as the barbarism, cruelty, and misrule of a few years back.' (1984, p511)

This is, surely, a comment which also points in the direction of a unified history[a+b]. It is a prescription for those who would intervene in the events of history[a] at the same time as it is a reminder that those who would write history[b] must take into account more than the determining import of material interests. It is a recipe for both making, and writing, history. It should be underscored, too, that for Dr Monygham a moral principle has both continuity and *force*; the novel's earlier suggestion that Don José Avellanos's liberal ideas are without any real purchase on events should, therefore, not be taken to imply that for Conrad (or for *Nostromo*) it is only material interests which are powerful. At the same time, Robert Holton is quite right to remind us that Conrad's ironic exposure of the limitations of the Blancos in *Nostromo* stops well short of any recognition of the native peoples as entitled to their own discourse of history. The narrative of *Nostromo* presents itself to the reader as able to perceive a historical totality of which the different characters of the novel can observe but a part. This 'totality' is however less than all-embracing.

I want now to look at *Nostromo* from a rather different perspective. *Nostromo* is itself an emplotment, although using this term about a work of fiction is admittedly more problematic than it is to use it about a work of history[b]. It is more problematic because even if one agrees that the historian, as Hayden White argues, takes a set of events, constructs them into a story, and then emplots this story in a particular way, the writer of fiction produces his or her events and story by implication at the same time as he or she emplots them. Few novelists first work out an idea of 'what really happened' and then seek to emplot this.[44] Nonetheless, the reader of *Nostromo* can, by treating the fictional world as real, to a considerable extent work out a tripartite map of what happened (events), why and how it happened (story), and how the narrative emplots this story. At the level of an analysis of the narrative of *Nostromo*, then, we can cast much light on the view of history[a] and history[b] endorsed by the novel.

One of the most striking aspects of the narrative of *Nostromo* is the way in which it makes problematic the very concept of 'event' through its manipulation of what narratologists call 'frequency', which refers to the relationship between the number of times an event *happens*, and the number of times it is *told*. In *Nostromo* Conrad manipulates frequency in such a way as continually to confuse the reader as to whether a particular event happened once, or happened many times.

In a very interesting study, Leona Toker has suggested that the uncertainty that such switches and indeterminacies produce on the reader is not accidental, and that the reader's inability to tell whether an action was repetitive, customary and unimportant – or unique and of great significance – mirrors a comparable uncertainty in the lives of the characters of the novel. Pamela H. Demory sees this element in the novel's construction as one of a number of techniques designed to deny 'temporal reference points' to the reader and thus make the narrative hard to follow. For her, '"What really happened" [in Nostromo] is unrecoverable'. *Nostromo* thus not only enters 'into the critical reevaluation of the nature of history that began in the early twentieth century', but

---

[44] Many issues relevant to this section are debated by Barbara Herrnstein Smith, Nelson Goodman and Seymour Chatman in their respective contributions to Mitchell (1981).

> Structurally and thematically, *Nostromo* undermines [traditional] common-place assumptions about the nature of history in the same way that certain historiographers are reevaluating assumptions about historical writing. (1993, p317)

For Demory, then, the view of history encouraged by a reading of *Nostromo* really is Hayden White's *avant la lettre*; for her, all attempts to trace 'what really happened' in the novel are doomed to failure. The reader can choose between a variety of interpretations which can be ranked only aesthetically and not by reference to the standard of an independent reality. Seen from this perspective, *Nostromo* thus enacts the impotence of modern historiography, doomed to produce stories which remain forever alienated from the reality which they claim to represent.

This seems to me to go too far. It is, in fact, not too hard to work out most of what 'really happened' in the novel. More than this: through its detailing of the interaction of larger forces and personal issues (from silver mines to romantic novels) we are also able to follow, more or less accurately, *why* and *how* what happened, happened. What the narrative's manipulation of frequency does, it seems to me, is temporarily to involve the reader in the misunderstandings and misperceptions of the characters of the novel. Once the novel is over the reader (and a perceptive character such as Dr Monygham) can work out both what has happened along with why and how it happened – although it is true that no character in *Nostromo* has so comprehensive an understanding of 'what happened' as has an attentive reader (or, ideally, re-reader) of the novel. But such under-standing is very much a *post facto* or after-the-event reconstruction; while events are unfolding both characters and the first-time reader are equally unable to construct a logic of history[a] which will allow for the accurate prediction of events. One could say, in other words, that *Nostromo* shares Marxism's belief in the possibility of writing a history[b] which will trace the unfolding of the dominance of the material basis (the phrase 'material interests' encompasses both this material basis and also its workings in the hearts and minds of those it affects). But Marxism also claims predictive power: given an understanding of the logic of historical development, the argument runs, human beings can combine to affect the course of history[a], they can write history[a+b]. About such a possibility, *Nostromo* is far less sanguine – perhaps partly because its denial of full personhood to the natives of Costaguana severely restricts the extent to which a comprehensive alliance of those involved in the region's history can be entered into.

What human beings *can* do, *Nostromo* would seem to suggest, is to commit themselves to 'the continuity and the force that can be found only in a moral principle' such that the workings of material interests are *not* allowed 'to impose the conditions on which alone they can continue to exist', but are forced to exist in conditions which are at least in part determined by human needs rather than by abstract and unfettered material interests. Such a commitment can guarantee no single outcome, as those closing lines of 'Spain' to which W. H. Auden was to take such great exception remind us. There will always be 'the defeated' in history[a]: life is not Hollywood and the good do not always win. But a world in which those in the right are guaranteed no victory is, Conrad suggests, preferable to a world in which material interests are allowed their victories on their own terms. Such an outlook has, at any rate, a moral strength and an integrity that seems to me to be infinitely superior to that of Hayden White's historiography. For White, at least as he expresses the matter in his *Metahistory*, plot structures 'represent an armory of relational models by which what would otherwise be nothing but chains of mechanical causes and events can be translated in moral terms' (see p41). Morality, in other words, is how we translate the mechanical processes of history into human terms – not how we influence or even alter these processes. In *Nostromo* Conrad is not optimistic about human beings' ability to control history[a]. But in this novel it is clear that morality is not – as it seems to be for Hayden White in *Metahistory* – a spectatorial sport. Human beings must try to do more than write history[b]; they must try to write history[a+b]. In seeking to understand the forces which determine history[a] they must attempt to humanize these forces. And the principles according to which they make this attempt can only be moral ones. The paradox of *Nostromo* is that Conrad is able to perceive this truth even though it is clearly quite beyond the reach of his imagination to consider that *all* human beings might be able to write history[a+b] – including those marginalized, disenfranchised and deprived of their very subjectivity by his narrative: the native Costaguanans.

II
Virginia Woolf, *Between the Acts*
History as Abortion

Although much of Virginia Woolf's fiction concerns itself with the passage of time and the workings of this process on human memory and experience, none of her full-length novels is so centrally concerned with the *production* of history – what I have referred to as history[b] – as is *Between the Acts*. Lucy Swithin's 'favourite reading' is *An Outline of History*, and after reading this text and its description of a prehistoric world full of monsters such as 'the iguanadon, the mammoth, and the mastodon', we are told that the sight of a thrush carrying a worm tempts her 'to continue her imaginative reconstruction of the past', and that 'she was given to increasing the bounds of the moment by flights into past or future' (1970, p9). The main events of the novel occur between her acts of reading this text. Lucy's imaginative reconstruction of the past does not go unchallenged in the novel, however, and Elizabeth Lambert has pointed out that a clash between the different ways in which she and her brother Bart 'appropriate the discourses of authority to make sense of their experience' remains in the novel, although it is more sharply drawn in Woolf's first draft *Pointz Hall* (1993, p83).

Moreover the pageant, which is the main public event around which the novel is structured, presents its audience – and the novel's readers – with its own outline of English history. Hardly anything in the novel is presented independently of a sense of its placing within a process of historical change or continuity: characters, house, locality, activities – all are set in a temporal context. But this 'placing' is seen as a problematic matter; the past is not straightforwardly available to characters' recuperation and display, but must be painstakingly searched for and carefully reconstructed.

This emphasis upon recapturing the past and charting the passage of time does not, however, detract from a very heightened awareness of the present moment. Indeed, 'sense of past' and 'sense of present' serve continuously to draw attention to each other, to set each other in relief. It is 'a June day in 1939', and the talk at the pageant is of the impending war; while Mr Streatfield is giving his closing address after the dramatic performance he is interrupted by 'Twelve aeroplanes in perfect formation like a flight of wild duck' (1970, p193). Giles Oliver suffers internal torments and frustrated fury at the seeming obliviousness of his companions to what is taking place across the English Channel, but he is by no means the only character affected by ominous current events. The novel's 'time present' was also the time present of its author, and its sense of history is as much inspired by the pressure of contemporary events as is W. H. Auden's 'Spain': times of crisis do not just make people think about the present, they encourage them to set this complex present in a context of more general historical development.

The first mention of the novel in Virginia Woolf's diary is in the entry for 12 April 1938, not long after Hitler's annexation of Austria. The same source gives 23 November 1940 as the day on which the novel (actually the first draft of the novel) was completed – soon after the Battle of Britain, which took place in the skies over south-east England and Woolf's Sussex residence. One diary entry describes her witnessing of a German plane disappearing among fir trees pursued by two British planes (see Bell 1984, pp133, 340, 312). Woolf's writing of *Between the Acts* took place during a time of constant worry about the threat of first war and then invasion (her membership of the Labour Party and, in particular, the fact that her husband, Leonard Woolf, was Jewish, would, they knew, guarantee that both would be persecuted by any occupying German army). The latter stages of the novel's composition were accompanied by the war at home: the defeat in France and the Dunkirk evacuation, the Battle of Britain, and the London Blitz, during which her own home was damaged and that of her sister was destroyed. Her diary entry for 17 October 1940 moves from discussing her work on the novel, to the air-raid siren, and to the comment, 'Every day seen against a very faint shade of bodily risk' (Bell 1984, p330). Hana Wirth-Necher reminds us that in a letter to Hugh Walpole written 29 September 1940, Woolf writes an X to mark the place at which her pen jumped out of her hand because a bomb had shaken the window so violently (see Nicolson and Trautmann 1980, p435).

Hana Wirth-Necher also argues that with 'every bomb that fell on London, with every donning of her gas mask, Woolf dug in deeper, as the manuscript absorbed the shock waves. Rather than retreating from artistic experimentation, Woolf invented literary strategies for registering the experience of war on the homefront, for resistance through art' (1994, p183). In particular, Wirth-Necher suggests that parallels can be drawn between the way in which Woolf depicts the war in her diary, and the way in which she structures the narrative of *Between the Acts*:

> The two major strains in her record of the war, therefore, are cognitive disorientation and reverse evolution. Her tendency is to describe the war as a play, at times with herself in the role of audience and at other times in the role of performer. At the same time, the war seems to have had the effect of stripping humanity to some primal state so that the end of civilization is a return to its beginning. Her impressions of the war, then, were influenced by Darwinian constructs that shaped so much of the literary and cultural discourse of her time. (1994, p186)

Thus the war serves not just as a backdrop to the writing of the novel, or to the experiences of its characters, but as originating force behind the particular form that its narrative assumes.

Virginia Woolf is not usually thought of as a postmodernist, and yet her view of what I have referred to as history[b] (that is, the process of representing the past in narratives) has many odd parallels with the historiography of Hayden White. In the world of *Between the Acts*, for example, one of the most important ways in which history[b] is constructed is through the mediation of art. Our view of the past is constructed for us by means of (among other things) the visions of artists of one sort or another. The historical pageant presents us with scenes from English history which all take their forms from representative genres of English literature, presented in pastiche form by the local actors. Ironically, when the main characters in the novel are called upon to display their acquaintance with the great works of English literature, they can only present garbled and inaccurate versions. Called upon to continue Hamlet's 'To be or not to be' soliloquy, Isa quotes from Keats's 'Ode to a Nightingale', a quotation which inspires William Dodge to misquote a line from the same poem (1970, p54). Many of the books in the library are 'shilling shockers' which bored 'week-enders' have bought to read on the three-hour journey to the village, and hardly reflect 'the anguish of a Queen or the heroism of King Harry' (1970, p16). The literary quotations which come to Giles's mind come in fragments, and he forgets the words (1970, p85).

We construct history[b] from history[a], the novel seems to suggest, by moulding events into patterns extracted from inadequately remembered literary works. Raw reality is too strong, too fragmentary, too unformed for us to be able to cope with it. When the pageant ends with the audience being forced to confront their own reflections in the mirrors held up in front of them by the performers, this glimpse of unmediated, unnarrated reality is too much for people:

> Ourselves! Ourselves!
> Out they leapt, jerked, skipped. Flashing, dazzling, dancing, jumping. Now old Bart . . . he was caught. Now Manresa. Here a nose . . . There a skirt . . . Then trousers only . . . Now perhaps a face. . . . Ourselves? But that's cruel. To snap us as we are, before we've had time to assume . . . And only, too, in parts . . . That's what's so distorting and upsetting and utterly unfair. (1970, p184)

If, as T. S. Eliot had it, humankind cannot bear too much reality, help is at hand in the form of art. Art softens the blow of immediacy and instead of disconnected flashes ('*All you can see of yourselves is scraps, orts and fragments*' [1970, p188]) it gives us the illusion of coherence and logical sequence. Human beings, seen from this perspective, are like the butterflies fooled by the trappings of art at the pageant: 'Red Admirals gluttonously absorbed richness from dish cloths, cabbage whites drank icy coolness from silver paper' (1970, p63). History[a] is actually *experienced* as a muddle of incoherent fragments which resemble Hayden White's disconnected 'events', but art helps us to construct a pleasing history[b], one which gives us a reassuring if perhaps false sense of a unified and logically coherent passage of time from past to present – and on to the future. Art, in this view of things, emplots reality for us in the most aesthetically satisfying manner – even when, paradoxically, our direct knowledge of art is as fragmented and incomplete as is reality itself.

If the pageant itself displays this process with reference to literature, other art forms are also involved in the transformations of reality into history[b]. Members of the audience use songs, again in fragments, as their own tickets for a journey back into the past:

> 'I remember . . .' she nodded in time to the tune. 'You remember too – how they used to cry it down the streets.' They remembered – the curtains blowing, and the men crying: 'All a blowing, all a growing', as they came with geraniums, sweet william, in pots, down the street.
> 'A harp, I remember, and a hansom and a growler. So quiet the street was then. Two for a handsom, was it? One for a growler? And Ellen, in cap and apron, whistling in the street? D'you remember? And the runners, my dear, who followed, all the way from the station, if one had a box.'
> The tune changed. 'Any old iron, any old iron to sell?' 'D'you remember? That was what the men shouted in the fog.' (1970, p158)

Paintings too perform the function of giving human beings a sense of contact with the past. But when *Between the Acts* moves to this particular art form, things become more complex:

> Two pictures hung opposite the window. In real life they had never met, the long lady and the man holding his horse by the rein. The lady was a picture, bought by Oliver because he liked the picture; the man was an

ancestor. He had a name. He held the rein in his hand. He had said to the painter:

'If you want my likeness, dang it sir, take it when the leaves are on the trees.' There were leaves on the trees. He had said: 'Ain't there room for Colin as well as Buster?' Colin was his famous hound. But there was only room for Buster. It was, he seemed to say, addressing the company not the painter, a damned shame to leave out Colin. (1970, p36)

One of the portraits is an ancestor, one is just 'a picture'. We are told the difference here, and it is one of which the characters in the novel are fully aware. Nevertheless the difference between these ostensibly similar portraits raises the crucial questions of reference and accuracy. How do we know, in general, whether what we are looking at is an ancestor or a picture? How do we tell the difference between the depiction of an extra-artistic reality, and a work of art which appears to be a depiction but which is, alas, only itself?

If we follow the strict logic of his argument in *Metahistory* we must assume that Hayden White's answer to such a question would be that we cannot. According to White's argument (see pp36–45), the portrait of the lady has the same ontological and representational status as history[b], as has the portrait of the gentleman; we may prefer one to the other on aesthetic grounds, but we cannot claim that one is to be preferred on the grounds of truth-to-reality. *Between the Acts* seems to take a more nuanced and (dare I say it?) sophisticated position. As history[b], the novel seems to say, one of the paintings enjoys undoubted priority. The gentleman is history, the lady is just a painting. But as art, the lady has all the advantage:

He was a talk producer, that ancestor. But the lady was a picture. In her yellow robe, leaning, with a pillar to support her, a silver arrow in her hand, and a feather in her hair, she led the eye up, down, from the curve to the straight, through shades of greenery and shades of silver, dun and rose into silence. The room was empty.

Empty, empty, empty; silent, silent, silent. The room was a shell, singing of what was before time was; a vase stood in the heart of the house, alabaster, smooth, cold, holding the still, distilled essence of emptiness, silence. (1970, pp36–7)

Initially, the phrase 'the lady was a picture' seems like an apology (I myself used the words 'just "a picture"'). But when repeated in the passage I have just quoted, 'the lady was a picture' seems much more like an admiring, even awestruck exclamation. Being 'a picture', the lady gives us something beyond a more-or-less accurate and pleasing representation of what was, it provides us with a sense 'of what was before time was'. History[b], the narrative seems to suggest here, has its realm, and art has its realm, and the two should not be confused with each other. Whereas the gentleman seeks to engage us in conversation, the lady has the effect of encouraging contemplation and aesthetic impartiality. A few pages further on we are told that when the assembled company looks at the lady 'she looked over their heads, looking at nothing. She led them down green glades into the heart of silence' (1970, p49). What is perhaps implied here is that while the painted gentleman speaks to those looking at his portrait from the past, the lady speaks from a standpoint that is neither past nor present. Art, if we follow this interpretation, effaces history[a]; it allows us to engage in a form of human intercourse that is outside history[a].

If that *is* the message of the two portraits, then it represents a classic example of the liberal-humanist view of art as discoverer of the essentially human hidden beneath the surface trappings of historical custom and convention. However, if such is the burden of the novel's concern with the two portraits, it does not represent the novel's final 'message' about either art or history (in both senses), or about the relation between the two.

I say this for two reasons. First, because *Between the Acts* continually reminds the reader that stories about the past, even when mediated by art, are not always received in the same pure and undeflected manner in which the lady imposes her aesthetic presence upon those who observe her portrait. It seems clear that Virginia Woolf deliberately makes the pageant a very impure form of art – impure in the sense that its performance does not reach the audience in unsullied form, but is combined by them with the trivial facts of their day-to-day existence, and with the real (as against the represented) people, situations and events all around them. Members of the audience are continually responding to actors rather than characters, they are affected by such things as sudden showers of rain and cows crying,[45] and they respond to what is performed in front of them in terms of their own personal concerns and histories:

> 'The Nineteenth Century.' Colonel Mayhew did not dispute the producer's right to skip two hundred years in less than fifteen minutes. But the choice of scenes baffled him.
> 'Why leave out the British Army? What's history without the Army, eh?' he mused. (1970, p157)

Every depiction leaves something out: the dog Colin is left out of the ancestor's portrait, the pageant has no room for the British army.

Miss La Trobe, the pageant's author and director, is mortified by what she perceives to be the failure of her vision to achieve a satisfactory embodiment in performance (it is worth pointing out that in this novel in which direct and implied references to abortion occupy strategic positions,

---

[45] Hana Wirth-Necher points out that 'In *A Room of One's Own*, Woolf had already demonstrated in both her rhetorical strategies and in her argument that interruption characterizes woman's writing and woman's experience as a creator, so that a series of interruptions in a work of art created by a woman is in keeping with her concept of woman's art' (1994, pp189–90). She also notes that all of the interruptions (Albert, the rain, the cow crying for her calf,) 'share qualities that are traditionally associated with women, namely identification with nature and its powerlessness in wartime' (1994, p189). In agreeing I would add that the lesson the audience (and the reader) learns from this is that we always humanize the texts of history[b] by opening them up to interrogation by the experiences of our daily lives.

La Trobe minus its first and last letters is an anagram of 'abort').[46] In spite of her attempts to imprison the attention of her audience, all sorts of distractions combine to free their imaginations in ways which are neither planned nor desired by Miss La Trobe.

Such personal or idiosyncratic understandings of the past are not, the novel suggests, necessarily based on misapprehensions or inaccuracies. We do not all see the same past when we look back because human experience is not homogeneous. Throughout *Between the Acts* we are reminded that England has always been divided in terms of both class and gender, and that such divisions inevitably lead to differences in the way in which its citizens have conceptualized their country and its history[a]:

> Only something over a hundred and twenty years the Olivers had been there. Still, on going up the principal staircase – there was another, a mere ladder at the back for the servants – there was a portrait. (1970, p7)

That ladder at the back has carried, the narrative implies, people as crucial to history[a] as those using the principal staircase, but their movements have been concealed from or invisible to many who have written histories[b]. The portrait is not for the servants. And at one striking point in the narrative it is as if the novel admits its own ignorance of the lives of the poor and underprivileged – and not just of those who lived in the past:

> And the local train, which met the express train, arrived by no means punctually, even if he caught the early train which was by no means certain. It which case it meant – but what it meant to Mrs. Sands, when people missed their trains, and she, whatever she might want to do, must wait, by the oven, keeping meat hot, no one knew.
> 'There!' said Mrs. Swithin, surveying the sandwiches, some neat, some not, 'I'll take 'em to the Barn.' As for the lemonade, she assumed, without a flicker of doubt, that Jane the kitchenmaid would follow after. (1970, p35)

The narrative is, at this point, both blind and perceptive. It recognizes its inability to penetrate into Mrs Sands's private thoughts, but at the same time it generalizes this inability – 'no one knew' – rather than perceiving that significant intersubjective understanding is typically possible only between members of the same social class. (Note how the narrative proceeds to penetrate without difficulty into Mrs Swithin's private thoughts in the second quoted paragraph: Woolf knows exactly what Mrs Swithin would assume in such a situation.)

My second reason for believing that *Between the Acts* is more than an apology for liberal humanism is that liberal-humanist anti-historicism is displayed in the novel as one view of history[a], rather than as truth itself:

[46] Patricia Maika suggests two other possibilities: that La Trobe is a (partial) anagram of Voltaire, and of the name of Albert, the village idiot (1984, p12).

'The Victorians,' Mrs. Swithin mused. 'I don't believe,' she said with her odd little smile, 'that there ever were such people. Only you and me and William dressed differently.'

'You don't believe in history,' said William. (1970, pp174–5)

Mrs Swithin believes, too, that it is the same swallows which, year after year, return to the barn (1970, pp101, 108). Her views do not remain un-challenged by other characters.

The novel does of course stress that there are continuities in history[a]; 'The Guide Book still told the truth. 1830 was true in 1939. No house had been built; no town had sprung up. Hogben's Folly was still eminent; the very flat, field-parcelled land had changed only in this – the tractor had to some extent superseded the plough' (1970, p52). But at the same time there are, in addition to the continuities, disruptions and alterations. Right at the start of the novel we are told that the site chosen for the cesspit is on the Roman road; moreover 'the house before the Reformation, like so many houses in that neighbourhood, had a chapel; and the chapel had become a larder, changing, like the cat's name, as religion changed' (1970, p32). History[a], from this perspective, involves both survivals and extinctions – extinctions as complete as those of the prehistoric monsters about which Mrs Swithin reads in her *Outline of History*. Sometimes the past survives only in scars, like those which, Bart claims, can be seen clearly marked from an aeroplane, those 'made by the Britons; by the Romans; by the Elizabethan manor house; and by the plough, when they ploughed the hill to grow wheat in the Napoleonic wars' (1970, p4).

If the novel as a whole comes to any conclusion concerning the respec-tive merits of Mrs Swithin's disbelief in 'history' and her husband's commitment to it, it is that both are right. Mrs Swithin herself realizes that 'she belonged to the unifiers; he to the separatists' (1970, p118) – a division which throughout Woolf's fiction is related to differences of gender. The reader is certainly led to consider whether both have some right on their side: there are both continuities and fractures in history[a]. When Mrs Swithin asks Isa about this matter, using Mr Streatfield's closing speech as her starting-point, Isa cannot decide in which way she inclines:

'Did you feel,' she asked, 'what he said: we act different parts but are the same?'

'Yes,' Isa answered. 'No,' she added. It was Yes, No. Yes, yes, yes, the tide rushed out embracing. No, no, no, it contracted. The old boot appeared on the shingle.

'Orts, scraps and fragments,' she quoted what she remembered of the vanishing play. (1970, p215)

Such indecision seems partly to have reflected Woolf's own. *Between the Acts* was written at what Woolf – and many others – saw as an extremely dark point in history. Although the novel is set just before the start of the Second World War its first draft was finished when the war was over a year old. The Woolfs saw the success of German fascism as quite likely, and they even had plans for a shared suicide, to be undertaken in the event of a successful German invasion. The war seemed like a confirmation of a human inability to change history[a], to build a world secure from war. At the same time Woolf certainly hoped that she was wrong, and that war was not an inevitable part of human existence, a hope which is perhaps most clearly expressed in the closing pages of the novel through Isa's consciousness: 'Love and hate – how they tore her asunder! Surely it was time someone invented a new plot, or that the author came out from the bushes' (1970, p215). This call for a new plot relates not just to our 'imaginative reconstruction of the past', the activity in which Mrs Swithin engages, but to our living of the present. Emplotments are not just things to help us to reconstruct the past, Woolf understands: they are also the means whereby we live the present. What Isa has to understand is that there is no author behind the bushes; she – like all of us – has to become the author of her own life.

As does Auden's 'Spain', *Between the Acts* implies that an understanding of contemporary history[a] cannot be achieved just by looking out at the public world, but by understanding the links between this public world and the inner worlds of those active in the public world. The character whose failure to understand this is a key element in the novel is Giles Oliver. Throughout the period of the narrative Giles is filled with rage against the brutalities being committed (we assume) by fascism on the continent of Europe. But at the same time his internal rage leads him to engage in acts of violence on a smaller scale, acts which suggest that fascism is not just 'in Europe' but is also in him:

> There, couched in the grass, curled in an olive green ring, was a snake. Dead? No, choked with a toad in its mouth. The snake was unable to swallow; the toad was unable to die. A spasm made the ribs contract; blood oozed. It was birth the wrong way round – a monstrous inversion. So, raising his foot, he stamped on them. The mass crushed and slithered. The white canvas on his tennis shoes was bloodstained and sticky. But it was action. Action relieved him. He strode to the Barn, with blood on his shoes. (1970, p99)

The 'monstrous inversion' of this 'birth the wrong way round' gives us the most horrifying image of abortion in the whole novel. The whole scene seems designed to convey Woolf's belief that a certain sort of masculinist rage at the horrors of fascism led to a mirroring of fascism's emotional mechanics in those attempting to oppose it.[47] Isa, Giles's wife, decides that

---

[47] Take, for example, the following comment in a letter written by Woolf's nephew Julian Bell to his mother, Woolf's sister Vanessa Bell. 'But there is one completely irrational side of my mind which can't accept things like fascist victories even in other countries, but wants to get out and do something. And intellectually and emotionally I have none of your horror of killing human beings as such – only when they are valuable or my friends' (Bell 1938, p167). The letter is dated 1 November 1936, but its publication in the 1938 memorial volume for Julian Bell means that Woolf could well have read it

'abortive' is the word that expresses her (1970, p15). It seems that their marriage is a sort of pageant expressive of the abortive history[a] of their times, one which corrupts both of them. The snake choking on the toad, then, represents abortive and self-destructive relationships both on the public and political level and also on the private and personal one. (William Dodge describes himself as 'a flickering, mind-divided little snake in the grass' and earlier Giles has characterized him as a 'toady' [1970, pp73, 60]. His abortive and self-devouring shame is of a kind with mankind's larger self-destructions of war.)

After his act of violence, Giles is (mentally) described by Isa as a 'Silly little boy, with blood on his boot' (1970, p111). A diary entry for 7 August 1938 gives us evidence of Woolf's association of masculine militarism with the activities of small boys: 'Yesterday I saw 6 tanks with gun carriages come clambering down the hill & assemble like black beetles at Rat Farm. Small boys playing idiotic games for which I pay' (Bell 1984, p160). Giles is so obsessed with the fascism that is over the channel that he is unaware of the fascism that is inside himself, a fascism that forms part of his masculine heritage in a patriarchal society.

The acts between which the pageant takes place are, among other things, two world wars. But the battle with which the novel ends is not one of country against country, it is a more personal conflict:

> Giles crumpled the newspaper and turned out the light. Left alone together for the first time that day, they were silent. Alone, enmity was bared; also love. Before they slept, they must fight; after they had fought, they would embrace. From that embrace another life might be born. But first they must fight, as the dog fox fights with the vixen, in the heart of darkness, in the field of night. (1970, pp218–19)

The vision of humanity expressed here is a pessimistic one which collapses culture into nature, and which sees warfare as as instinctively and inescapably human as the sexual urge. The sudden intertextual shock which comes from Woolf's citation of Conrad's 'heart of darkness' (which Woolf added at the final typescript stage) reminds the reader of what is perhaps the great modernist text, one which according to many interpretations links organized state brutality with a hopelessly corrupt human psyche.

The closing sentences in the novel, those which follow the above quotation, seem – at least at first – to assent to such pessimism. 'The house had lost its shelter. It was night before roads were made, or houses. It was the night that dwellers in caves had watched from some high place among rocks' (1970, p219). Giles and Isa seem to have become prehistoric cave-dwellers, the prisoners of their innate impulses and appetites, unchanged

---

and other similar expressions of her nephew's response to the frustrations engendered by the seemingly unstoppable fascist advance on continental Europe. Bell volunteered as an ambulance driver for the Spanish Republican forces, and was killed in Spain.

by centuries of culture, generations of civilization.[48] The last line of the novel does, however, hold out an unexpected hope: 'Then the curtain rose. They spoke' (1970, p219). If communication is possible then perhaps catastrophe can be headed off.

The balance of this conclusion – if my interpretation is correct – conforms with the balance of Miss La Trobe's concluding words for her pageant. Like Auden, Miss La Trobe (and, we assume, Woolf) points to a link between the individual psyche and acts of communal violence. '*Consider the gun slayers, bomb droppers here or there. They do openly what we do slyly. Take an example* (here the megaphone adopted a colloquial, conversational tone) *Mr. M's bungalow. A view spoilt for ever. That's murder'* (1970, p187). The connection is extended from negative to positive human attributes, from '*our kindness to the cat'* to '*the impulse which leads us – mark you, when no-one's looking – to the window at midnight to smell the bean'* (1970, p188). Like the 'fears' detailed in Auden's poem, the ones which made us respond to the medicine ad. and the brochure of winter cruises, Woolf's examples are trivial in comparison to her cited gun slayers and bomb droppers. What is however important is that both writers locate their human fears and impulses in cultural territory, rather than in the more biological territory implied by the final comparison of Isa and Giles to cavemen or fighting foxes. If culture constructs a human individuality which in turn projects its fears and impulses on to the world in (among other things) acts of collective brutality, then at least the possibility of constructing a better culture holds out some hope for the world.

That *Between the Acts* hesitates between a pessimistic biological determinism and a more optimistic view of the cultural construction of individuality reflects, no doubt, the divisions and contradictions in Woolf's own view of the history[a] of her own time – a history unfolding not just on the public stage but also in the hearts and minds of those living in and through the larger struggles of the 1930s.

---

[48] Woolf's diary entry for 17 August 1938 talks of Hitler's having a million men under arms and the threat of war, and comments: 'That is the complete ruin not only of civilisation, in Europe, but of our last lap. Quentin conscripted &c. One ceases to think about it – thats all. Goes on discussing the new room, new chair, new books. What else can a gnat on a blade of grass do? And I would like to write PH. [= *Pointz Hall*, the first title of *Between the Acts*]: & other things.' (Bell 1984, 162). 'Quentin' was Quentin Bell, Woolf's sister Vanessa Bell's younger, and by now her only surviving, son. Miss La Trobe's mention of '*this wall, the great wall, which we call, perhaps miscall, civilization'* (1970, p188) reflects a legitimate perception on Woolf's part that 'the complete ruin of civilisation' really was threatened by German fascism.

7

TRIVIAL PURSUITS: THE HISTORICAL ROOTS OF AMBIGUITY

Henry James, The Turn of the Screw

Two radically different views of the passage of the text through history are exemplified in, and by, Henry James's *The Turn of the Screw. Within* the world of the novella, on the one hand, the text of the governess's narrative passes through time apparently unsullied by any disfiguring contacts with the specificities of history or the demands of different readings. On the other hand so far as the novella's *actual* historical life is concerned we can witness a text buffeted by and seemingly at the mercy of a range of historical, cultural and critical forces, one which lives a chameleon existence which is apparently reflective of the changing human lives of which it is made a part. The text internal to the novella – the governess's manuscript – is portrayed as perpetually virginal, as much untouched by the life around it as the heroine of James's *What Maisie Knew* is innocent of the corruption lived out all around her. The text of the novella itself is, in contrast, more courtesan than virgin, forced to tolerate – if not to submit to – whatever rôle its readers want it to perform.

Let me start with the seemingly time-independent text of the governess's narrative. As Shoshana Felman has pointed out, it is '*death* itself which moves the narrative chain forward, which *inaugurates* the manuscript's *displacements* and the process of the *substitution* of the narrators' (1977, p128). The governess sends Douglas her manuscript 'before she died' (James 1966, p2), and Douglas passes this same manuscript on to the frame narrator 'before his death – when it was in sight' (1966, p4). The manuscript has thus been in Douglas's possession over twenty years when he announces its existence in the novella's frame narrative, and it recounts events which take place at least forty-eight years prior to the 'now' of the novella's opening sequence (see the Appendix, p225, for a representation of the time-scale of the whole novella).

In spite of this lapse of time the governess's manuscript seems like a little time capsule, a sort of scriptive fly in amber from which an unchanging sequence of events can be reconstituted. The manuscript has been in a locked drawer and has not been out for years, and the frame narrator even talks of Douglas as having 'broken a thickness of ice, the formation of many a winter' (1966, p2) by having revealed its existence. When Douglas reads the manuscript aloud to the assembled company he begins 'to read with a fine clearness that was like a rendering to the ear of the beauty of his author's hand' (1966, p6): even the manuscript's physical properties are translated without loss or alteration to those listening to its reading.

It is, moreover, revealing to note that the text of the governess's manuscript with which the reader makes acquaintance in his or her reading of *The Turn of the Screw* is depicted as having been untouched by Douglas's reading, for it pre-dates this reading by many years. An instructive contrast can be drawn between James's novella and another novella which achieved its first periodical publication a year later than did *The Turn of the Screw*: Joseph Conrad's *Heart of Darkness*, which was first published in 1899–1900. Both works open with a scene in which various individuals are gathered together in conversation, and in both cases this leads into an oral narrative delivered by one of those present. The difference is that the reader of *Heart of Darkness* is presented with what purports to be a transcription of Marlow's oral narrative – complete with interruptions from his listeners, remarks addressed directly to these same individuals, and a closing comment on the disposition of the members of the group by the frame narrator made once Marlow's narrative is completed. *The Turn of the Screw* presents us with a very significant modification of this narrative situation. The careless reader might well think that what we are given in James's novella is a transcription or account of Douglas's delivery of the governess's story, and indeed the final lines in the frame narrative seem almost to encourage this misapprehension:

> 'What's your title?'
> 'I haven't one.'
> 'Oh *I* have!' I said. But Douglas, without heeding me, had begun to read with a fine clearness that was like a rendering to the ear of the beauty of his author's hand. (1966, p6)

Immediately after this passage the text moves on to a presentation of the governess's narrative, and it is very easy to read on at this point under the mistaken belief that we are following Douglas's actual reading of the governess's manuscript. What we are in fact doing (seen in terms of the intrafictional world of the tale) is, just, reading the manuscript ourselves. Two pages earlier the frame narrative contains the crucial sentence: 'Let me say here distinctly, to have done with it, that this narrative, from an exact transcript of my own made much later, is what I shall presently give' (1966, p4). *Our* reading of the manuscript, in other words, is of something which is at least twenty years older than Douglas's recitation. Whereas in *Heart of Darkness* we are placed in the position of being one of Marlow's listeners, responding alongside others, in *The Turn of the Screw* we read the governess's manuscript rather than listen to its recital, and we read alone.

Now this has, I think, an important symbolic point. Our reading of the governess's manuscript is untouched by other readings, by the life of the manuscript subsequent to its initial composition. The manuscript is always the same manuscript – the one which the governess wrote; one logically independent of and prior to any other use which has been made of it. In Conrad's novella we are faced with something quite different. First because in *Heart of Darkness* there is no intrafictional written narrative, and second because the narrative we follow represents both *énoncé* and *énonciation*, both tale and telling. Such a combination stresses the text's dependence upon the circumstances of its telling; the reader of *Heart of Darkness* is confronted not with a rootless, unanchored or decontextualized narrative, but with a telling which is linked to the circumstances of its delivery and reception. James's novella, in contrast, presents the reader with a narrative seemingly independent of the circumstances of its telling, one which is linked to no extratextual time or place other than those of its birth, and one which moves on relentlessly over death after death, impervious to the fates of the human beings who assure its survival – a sort of Darwinian species trundling forward over the bodies of those who perpetuate it. Marlow's telling enables his listeners to use their knowledge of him, their observation of his manner of telling, as anchors or points of reference to be used as aids to response and interpretation – and the reader of *Heart of Darkness* is similarly able to rely upon the interaction between Marlow and his listeners for aid in arriving at and legitimating his or her own responses and interpretations. For the reader of *The Turn of the Screw* things are much harder. Douglas's preamble provides some contextualizing information, but at crucial points this is ambiguous or it contradicts what we read in the governess's account. We must deal with the governess's manuscript far more in terms of itself, cut off from any helpful details concerning its composition, performance or reception. (In contrast to the account of Marlow's narrative which we are given in *Heart of Darkness*, in *The Turn of the Screw* we are never told why the governess writes her account, for whom – if anyone – it was written, or how its perusal or recital were received.)

Once we turn from the intrafictional text of the governess's manuscript, and focus our attention on to the actual text which constitutes *The Turn of the Screw*, we confront a totally different situation. In this case it seems impossible for the modern reader to confront the text 'in itself'; we confront a text which is in part constituted by the stormy critical life which it has lived over the past century. Few literary works written during the past hundred years have generated so much literary-critical output as has James's novella, and few have been the focus of such sharp interpretative conflict. Much of this has centred on a fundamental split between two opposing interpretative camps: on the one hand those who believe that the governess should be understood to be a reliable witness and that her account of the threat posed by the ghosts of Peter Quint and Miss Jessel to the two young children is to believed, and on the other hand those who believe *The Turn of the Screw* to be concerned with the delusions of the mentally disturbed governess, delusions which lead her into greater and greater offences against the two children. The detail of these debates is too well known to need full recapitulation here, and although the intensity of critical exchanges on the subject has died down it is by no means dead.

Elliot M. Schrero has suggested that this critical debate can best be understood from a historical perspective. According to him, 'aside from the growing influence of psychoanalysis after the First World War, and, after the second, a general preoccupation with interpretation, the cause lies in the opacity of certain references in the tale – references formerly transparent but now darkened by cultural change' (1981, p261). Schrero is an 'apparitionist' – that is, he belongs to that camp which argues that a correct reading of James's novella takes the appearance of the two ghosts to Miss Jessel as actual rather than imagined. According to him, Miss Jessel is not to be read in historically inappropriate Freudian terms as a sexually repressed woman whose neuroses are displaced into hysterical imaginings; on the contrary, readers familiar with those 'specific cultural allegiances', which for James and his contemporaries 'controlled the play of textual meaning', would recognize that the novella addressed Victorian concerns about 'the roles of parents, servants, governesses, and children' (1981, p261). For Schrero, therefore, later critical fashion has obscured the important cultural context of the novella's genesis, a context without which James's work becomes impossible to interpret correctly.

Bruce Robbins has also insisted upon the importance of context: a context in which sex between the classes was almost universal but unspoken. He cites the evidence of an 'officer in the Indian Medical Service [who] wrote to Havelock Ellis as follows: "once at a club in Burma we were some twenty-six at table and the subject of first intercourse came up. All had been led astray by servants save two, whom their sister's governesses had initiated"' (Robbins 1984, p196, citing Smith 1966, pp49–50). It is worth noting the way in which agency is allotted in this account: it is those on a lower social scale who 'lead astray' the children of the middle and upper classes. In reality it is certain that most illicit sex between members of different social classes in late Victorian England involved the exploitation of lower-class women and girls by middle- and upper-class men. James's novella, like the unnamed officer in the Indian Medical Service, manages to make inter-class sex a matter of lusting menials and the innocent rich. Ideologically, *The Turn of the Screw* also does a thorough job in pinning the blame for promiscuity and corruption on the lower orders: whereas the uncle – whose type 'never, happily, dies out' (1966, p4) – is the innocent object of the desire of the governess who, Mrs Grose comments, is 'not the first' and 'won't be the last' (1966, p9) to be so attracted, both Peter Quint and Miss Jessel are active rather than acted upon in sexual terms. The uncle's philandering exists only on the margin of the text: the governess sees him 'all in a glow of high fashion, of good looks, of expensive habits, of charming ways with women', and remembers his town residence 'filled with the spoils of travel and the trophies of the chase' (1966, p4). His refusal to accept anything other than a purely financial obligation for the children leads to no overt condemnation: instead the responsibility for

Flora's and Miles's corruption is placed firmly on the shoulders of the lower orders.

If sex between the classes was as universal as Robbins suggests, it presumably made it easier for James to know in which direction his readers would respond to hints and suggestions in the narrative – of which more below. Robbins points out that the governess desires exactly what she condemns in her predecessor – a cross-class sexual relationship. This probably overlooks the fact that the governess's social status would have been considered to be much nearer to that of the uncle that was Miss Jessel's to that of Peter Quint, and that where there was marriage between different social classes it was generally found less socially offensive when the man belonged to the 'superior' class.

Schrero's views directly contradict those expressed by critics convinced that James's novella can fully be understood only by those able to set it into contexts of which even James was unaware. Thus Edmund Wilson, whose interpretation of the novella was modified twice over time and exists in three different versions, in his 'middle version' argues that even James himself, because of his own sexual blindnesses and repressions, was unaware of the fact that he had created a portrait of a governess whose sexual repressions led her to hallucinate the ghosts into existence (see the account in Slaughter [1966]).

The history of the work's reception, then, is a history which can be seen in two radically different ways. On the one hand we have a work which, because it moves further and further away from that complex of cultural codes within which its meaning becomes clear, is more and more misinterpreted by readers who apply inappropriate schemes of understanding to it. On the other hand we have a work which can be saved from its own ignorances, and from those of its creator, only by being subjected to the illumination of insights historically subsequent to its own creation and initial dissemination. Both of these accounts are, of course, quite different from the ahistorical life which the text *in* the work – the governess's manuscript – seems to enjoy. This text appears anachronistically New Critical in its independence of context, its implied total self-sufficiency.

If we are to reconcile these two very different pictures of the life of the text, we have, I think, to recognize their dependence upon each other. It is, in other words, precisely the lack of internal anchoring of the governess's tale which explains the promiscuity of the novella's interpretative life. We can go further. The chief critical disagreements centring on *The Turn of the Screw* are only partly the product of changing critical fashion and volatile cultural meanings. It is because the novella is so fundamentally (and studiedly) ambiguous that it has been buffeted by a succession of critical and cultural changes. This deliberate ambiguity is itself *achieved* by cutting the governess's narrative off from defining contextual information; at the same time it is *the product of* historically determinate conditions, as I shall hope to show. To express the paradox in a nutshell: history produces a retreat from history.

Given that half a century of argument had failed to settle the debate between the apparitionists and the non-apparitionists it is not surprising that two views of this quarrel should have emerged: first, that there was no way of resolving this disagreement as *The Turn of the Screw* was a fundamentally ambiguous text, and second, that this ambiguity was deliberate. But a formal and convincing demonstration of the work's root ambiguity had to await the development of a narratology with the technical resources to expose the means whereby this ambiguity was generated. Shlomith Rimmon's *The Concept of Ambiguity – the Example of James* (1977) builds upon such theoretical work as that of the Russian Formalists and the French Roland Barthes. Her analysis is extremely subtle and complex, and it encompasses many different aspects of James's text ranging from micro-elements (ambiguity at sentence level) to macro-elements (ambiguity caused by, for example, problems in the relationship between the frame narrative and the governess's manuscript). Rimmon stresses that for her, ambiguity is more than plurisignification; in her definition of the term not only does an ambiguous expression (i) have two or more distinct meanings in the given context, but (ii) these meanings are not reducible to each other or to some common denominator, nor are they subsumable in any larger unit of meaning within which they can be reconciled, (iii) the different meanings are mutually exclusive, and (iv) hence an ambiguous expression 'calls for choice between its alternative meanings, but at the same time provides no ground for making the choice' (1977, p17).

Rimmon's definition of ambiguity places it very close to the concept of the double-bind. In both cases the victim – the person who experiences ambiguity or double-bind – is locked into an endless loop of affirmation and denial, unable to appeal to a different level of legitimation so as to be able to break the equal but conflicting claims of mutually exclusive clues or assertions. It is therefore not surprising to find that much of the debate between the apparitionists and the non-apparitionists restricts itself to the level of the governess's, or to the novella's, fictional world. Such a restriction, even when entered into voluntarily, almost inevitably leads to a treatment of the events recounted by the governess as if they were not fictional but real, and to a subsequent critical strategy reminiscent of that associated with A. C. Bradley's Shakespearian analyses. Anthologies of criticism directed towards *The Turn of the Screw* are full of examples of such analysis, analysis which indeed calls to mind L. C. Knights's ironic use of the title 'How Many Children Had Lady Macbeth?'. Here is a representative example from a book entitled *An Anatomy of 'The Turn of the Screw'*, by Thomas Mabry Cranfill and Robert Lanier Clark Jr. (1965). The two authors point out, correctly, that James's text gives no information concerning the whereabouts, or activities, of the governess after the death of Miles and before she joined the Douglas family – a period of about ten years (actually less: see the Appendix, p225). They comment as follows.

> Nonapparitionists might guess that she had passed the decade in a nursing home for the mentally deranged, repairing her shattered nerves and turning herself from virtual lunatic into a most charming person.

At any rate, she had never told anyone her story. Even if one argues, with the apparitionists, that the demons which haunted her were sterling, bona-fide ghosts, how could her history recommend her to any future employer? Besides, what woman is willing to bare the details of a frustrating, one-sided love affair?

She was, Douglas goes on to say, 'the youngest of several daughters of a poor country parson.' These words provide an interesting if brief revelation of her background that might invite the attentive reader to all sorts of speculation. (1965, p23)

And speculation, of course follows. We are asked to wonder whether she was doomed perpetually to wear clothes handed down from elder sisters, whether she was spoiled or bullied, whether she spent her childhood in genteel poverty – and so on, and so on. We are back to 'The Girlhood of Shakespeare's Heroines' with a vengeance: treating the story of the novella as if it were an account of real lives and experiences.

There is plenty of evidence to suggest that James himself was consciously committed to encouraging his readers to treat his fictions in this manner. In her very enlightening study *Henry James: History, Narrative, Fiction* (1993), Roslyn Jolly shows how James remained convinced for most of his writing life that fiction could made socially and intellectually respectable only by means of an alliance with the high esteem enjoyed by the discipline of history. In the face of numerous attacks on the moral and intellectual value of fiction, James insisted that fiction had, as it were, to disown its fictionality and to lay claim to the status of history. In his *The Art of Fiction* (1884), for example, James sets out to confront the 'old superstition about fiction being "wicked"', only 'a "make-believe"', and he counters that the 'only reason for the existence of the novel is that it does attempt to represent life'. He adds: 'When it relinquishes this attempt, the same attempt that we see on the canvas of the painter, it will have arrived at a very strange pass' (1951, p393). For James, there is only one way forward for he or she who would defend fiction, which is

to insist on the fact that as the picture is reality, so the novel is history. That is the only general description (which does it justice) that we may give of the novel. But history also is allowed to represent life; it is not, any more than painting, expected to apologize. The subject-matter of history is stored up likewise in documents and records, and if it will not give itself away, as they say in California, it must speak with assurance, with the tone of the historian. (1951, p394)

What James means by fiction's 'not giving itself away', he goes on to make clear, is that the novelist must not – as James claims that Anthony Trollope does – break in to the narrative in his or her own voice, revealing that indeed the novel is only 'a "make-believe"'. 'Such a betrayal of a sacred office seems to me', James confesses, 'a terrible crime' (1951, p394).

James's position here is replete with paradox, for, as Roslyn Jolly points out, in attempting to legitimize fiction by allying it with history, James 'worked with, rather than against, the whole philosophical, social, and political complex of hostility to fiction in English culture' (1993, pvi). She quotes tellingly from James's 1883 essay 'Anthony Trollope':

> It is impossible to imagine what a novelist takes himself to be unless he regards himself as an historian and his narrative as a history. It is only as an historian that he has the smallest *locus standi*. As a narrator of fictitious events he is nowhere; to insert into his attempt a backbone of logic, he must relate events that are assumed to be real. (Edel and Wilson 1984 1, p1343)

Assuming the events of a novel to be real is, of course, precisely the category of error for which the New Critics admonished A. C. Bradley and others, and it is also just that critical procedure which has locked generations of commentators on *The Turn of the Screw* in a critical double-bind. So long as we assume the events narrated by either the frame narrator or the governess, or both of them, to be true, then we sign away our ability ever to stop a perpetual oscillation between opposing and contradictory interpretations, an oscillation as neurotic as that into which the fictional governess falls. Thus both 'apparitionists' and 'anti-apparitionists' share a common assumption more fundamental than their disagreement about the status of the ghosts in the novella; as Roslyn Jolly puts it,

> the long-running opposition between 'ghostly' and 'psychological' readings masked the essential similarity of their aims. Whether affirming the reality of the ghosts or arguing that they are the product of the governess's imagination, whether confirming the story as apparent from her account or retelling it with a commentary, both groups of critics express the desire to establish 'what happens', to retrieve an authentic story of character and event. (1993, p102)

Ironically, by treating the fictional world as real, such critics imply a real world that is like the deconstructionist text – lacking any means to validate any of its own contradictory assertions. Or, to put it another way: that 'ceaseless play of the signifier' which deconstructionists have claimed is universal is, I would argue, only to be found in situations in which text-independent evidence (or, as the governess would say, 'proof') is lacking. In the real world there is, whatever Jacques Derrida claims to the contrary, something outside the text – for example, that water under which Joseph Conrad recommended that the head of Yamsi's manager be held for a while. But once we treat a literary text as a historical text we immediately lock ourselves into a world which really is constituted by and limited to the text, a text we are unable to leave. In such a situation the play of signifiers – as the history of criticism of *The Turn of the Screw* demonstrates – is indeed ceaseless. What James presents as a movement towards history is actually a flight from history – the history of the literary work's creation, dissemination and reception.

Early on in this book I referred to a method of validation called by historians 'triangulation', one which matches personal testimony about a historical event with other forms of evidence including historical documents (see p28). Triangulation involves, essentially, the use of different forms of evidence to ensure that error and falsity can be detected. But it is a method which cannot be applied to the world of a fictional work in unmodified form, because the evidence *in* a fictional work, unlike the different sorts of evidence used in triangulation, may have exactly the same status as evidence and thus cannot be used to test itself. The testimony of a holocaust survivor and the evidence of a document produced by a Nazi concentration camp official have different origins and represent alternative sources of documentation. In contrast, a sentence from the frame narrative of *The Turn of the Screw* and a sentence from the governess's manuscript have, essentially, the same truth value; they cannot be used to resolve a problem in that world in the way that 'triangulated' evidence from the real world can. What James's theory of fiction lacks is a concept of the way in which fiction represents life which is different from, rather than adopted from, the armoury of the historian: it lacks a theory of the mediations by which life is transformed into art, and by which art feeds back into life.

Thus contrary to what James claims in 'The Art of Fiction', the defender of fiction must admit, rather than conceal, the 'make-believe' nature of fiction. This is not to impose an anachronistically postmodernist frame of reference on to premodernist literature: I am not saying that a work of fiction has to display its own fictionality, nor that a novel reader must never sink into an acceptance of 'the world' of the novel while he or she is reading it. What I am saying, however, is that some interpretative problems cannot be solved from within this world; some can be resolved only by observing them from outside of its boundaries. This is in no way to diminish fiction: it is to accept it as what it is; not to deny that fiction represents life, but to adopt a defensible starting-point from which we may investigate exactly *how* and in what variety of ways the novel represents life. The life which *The Turn of the Screw* represents cannot adequately be revealed by our assuming that, as James comes near to suggesting in 'The Art of Fiction', there is no difference between what in his fiction he is doing (and Anthony Trollope should be doing), and what Gibbon or Macaulay have done. Such a mistaken analogy between the writing of fiction and the writing of history merely encourages us to treat fiction as bad, or failed, history – precisely the message that a half century of critical disagreement about *The Turn of the Screw* might suggest to the cynical historian.

But even those who believe that they are escaping from the double-binding effect of imprisonment within the fictional world of the novella may succeed in escaping only so far as to James's own comments on the story, comments which half a century of argument has also failed to prove helpful in resolving the novella's ambiguities. If escape is sought, it must be to a level of explanatory evidence which explains rather than perpetuates the ambiguity of James's text.

Shlomith Rimmon's account is very considerably strengthened by the fact that it does not limit itself to *The Turn of the Screw*, but also includes detailed analyses of the ambiguity of 'The Figure in the Carpet', 'The Lesson of the Master', and *The Sacred Fount*. Were her case limited to the one novella there might always remain a possibility that, as Schrero argues, the text is ambiguous to us, and to us alone, because ambiguity-resolving contextual details have been lost in the passage of time. To misquote Wilde, to produce one ambiguous text without intending so to do might be dismissed as unfortunate, but to produce four begins to look like careless-ness. We know, however, that James was the least careless of authors, and this alone argues strongly if not conclusively that the ambiguity of *The Turn of the Screw* (an ambiguity which, as Rimmon points out, because it remains unresolved makes of the novella a perfect example of what Tzvetan Todorov has defined as the 'pure fantastic' [Rimmon 1977, p119]) is fully conscious and deliberate on James's part.

I will now give some examples of Rimmon's analysis, and then add some comments concerning the frame narrative and its relationship to the governess's tale. I would then like to suggest how all of these matters can be fully illuminated only by a criticism which is historicist and which has some insight into the nature of historical determination.

A good example of Rimmon's painstaking analysis is given in her treatment of the following passage from the final page of the novella. In this final scene the governess tries to wrest a proof from Miles that he sees the apparition of Peter Quint, observed by the governess peering in through the window:

> I was so determined to have all my proof that I flashed into ice to challenge him. 'Whom do you mean by "he"?'
> 'Peter Quint – you devil!' His face gave again, round the room, its convulsed supplication. '*Where?*'
> They are in my ears still, his supreme surrender of the name and his tribute to my devotion. 'What does it matter now, my own? – what will he *ever* matter? I have you,' I launched at the beast, 'but he has lost you for ever!' (1966, p88)

Rimmon comments on this passage as follows:

> As has so often been remarked, Miles's 'you devil!' may refer either to Peter Quint or to the governess. The governess, of course, chooses the first possibility, taking it as an expression of the boy's complete rejection of evil. But the cry can also be directed against the governess, accusing her of infernally instilling a consciousness of evil into an innocent soul.
> Similarly, the governess's 'I have you, . . . but he has lost you for ever!' may be addressed either to Miles or to Quint. If it is addressed to Miles, it expresses the governess's feeling of victory: it is she who now possesses the child, and the devil has lost him forever. On the other hand, if the words are addressed to Quint, they mean that the governess has now become possessed by the devil ('I have you'), thus freeing Miles, who has consequently lost Quint forever. This double possibility is sustained by the

two meanings of 'I launched at the beast.' If *launch* means 'throw oneself', then 'I have you' is addressed to Miles. If, on the other hand, *launch* signifies 'say vigorously', the whole speech is addressed to Quint, the 'beast'. (1977, p165; Rimmon acknowledges West 1964, pp286–7)

Rimmon makes a useful distinction between what she dubs 'singly directed clues' and 'doubly directed clues' in the novella. Ambiguity results when a number of singly directed clues point in different directions without our being able to decide on which of these we are to place our trust, or when we are unable to decide how to interpret a doubly directed clue. It is palpable that each clue which seems to point unambiguously in one direction is soon followed by another clue pointing unambiguously in the opposite direction. One of the most striking examples of this follows the governess's ill-fated confrontation of Flora with the name of Miss Jessel. Mrs Grose's response to this would seem to confirm the hypothesis of the hallucinationists, denying all the moral support for the governess's belief in the reality of the apparitions which the governess has earlier claimed that Mrs Grose has granted her:

'She isn't there, little lady, and nobody's there – and you never see nothing, my sweet! How can poor Miss Jessel – when poor Miss Jessel's dead and buried? *We* know, don't we love?' – and she appealed, blundering in, to the child. 'It's all a mere mistake and a worry and a joke – and we'll go home as fast as we can!' (1966, p72)

To the reader wrestling between the two ways of interpreting the novella this would seem to damage the governess's credibility so fundamentally as to render the non-apparitionist interpretation highly likely – especially as the governess has already claimed a number of times that she enjoys Mrs Grose's support. But a few pages later Mrs Grose undercuts the whole force of this outburst:

She held me a moment with heavy eyes, then brought out the rest. 'Your idea's the right one. I myself, Miss –'
'Well?'
'I can't say.'
The look she gave me with it made me jump at possibilities. 'You mean that, since yesterday, you *have* seen –?'
She shook her head with dignity. 'I've *heard* – !'
'Heard?'
'From that child – horrors! There!' she sighed with tragic relief. 'On my honour, Miss, she says things – !' (1966, p77)

Such oscillation is – to use the governess's phrase from the opening of her narrative – 'a succession of flights and drops, a little see-saw of the right throbs and the wrong' (1966, p6), except that the reader of *The Turn of the Screw* is never able to determine unambiguously whether he or she is dealing with the right throb or the wrong throb. As Rimmon puts it,

> Trying to make up his mind whether the situation at Bly corresponds to the governess's ghost-ridden account or to Mrs. Grose's sealed-eye description, the reader is bound to realize that James gives him no independent information on which to base his decision. There is no independent dramatization of an encounter between either of the ghosts with any other member of the household, particularly the children, whom the governess believes to be in constant touch with the evil apparitions. Everything we hear about the ghosts (and for that matter, about everything else) comes from the governess, and there is no external source which could help us to decide whether the communications she attributes to the children are real or merely a figment of her own imagination. The reader is thus made aware of an informational gap at the core of the narrative. (1977, pp126–7)

The reader witnesses the governess lying (when she reports to Mrs Grose what Miss Jessel has said to her while the family is at church – a scene which has already been described differently to us by the governess; one of these accounts, to the reader or to Mrs Grose, must be false), and so nothing in her narrative can be relied upon as unimpeachable. Yet the prologue delivered by the frame narrator offers no basis for resolving the ambiguities of the governess's account.

A further complication is that James is (untypically) quite explicit about one thing: that in *The Turn of the Screw* his intention was to encourage the reader to respond creatively to suggestions in the text. This is stated quite unambiguously in his preface to the New York edition of the novella (reprinted in the Norton Critical Edition):

> There is for such a case no eligible *absolute* of the wrong; it remains relative to fifty other elements, a matter of appreciation, speculation, imagination – these things moreover quite exactly in the light of the spectator's, the critic's, the reader's experience. Only make the reader's general vision of evil intense enough, I said to myself – and that already is a charming job – and his own experience, his own imagination, his own sympathy (with the children) and horror (of their false friends) will supply him quite sufficiently with all the particulars. Make him *think* the evil, make him think it for himself, and you are released from weak specifications. (1966, pp122–3)

A few lines further on James is even more explicit: 'my values are all blanks save so far as an excited horror, a promoted pity, a created expertness . . . proceed to read into them more or less fantastic figures' (1966, p123). Such a passing of the buck to the reader seems to be a part of James's love affair with indeterminacy. It also puts the reader in the position of the characters in the novella, and encourages him or her to respond as do Mrs Grose and the governess. To use Mrs Grose's words: 'And afterwards I imagined – and I still imagine. And what I imagine is dreadful' (1966, p33). But what is dreadful to Mrs Grose may not be dreadful to the governess, and what one reader imagines as dreadful may be less so to another.

Let me turn now to the novella's few opening pages which are delivered by an anonymous frame narrator. As with the double-bind, what we are presented with in the frame narrative is a set of clues which offer contradictory evidence for the reader interested in resolving the ambiguities of the governess's tale. The most striking of these is Douglas's account of the governess's predecessor – Miss Jessel: 'There had been for the two children at first a young lady whom they had the misfortune to lose. She had done for them quite beautifully – she was a most respectable person – till her death, the great awkwardness of which had, precisely, left no alternative but the school for little Miles' (1966, p5). Now we have to remember that Douglas's information must by his own account have come from one of two sources: either from the governess's manuscript, or from information imparted to him in person by the governess. But this information about Miss Jessel directly contradicts what the governess says of Miss Jessel in her narrative. Are we to assume that subsequent to writing her account the governess enjoys a change of heart, recognizes that indeed Miss Jessel was someone who did 'quite beautifully' for the children, and so informs Douglas? The other alternative we have is to read the entire paragraph in which this statement occurs as Free Indirect Discourse, representing not the governess's views but the uncle's statement of his views to the governess. This is not impossible, but it is immediately rendered less likely by the fact that the following paragraph opens with the words, 'So far had Douglas presented his picture when someone put a question'.

A few lines further on, Douglas is asked of what the former governess died: 'Our friend's answer was prompt. "That will come out. I don't anticipate."' But of course it does not come out, and it is the reader who is forced if not to anticipate at least to speculate – as does Mrs Grose.

A similar problem occurs in relation to Douglas's earlier claim that the story will not tell with whom the governess was in love, at least 'not in any literal vulgar way' (1966, p3). But the governess's manuscript certainly does tell the reader, pretty explicitly, that the governess was in love with the children's uncle. Has Douglas forgotten what is in the manuscript? Or is this a hint that the governess was 'really' in love not with the uncle but with someone else – Miles, for example?

Such questions are the first signs that one is again falling into the double-binding trap of treating the evidence in James's pages as equivalent to real-world evidence, and assuming that just as there must be a full reality behind a non-fictional account, so too behind a fictional account such as that we are faced with in *The Turn of the Screw* there must be a full reconstructible reality as rich as that which we could assume existed behind a non-fictional, historical narrative.

If evidence is needed that this cannot be the case, then we can show that even the time-scale of the days covered in the tale's frame narrative is presented in varied and mutually exclusive ways. At one point in the account given by the anonymous 'I' narrator we are told that from 'day one' of the opening of the frame narrative to the evening when the governess's manuscript is read aloud by Douglas, four days pass. ('Poor

Douglas, before his death – when it was in sight – committed to me the manuscript that reached him on the third of these days and that, on the same spot, with immense effect, he began to read to our hushed little circle on the night of the fourth' [1966, p4].) A page earlier, we have been told that Douglas will receive this manuscript with the second post on 'Thursday'. We thus have a sequence ranging from Tuesday (the Christmas Eve of the opening), through to the Friday on which the story is read.

But other information in the frame narrative contradicts this time-scale. We are told that a letter is sent to Douglas's London apartments 'the next day' after Christmas Eve. The evening of the same 'next' day (i.e. Christmas Day[49]), Douglas gives his 'few words of prologue' (1966, p4), and he starts to read the governess's story 'the next night' (1966, p6). This gives us a sequence not of four days but of three. These two time-scales are, like rival emplotments of historical events according to Hayden White, impossible to rank by means of their greater or lesser fidelity to an independent reality. There just is no '*hors texte*' to which to appeal.

Is this carelessness on James's part? Or an extra joke at the reader's expense, an inconsistency which rams home the lesson of the master that we will never find certainty so long as we limit ourselves to the information provided by the text? Given James's deserved reputation as an extremely careful and studied writer, the latter would appear to be the more likely – especially as this is not the only puzzling element in the frame narrative. One to which I have drawn attention elsewhere concerns the gender of the 'I' narrator. Nearly every commentator on James's novella refers to the frame narrator as 'he'. This appears to be because there are a number of dismissive remarks aimed at 'the women' in the gathering. ('"Oh how delicious!" cried one of the women' [1966, p2], starts the ball rolling on the second page of the novella.) At one time it *sounds* as though all of the ladies will depart before Douglas reads the story, so that this reading will be to an all-male gathering:

> 'You'll all meet me here?' He looked us round again. 'Isn't anybody going?' It was almost the tone of hope.
> 'Everybody will stay!'
> '*I* will – and *I* will!' cried the ladies whose departure had been fixed. (1966, p3)
> The departing ladies who had said they would stay didn't, of course, thank heaven, stay: they departed, in consequence of arrangements made, in a rage of curiosity, as they professed, produced by the touches with which he had already worked us up. (1966, p4)

In what is a classic example of James's ambiguity, 'the departing ladies' can mean either 'the ladies, (all of them) who were departing', or 'those among the ladies who were departing'. The general tone of apparently masculine sneering leads most readers, I think, to assume that the former meaning is

---

[49] For those wondering, yes, there were postal services on Christmas Day in Britain then.

the one to be taken. But it clearly is not, as when Douglas starts reading, 'one of the ladies' (1966, p6) asks a question.

It is doubtless this attitude of dismissal towards some or all of the ladies present which leads most critics of *The Turn of the Screw* to assume that the 'I' narrator is a man. But in 1965 A. W. Thomson revealed that his own reaction to the frame narrative had led him to assume that the opposite was 'fairly obviously' the case – a reminder that so far as literary works are concerned, readers' assumptions are not always universal:

> And there is one other point which should be made here, which is that the narrator of the prologue[50] is fairly obviously a woman. Her reaction to Douglas's description of the governess's aristocratic and fascinating employer – 'One could easily fix his type; it never, happily, dies out' – is probably as final as such suggestion could be. As for the nature of Douglas's relations with the narrator, it may not be important that she speaks of him as 'poor Douglas', but it is to her in particular that he tells the story – or at least to her that he seems to appeal for confirmation of his decision to send for the manuscript and break this silence of forty years – and it is to her that he will bequeath the manuscript not long before his death. And on at least one occasion James shows us Douglas singling out the narrator ('"You'll easily judge," he repeated; "*you* will"') as if whatever understanding there was between them would make it appropriate that he should tell it to her. (1965, p35)

The truth surely is that here again James seems deliberately to scatter conflicting and contradictory clues; it is not just that he fails to let us know whether the frame narrator is male or female, but that he actually encourages us to make assumptions in both directions. Thomson's word 'suggestion' is just right: there are suggestions in the novella's opening pages both that the frame narrator is a man and also that the frame narrator is a woman.

Of course, depending upon which of James's suggestions is effective, other implications remain to be responded to. Given that Douglas's behaviour towards the frame narrator suggests that their relationship enjoys a high level of intimacy, and quite possibly has an erotic or sexual component, then those readers who assume that the frame narrator is male are likely to perceive a homoerotic component in the frame narrative, one which will make it more likely that they will perceive the relationships between, respectively, Peter Quint and Miles, and Miss Jessel and Flora, as also of a homoerotic nature. Readers who, in contrast, believe the frame narrator to be a woman, are likely to be more receptive to later suggestions concerning the governess's heterosexual impulses – both towards the uncle and also towards Miles. (A celebrated passage towards the end of the governess's narrative has her comparing herself and Miles to 'some young

---

[50] Thomson's terminology is a little confusing here. In the novella it is Douglas who delivers 'a few words of prologue' to the assembled gathering. But by 'the narrator of the prologue' Thomson clearly means the narrator of the opening frame narrative.

couple who, on their wedding journey, at the inn, feel shy in the presence of the waiter' [1966, p81]. The shock effect of this is, as many commentators have pointed out, given an additional turn of the screw by her referring to the maid as 'the waiter' in her next sentence.) It is by no means accidental that the word 'suggestive' can have a specifically sexual set of meanings. Many of the character names in the novella are sexually suggestive. 'Quint' runs together 'quim' and 'cunt'; 'Flora' suggests the possibility of defloration, and 'Jessel' may suggest 'Jezebel' – 'Jessie' is apparently still a slang term for Jezebel in certain regional British dialects, and according to Partridge 'Jezebel' is a slang term for the penis. (In Northern Ireland, according to one source, 'She's in her Jezabels' means 'She's in a state of undress' [= déshabillé]! See McKendry [1991], p28.) And of course the word 'screw' itself has a widely known sexual meaning.

It seems to me that the case for the ambiguity of *The Turn of the Screw* (as defined by Rimmon) is unassailable. But such a conclusion leads us in two ways, and both require us to consider the life of this text as it has been lived in culture and history. In one direction, only changing cultural expectations can explain why different generations of readers and critics have attempted to resolve James's ambiguities in the historically variable ways in which they have so done. In another direction, only an investigation into the detail of James's own position in the culture of late Victorian England, and into the detail of his own background in the United States and England, can explain why he should have wanted to produce not one but several works all characterized by an ambiguity whose consistency is rare in the history of English fiction.

James may have written only four works which conform to the requirements of what Todorov calls the 'pure fantastic'. But his fiction is, more generally, characterized by an obsession with indeterminacy, by the attempts of individuals to resolve puzzles without reaching out beyond the confines of their disengaged and normally private or secret consideration of these puzzles. In this James's work is again strikingly different from that of his contemporary, Joseph Conrad. Consider, for example, one key scene in Conrad's *The Secret Agent*. Following a totally unexpected but bungled bomb attack on the Greenwich Observatory, the police are baffled but under considerable political pressure to solve the mystery of who is responsible for the outrage. In charge of the investigation is the Assistant Commissioner, who feels hamstrung by his being restricted to his desk:

> Crossing over to his desk with headlong strides, he sat down violently. 'Here I am stuck in a litter of paper,' he reflected, with unreasonable resentment, 'supposed to hold all the threads in my hands, and yet I can but hold what is put in my hand, and nothing else. And they can fasten the other ends of the threads where they please.' (1990, p91)

His response is, in fact, to quit his desk, to leave his rôle as observer, as trader in second-hand information, and to go out into the city to investigate the mystery at first hand. His investigation is successful: he manages to bring the culprit to book. Those readers who remember my much earlier (p15) quotation from Conrad's *The Shadow-Line* in which a dismissive comment is made about those shore officials who deal only with reality at second hand, will realize that Conrad's contempt for a life lived at a distance from physical reality, dealing with its demands only through mediations contemplated away from the heat of battle, is as consistent as is James's preference for and valorization of such a life.

In other words, the Assistant Commissioner's frustrated abandoning of his desk, his movement outwards from contemplation to engaged participation, is thoroughly un-Jamesian. Throughout his fiction James's constant tendency is to prize detached contemplation over 'vulgar' participation, to rank the rôle of observer higher on all counts than that of player in the field. To contemplate action at a remove is 'fine'; to attempt better to understand it by direct involvement is 'vulgar'. For James, going out to see directly where the Assistant Commissioner's 'threads' are fastened would surely have been seen as vulgar: how much better to remain in ignorance, perpetually considering the implications of their different possible fastening-points! Trying to imagine *The Secret Agent* as it might have been written by Henry James is an awe-inspiring task, but we can at least feel fairly confident that a Jamesian narrator would have preferred to luxuriate in the ignorance of the authorities rather than to have a character prepared to leave his desk to end it.

The pattern is already apparent in James's first (if one ignores the short *Watch and Ward*) major novel – *Roderick Hudson*. In this work the rich Rowland Mallet, a man of fine but passively utilized sensibilities is quizzed by the serious and morally firm Mary Garland:

> Then noticing that he had spoken jestingly she glanced at him askance, though with no visible diminution of her gravity. 'Don't you know how to do anything? Have you no profession?'
> Rowland shook his head. 'Absolutely none.'
> 'What do you do all day?'
> 'Nothing worth relating. That's why I am going to Europe. There at least if I do nothing I shall see a great deal; and if I am not a producer I shall at any rate be an observer.' (1986, pp97–8)

Realizing that such an admission puts him in a bad light with Mary he insists, shortly after this exchange, that 'I am not frivolous' (1986, p99). Indeed, if the plot of *Roderick Hudson* can be said to demonstrate anything it is that engagement in – rather than contemplation of – the world leads to just such frivolousness: while Mallet retains his moral equilibrium the painter Roderick Hudson, who does so commit himself to living rather than to merely observing life, destroys himself.

In varying ways much of James's fiction devotes itself to a defence of those who by necessity or choice are observers and not producers. The detached observer typically occupies the rôle of moral centre in James's fiction – to the extent that a refusal to 'find things out' by actually confronting reality directly as does Conrad's Assistant Commissioner is taken as token of sensibility and moral superiority. As Ralf Norrman has sarcastically (and perhaps with a little irritability) expressed it, 'Utterances in James should preferably not be uttered. Wills should not be read, instead one should speculate over their contents (*The Ivory Tower*). Letters should not be opened and read; it is much better to throw them unopened into the fire (*The Wings of the Dove*) or give them unopened to a friend ('Eugene Pickering'). That way one knows their contents much better than by reading them' (1982, p129). He remarks, further:

> In his parody 'The Mote in the Middle Distance' Max Beerbohm made the two children, Keith Tantalus and his sister, decide *not* to peer into their Christmas stockings. Beerbohm has indeed caught the essence of James's world. If Keith and his sister *did* peer, their speculations, fantasies etc. would be checked against reality and that is always the great risk in James. If you do *not* utter utterances you can (can you?) live on in the belief that whatever you make other people out to have understood you as silently 'saying' – or them to have been on the point of saying, etc. – is true. If you do *not* read letters you can think (can you?) that you know what their contents are. If you do *not* read wills you can yourself (can you?) create their contents verbally.
>
> One way to ensure that language has power over reality is to see to it that whatever has been imagined verbally is never checked against reality. Therefore you must not utter utterances, must not read letters, must not break the seal of wills etc. (1982, pp129–30)

From this perspective it can be calculated that what James does to the reader of *The Turn of the Screw* is to force him or her into such a rôle of uninvolved observer. Like the heroine of another of James's tales, the reader is 'in the cage', locked in the textual prison-house, able to oscillate eternally between different readings without any danger of reality confronting one with the real state of affairs, spared for ever the vulgarity of the Assistant Commissioner's flight from 'a litter of paper' to a first-hand reality. For the reader of James's fiction, paper is very often all we get. And given that we may all be responding differently to James's hints and suggestions, we can never be sure that we all have the same bits of paper.

Now given the difference that I have posited between Conrad and James we are unlikely to be able to explain James's idiosyncratic flight from vulgar reality by a crude appeal to a monolithic 'historical reality'. Both James and Conrad were – in 1898 – expatriates of nearly the same age living in England. Why should these two writers have valued detached contemplation so very differently?

Two separate but related questions are involved in this query. The obvious question relates to those elements in the two writers' personal histories – elements generated by an interplay between their individual circumstances and wider social and cultural forces – which led them to such different attitudes towards involvement in and detachment from life. But a writer does not just pour out a vision of the world to a passively receptive audience. Publication, especially by writers seeking for a wider readership, involves anticipation of and response to the expectations and needs of readers. Had James and Conrad based structuring configurations of human behaviour in their fiction on what were merely idiosyncratic or personal patterns of response it is unlikely that their fiction would have attracted many readers at the time of initial publication, or that it would have continued to be deemed worthy of serious attention. A writer has to build on his or her personal experience, but unless this experience can produce patterns or problems which strike chords in readers it is unlikely to result in art which captures a public.

Thus Conrad's life, prior to his beginning to write fiction, of sustained and direct physical, mental and emotional engagement with the world during his time as a working seaman, is doubtless highly relevant to the fact that such engagement (of the sort manifested by the Assistant Commissioner in *The Secret Agent*) is never dismissed as 'vulgar' in the pages of his fiction. In contrast, James, unlike two of his brothers, had not fought in the American Civil War, but had, rather, lived a life in which contemplation rather than engagement had been the norm. In his major study of the James family, *The Jameses: A Family Narrative* (1991), R. W. B. Lewis stresses that the particular example of James's brother Wilky, who achieved fame as one of the officers commanding the first Black unit of soldiers to fight in the Civil War (the subject of the 1989 film *Glory*), was particularly significant for Henry. Lewis argues that 'it was the example of Wilky that gave the watchful Henry the sharpening sense of two fundamentally different ways of taking life – Wilky's way and his', and he quotes, tellingly, James's own autobiographical comment that 'one way of taking life was to go in for everything and everyone, which kept you abundantly occupied, and the other way was to be as occupied, quite as occupied, just with the sense and the image of it all' (1991, p84). In Lewis's opinion, the experience of *not* having served as a soldier in the Civil War became crucial for Henry James:

> Before the figures of those who had fallen in battle, Henry felt, or came to feel, a becoming humbleness. They seemed to him to have the power of 'facing us out, quite blandly ignoring us, looking through or straight over us at something they partake of altogether but that we mayn't pretend to know.' This was the locus of Henry's immediate and his long-range response: regret – not guilt – at having failed to acquire the knowledge of combat, violence, death. In talking of his younger brothers and their letters from the front, he put it more personally: that the effect of them coalesced into 'the single sense of what I missed, compared to what the authors of our bulletins gained, in wondrous opportunity of vision, that is *appreciation of the thing seen* – there being clearly such a lot of this, and all of it, by my conviction, portentous and prodigious.' (1991, p158; the quotations are again from James's autobiographical writings)

James's quoted comments display an extraordinary ideological sleight-of-hand, a doubling back which allows him to recuperate the initially admitted inferiority. For whilst the reader initially expects that James's 'humbleness' will be that of the man of contemplation for the man of action, by a piece of dazzling recuperative footwork this is undercut by his envy of his brothers being expressed in terms of their 'wondrous opportunity of vision', their *'appreciation of the thing seen'*. The measure of importance, in other words, is again that of *contemplative* fullness: action and engagement are valued because of what they enable the actor to *see*, and not in terms of what they allow the actor to do or to achieve.

The recurrent figure of the uninvolved observer in James's work serves, then, to valorize and to celebrate what is presented as the supreme good: *seeing* in as full and as sensitively complex a manner as possible. To dismiss action as vulgar is, indirectly, to exculpate James from the charge that by failing to engage directly in the Civil War he condemned himself to a life lived less fully than it might have been. Such a suspicion is never so very far beneath the surface in James's fiction, it is true, and with a character such as Lambert Strether in *The Ambassadors* it is granted perhaps the most overt admission that it gets in the pages of his fiction. But in a work such as *The Turn of the Screw* the association of subtlety and moral firmness with disengaged observation and unspecific suggestion, and of vulgarity and crudeness with engagement and unambiguous statement, both serve as justifications for the choice made by, or for, James: to look at rather than to participate in life, to be an observer rather than a producer.

If disengagement was something which distinguished James from at least two of his brothers so far as the matter of the Civil War was concerned, it was also something which united him with his generation of family members in questions of money. James's grandfather, as Lewis establishes, was not just a very rich man but was, at the time of his death, probably one of the three richest men in the United States. Lewis reports that in the 1830s the fortune of the older William James was reputed to be second only to that of John Jacob Astor (1991, p30). The fortune was new money, built up by James's grandfather more or less from nothing. But after his death the family became, instead of producers of new wealth, rentiers living off inherited capital. Lewis again quotes tellingly from Henry James's autobiographical writings, in which James speaks of the complete rupture with his grandfather's tradition and attitude which the '"sudden collective disconnectedness" of the later Jameses "from *the* American resource of those days", the resource of business' (1991, p13) was to constitute. According to Lewis, however,

> the phenomena of money and business agitated the Jamesian mind, in the generations after the Albany grandfather, to a degree which it is difficult, or even impossible, to match elsewhere in our literary and intellectual history.
>
> What these Jameses did was to displace the language and the motifs of the money world into other realms of discourse: into theology, philosophy, psychology, literature; and to entangle them with other urgencies of experience. (1991, p13)

The comment is thought-provoking, and helps to suggest how James's personal concerns and moulding influences could be translated into forms which struck chords with a wider reading public.

The period of James's fictional career is the period in which national and international finance capital achieves a pre-eminence significant enough to challenge the less mobile strength of industrial capital. In other words, this is the period in which – as Martin Decoud has it in Conrad's *Nostromo* – the 'speculations of grave and reverend persons in England' lead to the activities of bands of adventurers. As Decoud notes: 'That is history' (see p187), and indeed by the turn of the century the detached manipulation of capital had become a more potent factor in human history than movements initiated on a merely local basis and carried out in person by those involved. The age of imperialism is the age of the disengaged manipulation of human history by those controlling (or controlled by) material interests. One of the reasons why James's detached observers are so relevant to late nineteenth-century America and Britain is that this is the age of the speculator, the man (and not the woman) who observes and interferes without physically being present at what he initiates and controls.

We can perhaps risk a generalization and say that while Conrad's characters typically do things without seeing what the implication of this doing is, James's characters typically see complex chains of causal and non-causal connections and influences without being able to do much to intervene in these processes. Both writers can therefore be said to reflect different aspects of a world in which seeing and doing are being torn apart by the increasingly highly mediated nature of the relationship between observation and engagement ushered in by the age of imperialism. If we consider a novel such as E. M. Forster's *A Passage to India*, and we consider the difference between a shrewd observer such as Fielding and a dim colonial administrator such as Ronny Heaslop, we may recognize in one novel two aspects of the British Empire in the late nineteenth and early twentieth centuries. We may also guess that perhaps men such as Fielding might find much to enjoy in the novels of James, and men such as Ronny (or, at least, those like him but a little less stupid) might find much to which they could relate in the novels of Conrad.

James's disengaged observers are typically without power. The marginal social status of the governess in *The Turn of the Screw* fits her perfectly for the rôle of Jamesian observer, an observer whose only claim to power or moral force lies in his or her *knowledge* – like the telegraph girl in 'In the Cage'. In both of these cases the observer is denied power through social and economic placings and exclusions, but other forms of disempowerment are possible in the Jamesian fictional world: age, bad health, gender, lack of sexual attractiveness – all can render the Jamesian observer powerless, can deny him or her any controlling purchase on life other than that of seeing or knowing. And all serve to create a node of experience reflective of that of the intelligentsia in James's day: able to observe, to analyse, to comment, to hypothesize – but not to intervene, not to change. Such intervention is typically situated in a colonial context; precisely that context, in fact, in which Conrad's characters typically attempt to gain a purchase on the world, and the context in which the grandparents of Miles and Flora, the parents of the so-attractive uncle, have made their money. James spells out these complex socio-economic relationships very precisely:

> He [the uncle] had been left, by the death of his parents in India, guardian to a small nephew and a small niece, children of a younger, a military brother whom he had lost two years before. (1966, p5)

James's military brother Wilky had died in 1883, and had left his brother Henry – like the uncle, 'a lone man without the right sort of experience' – not with the responsibility of looking after two small children, but with the task of dealing emotionally and psychologically with the legacy of his so-very different life.

But if James's fictional vision clearly springs from what Raymond Williams would term a particular 'structure of feeling', the structure of feeling cannot fully be understood independently of larger social and economic movements in a world increasingly dominated by imperialism. Thus in speaking of their creator's sense of exclusion from direct involvement in life, and especially through their attempt to valorize such a lived perspective, James's fictional works reach out to a whole range of readers who are similarly condemned to a spectatorial relationship with the forces of historical change. If Conrad's *Nostromo* shows us human beings who are directly involved in historical events they neither understand nor planned for, and James's fiction recurrently depicts detached observers who attempt to see and understand without being able to intervene or change, then we should realize that both present a view of reality in which there is a sharp division between those who see and understand and those who are involved in events they do not understand. So different in so many ways, the fiction of both James and Conrad is at one in its belief that action and contemplation are typically mutually exclusive options. It is in *Nostromo* that we can read the following lines, but they express a sentiment with which James seems to have been in agreement: 'Action is consolatory. It is the enemy of thought and the friend of flattering illusions. Only in the conduct of our action can we find the sense of mastery over the Fates' (1984, p66). It is, we should note, only 'the sense' of mastery – not mastery itself.

In James's fiction, however, the issue of the ways in which social class constrains or enables vision, and is associated with directness or indeterminacy, literalness or periphrasis, looms much larger than it does in Conrad's work. The reason why, as Ralf Norrman puts it, letters should not be opened or read in the world of Henry James, is that such a prohibition serves to valorize the blind speculations of those readers who have themselves to guess at the processes by which the world is manipulated. Such readers can rest assured that James's stories 'won't tell . . . not in any literal vulgar way', but will patronize them by allowing them to associate real power with vulgarity:

Flora continued to fix me with her small mask of disaffection, and even at that minute I prayed God to forgive me for seeming to see that, as she stood there holding tight to our friend's dress, her incomparable childish beauty had suddenly failed, had quite vanished. I've said it already – she was literally, she was hideously hard; she had turned common and almost ugly. 'I don't know what you mean. I see nobody. I see nothing. I never *have*. I think you're cruel. I don't like you!' Then, after this deliverance, which might have been that of a vulgarly pert little girl in the street . . . (1966, pp72–3)

Speaking directly is what the lower classes do, and it goes along with their inability to *see*. Beauty is the prerogative of disempowerment and blindness, of understanding without *knowing* – in the manner of Maisie. The position of the marginally placed governess, who lacks both the power of the uncle and also that ability to speak without circumlocution enjoyed by the lower orders, reflects that of the disempowered intelligentsia of James's day. As a number of critics have pointed out, the governess's view of her life at Bly is highly literary, charged with references and allusions to works such as *Jane Eyre*, *The Mysteries of Udolpho*, and *Amelia*. Mrs Grose, in contrast, is illiterate. And as the governess sees Peter Quint 'as I see the letters formed on this page', the link drawn between reading and seeing ghosts should prepare us for the fact that Mrs Grose will see neither Peter Quint nor Miss Jessel. Once again, seeing (rather than acting, or stating 'literally') is valorized and associated with culture and refinement.

Shoshana Felman refers tellingly to a letter written by James to H. G. Wells in which James writes that 'The difficulty itself is the refuge from the vulgarity', and to his preface to the New York edition of the novella, in which he comments:

> Portentous evil – how was I to save that, as an intention on the part of my demon-spirits, from the drop, the comparative vulgarity, inevitably attending, throughout the whole range of possible brief illustration, the offered example, the imputed vice, the cited act, the limited deplorable presentable instance? (1966, p122)

Felman draws the essential point as follows:

> What is vulgar, then, is the '*imputed* vice', the 'offered example', that is, the explicit, the specific, the unequivocal and immediately referential 'illustration.' *The vulgar is the literal*, insofar as it is unambiguous: 'the story won't tell; not in any *literal, vulgar* way.' The literal is 'vulgar' because it *stops the movement* constitutive of meaning, because it blocks and interrupts the endless process of metaphorical substitution. The vulgar, therefore, is anything which misses, or falls short of, the dimension of the symbolic, anything which rules out, or excludes, meaning as a loss and as a flight, – anything which strives, in other words, to eliminate from language its inherent silence, anything which misses the specific way in which a text *actively* 'won't tell.' (1977, p107)

The endless play of mutually exclusive possibilities in *The Turn of the Screw* is, then, for the reader who accepts his or her imprisonment within the world of the fiction, not something by which he or she is expected to become frustrated. On the contrary, as we travel the endless loop of alternative interpretations, oscillating between apparitionist and non-apparitionist viewpoints, we should remind ourselves that our ability to maintain such an endless hesitation between alternatives *guarantees our gentility*. We are doing what the vulgar cannot, and we are not doing what they must do in their forced daily concern with 'the limited deplorable presentable instance'. We may have no power actually to influence what goes on in the world, but we *see* so much more than those who do. Certainty is a privilege or a curse granted only to the rich uncles or the illiterate Mrs Groses of the world. To lack it, but to be capable of fine discriminations in one's detached observations of the world is to belong to that social fraction James occupied and to which he made his literary appeal. *The Turn of the Screw* is product of, and panacea for, those who have leisure to observe the world but no power to change it. There is an old joke which has Queen Victoria, referring to the sex act, ask Prince Albert if the working classes also 'do it'. When he answers in the affirmative, the Queen responds decisively: 'It's far too good for them'. What James seems to think is too good for the lower orders is, however, not doing it (sex – or anything else), but thinking about doing it.

Those who have argued that *The Turn of the Screw* depends for its intended effect upon a widespread sexual exploitation of lower-class women by middle- and upper-class men are probably right. James may have left blanks, but he knew how most of his readers would fill them in. The paradox is, however, that there is a deeper historical reality than this to which the novella appeals, one which admittedly rests upon the possibility of such exploitation but which calls it up only to renounce it. It is delayed or denied gratification which is the mark of refinement for James, a mark validated for him by its association with that intelligentsia to which he belongs – an intelligentsia for which renunciation was a necessity which was turned into a virtue, a mark of caste.

Appendix: The Time-scale of *The Turn of the Screw*

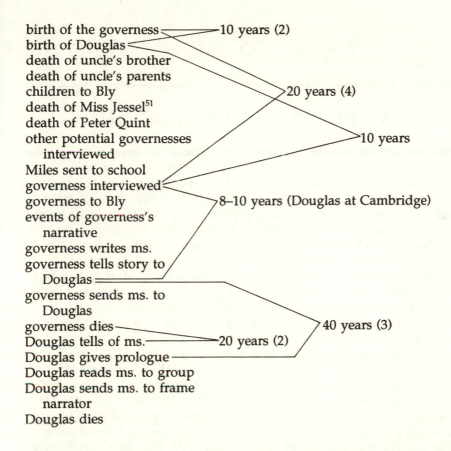

birth of the governess
birth of Douglas
death of uncle's brother
death of uncle's parents
children to Bly
death of Miss Jessel[51]
death of Peter Quint
other potential governesses
    interviewed
Miles sent to school
governess interviewed
governess to Bly
events of governess's
    narrative
governess writes ms.
governess tells story to
    Douglas
governess sends ms. to
    Douglas
governess dies
Douglas tells of ms.
Douglas gives prologue
Douglas reads ms. to group
Douglas sends ms. to frame
    narrator
Douglas dies

10 years (2)
20 years (4)
10 years
8–10 years (Douglas at Cambridge)
40 years (3)
20 years (2)

Numbers in brackets refer to the Norton edition of *The Turn of the Screw* (James 1966).

[51] Miss Jessel may die before or after Peter Quint. Mrs Grose says of Quint that after the master's departure 'last year' he was 'alone with *us*' (1966, p24), but Miss Jessel's mourning might suggest that she survived him. Her death takes place 'at the end of the year' (1966, p13); the year is not specified, but it is presumably also 'last year'.

8

A TENTATIVE CONCLUSION

Cunning passages rarely have neat conclusions, and this book is no exception. Rather than a neat conclusion I have tried to provide help in negotiating some of the twists and turns involved in plotting the cunning passages of literary works: both the ones they contain, and the ones they trace. There are certain issues, however, which I would like to underscore in these final pages.

I started this book by declaring – or confessing – my Marxism. I remain convinced that any serious theory of history needs some conception of the relative strength enjoyed by the myriad possible forces and influences which can direct and determine the path of human society. Marxism's insistence upon the ultimate dominance of economic factors in such direction and determination is such a theory, and in my opinion enjoys more proven explanatory force than any rival. At the same time, Marxists have devoted increasing attention to the problematic issue of the mediations through which such economic forces pass before exerting their influence. Chief amongst such mediating stages is that of ideology. I hope that my chapter on the literature of the *Titanic* has gone some way towards displaying the manner in which class interests present themselves in disguised and transformed forms when faced with what is perceived as a threat to themselves.

But a belief in the ultimate sovereignty of economic forces in the development in human society does not necessarily make a quietistic surrender to such forces inevitable. Such a surrender – as Joseph Conrad's *Nostromo* reminds us – is an abdication of our moral responsibility. A realistic political agenda must needs seek to yoke these forces to our own moral priorities; to subdue rather than to ignore, or to capitulate to, them.

Human beings face the past both as scavengers and as fellows. We are scavengers inasmuch as we want to take what is useful from the past, to learn from and build on what the past has to offer us. We are fellows inasmuch as we recognize the humanity of those who have gone before us and to the extent that we manifest a non-exploitative and non-instrumental interest in their lives and experiences. Distinguishing between ourselves as scavengers and ourselves as fellows is not necessarily straightforward, and may indeed be impossible: learning more about the humanity of others is never entirely without use to us in the present. That said, my tentative conclusion is that a work of literature is valuable to the extent that it puts us in contact with what lies outside the text – even, or especially, when it does this by forcing our concentrated moral and intellectual attention on to what is in the text. Sometimes, it is true, our responses to literature lead to such contact only when we are led to consider just what it is that literary works leave out. But many of the literary works at which I have looked either address, or direct attention to, such absences. My discussion has often been led to a consideration of those people and those experiences that exist beyond the limits of various officially sanctioned histories: the steerage passengers of the *Titanic*, Auden's 'poor in their fireless lodgings', the 'natives' of Conrad's Costaguana, the lower orders in Woolf's *Between the Acts* and James's *The Turn of the Screw*. The more these works are themselves involved in such a direction of our attention, the more valuable I believe them to be.

All histories are selective, and the writers and critics of literary works are just as subject to those ideological pressures which trim off awkward aspects of experience – the ones which do not fit the patterns preferred by those in power – as is anyone else. Hardy's response to the loss of the *Titanic* is no more ideologically innocent than is Conrad's decision concerning the subject positions he will recognize in *Nostromo*. Indeed, there is a case to be made that Conrad confronts and opposes ideological obfuscation more directly and more successfully in his essays on the *Titanic* disaster than in a work of fiction such as *Nostromo*. Literature does not live in a universe miraculously swabbed clean of ideology. But it can enter into those conflicts which are themselves constitutive of ideologies and counter-ideologies, and can display such conflicts for those readers willing to approach literary texts as records of complex and changing engagements with historical realities – and as the means whereby more challenging and creative engagements can be negotiated. At the present time it is, I believe, those critics who are known as cultural materialists who are plotting and extending such exploratory work with most sophistication and commitment.

The writer and the historian share a common desire to represent realities which are, or will be, unavailable for direct scrutiny by their readers. Both have to negotiate and map the cunning passages of history in cunning passages of their own, and, as we have seen, both recognize that deciding what is left in and what is left out is far from easy or straightforward. Both give us pictures, but like the paintings in Woolf's *Between the Acts*, these pictures may testify to different criteria of what is important. It would be easy to say that whereas art takes us into the past, history displays the past for us – except that a good historian can also take us into the past and a good poet or novelist can (as do Enzensberger, Conrad and Woolf) cause us to step back and consider more general questions relating to the portrayal of the past.

Writing about the *Titanic* disaster and its aftermath, Joseph Conrad made the wry comment that '[s]ome people can only learn from that sort of experience which comes home to their own dear selves' (1921b, p333).

Conrad knew, before Derrida was even born, that some people have difficulty seeing non-textual realities through or beyond texts, are unable fully to share those human experiences which are depicted in or constitutive of literary works. But it is because literary works provide experiences which do, classically, come home to their readers' own dear selves that – their textuality notwithstanding – they are often able to open up veins of history before which the quarryings of historians stop short. It is also, incidentally, why people in power tend to take works of literature seriously.

In reading books we are helped to read ourselves; as what we are reading comes home to us, we see ourselves displayed in the forms and patterns our response assumes. Because the turn to history in literary studies has helped to expose the multitude of ways in which literary works intervene in and grow out of history, it is a development which has helped to remind us of our own historicity, our own interactive involvement in a world of ceaseless change. We are thus helped to progress beyond a passive attitude to both art and life, helped to realize or to remember that neither art nor life are spectator sports. The answer to textualism is not to collapse the aesthetic back into history, to claim that everything is outside the text. It is, rather, to see texts – and especially literary texts – as complex sites and records of a human engagement with history, as well as a means whereby this engagement can be refined and extended.

After decades of literary criticism dominated by the formalisms of the New Critics, the structuralists, and the post-structuralists, the achievements of New Historicism and, especially, of cultural materialism, are allowing students of literature not just to observe but to take part in the social struggles that literature arises from and gives access to. The opportunity should be grasped. The doors to the ivory towers filled with the prisoners taken by fifty-seven varieties of formalism have been unlocked. Let's take a look outside.

SELECT BIBLIOGRAPHY

ALTHUSSER, LOUIS 1969: *For Marx*. Ben Brewster (tr.). London: Allen Lane. (First published in French 1963.)

ARMSTRONG, TIM 1992: 'Hardy, Thaxter, and History as Coincidence in "The Convergence of the Twain"'. *Victorian Poetry* 30, pp29–42.

AUDEN, W. H. 1937: *Spain*. London: Faber and Faber.

—— 1966: *Collected Shorter Poems*. London: Faber and Faber.

BARKER, FRANCIS and HULME, PETER 1985: '"Nymphs and Reapers Heavily Vanish": The Discursive Con-texts of *The Tempest*'. In John Drakakis (ed.), *Alternative Shakespeare*. London: Methuen, pp191–205.

BARRETT, MICHÈLE 1991: *The Politics of Truth: From Marx to Foucault*. Oxford: Polity Press.

BARTHES, ROLAND 1973: *Mythologies*. Annette Lavers (ed. and tr.). Frogmore: Granada. (First published in French 1972.)

BELL, ANNE OLIVER (ed.) 1984: *The Diary of Virginia Woolf*. Volume Five 1936–1941. New York: Harcourt Brace Jovanovich.

BELL, QUENTIN (ed.) 1938: *Julian Bell: Essays, Poems and Letters*. London: Hogarth Press.

BRADY, PHILIP 1989: 'Watermarks on the Titanic: Hans Magnus Enzensberger's Defence of Poesy'. *Publications of the English Goethe Society* 58, pp3–26.

BRANSON, NOREEN and HEINEMANN, MARGOT 1971: *Britain in the 1930's*. New York: Praeger.

BRENNER, HENRY 1932: *Titanic's Knell*. St Meinrad, Indiana: The Raven.

BRIDGEN, JOHN 1990: 'Frank McEachran (1900–1975): An Unrecognized Influence on W. H. Auden'. In Bucknell and Jenkins (1990), pp117–33.

BRONSON, BERTRAND H. 1958: *Samuel Johnson: Rasselas, Poems, and Selected Prose*. New York: Holt, Rinehart and Winston.

BROWN, EMERSON, JR. 1994: 'The Ruthless Artistry of Hardy's "Convergence of the Twain"'. *Sewanee Review* 102, pp232–43.

BROWN, RICHARD 1983: *Voyage of the Iceberg: The Story of the Iceberg That Sank the Titanic*. Toronto: James Lorimer.

BROWNING, CHRISTOPHER R. 1992: 'German Memory, Judicial Interrogation, and Historical Reconstruction: Writing Perpetrator History from Postwar Testimony'. In Friedlander (1992), pp22–36; 338–40.

BUCKNELL, KATHERINE and JENKINS, NICHOLAS (eds) 1990: *W. H. Auden 'The Map of All My Youth': Early Works, Friends and Influences*. Auden Studies 1. Oxford: Clarendon Press.

BUTLER, MARILYN 1982: *Romantics, Rebels and Reactionaries: English Literature and its Background 1760–1830*. New York: Oxford University Press.

CAMPBELL, LILY B. 1947: *Shakespeare's Histories: Mirrors of Elizabethan Policy*. San Marino: Huntingdon Library.

CHAMBERS, ROSS 1984: *Story and Situation: Narrative Seduction and the Power of Fiction*. Theory and History of Literature, vol. 12. Minneapolis: University of Minnesota Press.

CHASE, RICHARD (ed.) 1950: *Herman Melville: Selected Tales and Poems*. New York: Holt, Rinehart and Winston.

CONNOLLY, CYRIL 1975: 'Some Memories'. In Spender (1975), pp68–73.

CONRAD, JOSEPH 1921a: 'Some Reflections on the Loss of the *Titanic*'. In *Notes on Life and Letters*. London: Dent, pp287–307.

—— 1921b: 'Certain Aspects of the Admirable Inquiry Into the Loss of the *Titanic*'. In *Notes on Life and Letters*. London: Dent, pp309–34.

—— 1921c: 'Henry James: An Appreciation'. In *Notes on Life and Letters*. London: Dent, pp13–23.

—— 1947: *Almayer's Folly: A Story of an Eastern River*. London: Dent.

—— 1950: *Within the Tides*. London: Dent.

—— 1983: *Lord Jim*. World's Classics edition. John Batchelor (ed.). Oxford: Oxford University Press.

—— 1984: *Nostromo*. World's Classics edition. Keith Carabine (ed.). Oxford: Oxford University Press.

—— 1985: *The Shadow-Line*. World's Classics edition. Jeremy Hawthorn (ed.). Oxford: Oxford University Press.

—— 1986: *Victory*. World's Classics edition. John Batchelor (ed.). Oxford: Oxford University Press.

—— 1990: *The Secret Agent: A Simple Tale*. Bruce Harkness and S. W. Reid (eds), Nancy Birk (assistant ed.). The Cambridge Edition of the Works of Joseph Conrad. Cambridge: Cambridge University Press.

—— 1994: *Almayer's Folly: A Story of an Eastern River*. David Leon Higdon and Floyd Eugene Eddleman (eds). The Cambridge Edition of the Works of Joseph Conrad. Cambridge: Cambridge University Press.

COOK, ELIZABETH (ed.) 1990: *John Keats*. The Oxford Authors. Oxford: Oxford University Press.

COSTELLO, MARY 1993: *Titanic Town*. London: Mandarin. (First published 1992.)

COWARD, NOËL 1933: *Cavalcade*. New York: Grosset and Dunlap. (First published in Britain 1932.)

COX, JEFFREY N. and REYNOLDS, LARRY J. (eds) 1993: *New Historical Literary Study: Essays on Reproducing Texts, Representing History*. Princeton, N.J: Princeton University Press.

CRANFILL, THOMAS MABRY and CLARK, JR., ROBERT LANIER 1965: *An Anatomy of* The Turn of the Screw. Austin: University of Texas Press.

CUSSLER, CLIVE 1976: *Raise the Titanic!* New York: Viking Press.

DAVENPORT, ARNOLD 1958: 'A Note on "To Autumn"'. In Kenneth Muir (ed.), *John Keats A Reassessment*. Liverpool: Liverpool University Press, pp95–101.

DAVIE, MICHAEL 1987: *Titanic: The Death and Life of a Legend*. New York: Knopf.

DEMORY, PAMELA H. 1993: '*Nostromo*: Making History'. *Texas Studies in Literature and Language* 35(3), pp316–46.

—— 1994: '*Nostromo* and *Don Quixote*: The Fiction of True History'. *Joseph Conrad Today* XVIII(3–4), p2.

DE SELINCOURT, E. 1944: *The Poetical Works of William Wordsworth*. Vol. 2. Oxford: Clarendon Press.

DJWA, SANDRA and MOYLES, R. G. (eds) 1989: *E. J. Pratt: Complete Poems. Part One*. Toronto and London: University of Toronto Press.

DRAKAKIS, JOHN (ed.) 1992: *Shakespearian Tragedy*. Harlow: Longman.

EAGLETON, TERRY 1985: 'Ideology and Scholarship'. In Jerome J. McGann (ed.), *Historical Studies and Literary Criticism*. Madison: The University of Wisconsin Press, pp114–25.

EDEL, LEON and WILSON, MARK (eds) 1984: *Henry James: Literary Criticism*. 2 vols. 1: *Essays on Literature, American Writers, English Writers*; 2: *French Writers, Other European Writers, the Prefaces to the New York Edition*. New York: Library of America.

ENGELS, FREDERICK 1956: Letter to Minna Kautsky, 26 November, 1885. In Karl Marx and Frederick Engels, *Literature and Art*. Bombay: Current Book House.

ENZENSBERGER, HANS MAGNUS 1989: *The Sinking of the Titanic: A Poem*. (Tr. by the author.) London: Paladin. (First published in German 1978, and in English 1981.)

ERMARTH, ELIZABETH DEEDS 1992: *Postmodernism and the Crisis of Representational Time*. Princeton, N. J. : Princeton University Press.

EVERETT, MARSHALL (ed.) 1912: *Wreck and Sinking of the Titanic: The Ocean's Greatest Disaster*. L. H. Walter. (Title on cover: *Story of the Wreck of the Titanic: The Ocean's Greatest Disaster*. No place of publication given.)

FANON, FRANTZ 1963: *The Wretched of the Earth*. Constance Farrington (tr.). New York: Grove.

FELMAN, SHOSHANA 1977: 'Turning the Screw of Interpretation'. *Yale French Studies* 55/56, pp94–207.

FELPERIN, HOWARD 1990: *The Uses of the Canon: Elizabethan Literature and Contemporary Theory*. Oxford: Clarendon Press. (Repr. with corrections 1992.)

FISHER, CLIVE 1992: *Noël Coward*. New York: St Martin's Press.

FOGEL, AARON 1985: *Coercion to Speak: Conrad's Poetics of Dialogue*. Cambridge, Mass.: Harvard University Press.

FOUCAULT, MICHEL 1972: *The Archaeology of Knowledge*. A. M. Sheridan Smith (tr.). London: Tavistock. (First published in French 1969.)

—— 1980: 'What is an author?' (First published in English 1977, in Donald F. Bouchard [ed]., *Language, Counter-memory, Practice: Selected Essays and Interviews*. New York: Cornell University Press.) In J. V. Harari (ed.), *Textual Strategies: Perspectives in Post-structuralist Criticism*. London: Methuen, pp141–60.

—— 1994: *The Order of Things: An Archaeology of the Human Sciences*. New York: Vintage Books. (First published in French 1966.)

FREEMANTLE, ANNE 1975: 'Reality and Religion'. In Spender (1975), pp79–92.

FRIEDLANDER, SAUL (ed.) 1992: *Probing the Limits of Representation: Nazism and the 'Final Solution'*. Cambridge, Mass./London: Harvard University Press.

FROW, JOHN 1986: *Marxism and Literary History*. Oxford: Blackwell.

GARDNER, MARTIN 1986: *The Wreck of the 'Titanic' Foretold?*. Buffalo, New York: Prometheus Books.

GARROD, H. W. 1926: *Keats*. Oxford: Clarendon Press.

GEERTZ, CLIFFORD 1973: *The Interpretation of Cultures*. New York: Basic Books.

GINZBURG, CARLO 1992: 'Just One Witness'. In Friedlander (1992), pp82–96.

GOLDMANN, LUCIEN 1964: *The Hidden God*. Philip Thody (tr.). London: Routledge and Kegan Paul.

GREENBLATT, STEPHEN J. 1982: *The Power of Forms in the English Renaissance*. Norman, Okla.: Pilgrim Books.

—— 1988: *Shakespearian Negotiations*. Berkeley and Los Angeles: University of California Press.

GRENNEN, JOSEPH E. 1988: 'Hardy's Lines on the *Titanic*: A View from a Technical Stance'. *Colby Library Quarterly* 24(4), pp197–204.

HANSEN, ERIK FOSNES 1990: *Salme ved Reisens Slutt*. Oslo: J. W. Cappelens Forlag.

HARDY, THOMAS 1975: *Tess of the D'Urbervilles: A Pure Woman*. The New Wessex Edition. London: Macmillan.

HART, HENRY 1986: *The Poetry of Geoffrey Hill*. Carbondale/Edwardsville: Southern Illinois University Press.

HARTMAN, GEOFFREY 1975: 'Poem and Ideology: A Study of Keats's "To Autumn"'. In Geoffrey Hartman, *The Fate of Reading*. Chicago: University of Chicago Press, pp124–46.

HAWTHORN, JEREMY 1973: *Identity and Relationship: A Contribution to Marxist Theory of Literary Criticism*. London: Lawrence and Wishart.

—— 1990: *Joseph Conrad: Narrative Technique and Ideological Commitment*. London: Edward Arnold.

—— 1994a: *A Glossary of Contemporary Literary Theory*. (Second edn.) London: Edward Arnold.

—— 1994b: 'Joseph Conrad's Theory of Reading'. In Andrew Kennedy and Orm Øverland (eds), *Excursions in Fiction: Essays in Honour of Professor Lars Hartveit on his 70th Birthday*. Oslo: Novus Press, pp89–107.

HEALY, THOMAS 1992: *New Latitudes: Theory and English Renaissance Literature*. London: Edward Arnold.

HILL, GEOFFREY 1958: 'The Poetry of Allen Tate'. *Geste* (Leeds) 3(3), pp8–12.

—— 1959: *For the Unfallen: Poems 1952–1958*. London: André Deutsch.

—— 1985: *Collected Poems*. Harmondsworth: Penguin.

HOBSBAWM, ERIC 1989: *The Age of Empire: 1875–1914*. New York: Vintage Books. (First published 1987.)

HOLDERNESS, GRAHAM 1992: *Shakespeare Recycled: The Making of Historical Drama*. Hemel Hempstead: Harvester Press.

HOLTON, ROBERT 1994: *Jarring Witnesses: Modern Fiction and the Representation of History*. Hemel Hempstead: Harvester Wheatsheaf.

HOUGH, GRAHAM 1970: 'Criticism as a Humanist Discipline'. In Malcolm Bradbury and David Palmer (eds), *Contemporary Criticism*. Stratford-Upon-Avon Studies 12. London: Edward Arnold, pp39–59.

HYNES, SAMUEL 1976: *The Auden Generation*. London: The Bodley Head.

ISER, WOLFGANG 1974: *The Implied Reader: Patterns of Communication in Prose Fiction from Bunyan to Beckett*. London: The Johns Hopkins University Press.

JACKSON, BRUCE 1974: *'Get Your Ass in the Water and Swim Like Me': Narrative Poetry from Black Oral Tradition*. Cambridge, Mass.: Harvard University Press.

JACKSON, J. R. DE J. 1989: *Historical Criticism and the Meaning of Texts*. London: Routledge.

JAMES, HENRY 1951: *The Art of Fiction*. First published 1884. In Morton Dauwen Zabel (ed.), *The Portable Henry James*. New York: Viking Press, pp391–418.

—— 1966: *The Turn of the Screw*. Robert Kimbrough (ed.). Norton Critical Edition. New York: Norton.

—— 1986: *Roderick Hudson*. Geoffrey Moore (ed. and intr.). Harmondsworth: Penguin.

JAMESON, FREDRIC 1972: *The Prison House of Language*. Princeton, N. J.: Princeton University Press.

JAY, MARTIN 1992: 'Of Plots, Witnesses, and Judgments'. In Friedlander (1992), pp97–107.

JENKINS, NICHOLAS (ed.) 1990: 'Eleven Letters from Auden to Stephen Spender'. (Includes an introduction, the text of the letters, and an appendix: 'Auden and Spain'.) In Bucknell and Jenkins (1990), pp55–93.

JOHNSON, PAULINE 1984: *Marxist Aesthetics: The Foundations Within Everyday Life for an Enlightened Consciousness*. London: Routledge.

JOLLY, ROSLYN 1993: *Henry James: History, Narrative, Fiction*. Oxford: Clarendon Press.

KERMODE, FRANK 1988: *History and Value*. Oxford: Clarendon Press.

—— 1990: *Poetry, Narrative, History*. Oxford: Blackwell.

KERN, STEPHEN 1983: *The Culture of Time and Space 1880–1918*. Cambridge, Mass.: Harvard University Press.

KETTLE, ARNOLD 1979: 'W. H. Auden: Poetry and Politics in the Thirties'. In Jon Clark, Margot Heinemann, David Margolies and Carole Snee (eds), *Culture and Crisis in Britain in the 30s*. London: Lawrence and Wishart, pp83–101.

—— 1988: *Literature and Liberation: Selected Essays*. Graham Martin and Dipak Nandy (eds). Manchester: Manchester University Press.

KNIGHT, G. WILSON 1944: *The Olive and the Sword*. Oxford: Oxford University Press.

LACAPRA, DOMINICK 1983: *Rethinking Intellectual History: Texts, Contexts, Language*. Ithaca, N. Y. and London: Cornell University Press.

LAMBERT, ELIZABETH 1993: 'Evolution and Imagination in *Pointz Hall* and *Between the Acts*'. In Vara Neverow-Turk and Mark Hussey (eds), *Virginia Woolf: Themes and Variations. Selected Papers from the Second Annual Conference of Virginia Woolf*. New York: Pace University Press, pp83–9.

LANCHESTER, JOHN 1995: 'Concierge'. *London Review of Books* 17(22), pp3–7.

LERNER, LAURENCE 1993: 'Against Historicism'. *New Literary History* 24, pp273–92.

LEVINSON, MARJORIE 1988: *Keats's Life of Allegory: The Origins of a Style*. Oxford: Blackwell.

LEWIS, R. W. B. 1991: *The Jameses: A Family Narrative*. New York: Farrar, Straus and Giroux.

LIPSTADT, DEBORAH 1994: *Denying the Holocaust*. Repr. with a new introduction by the author. New York: Plume Books. (First published 1993.)

LORD, WALTER 1955: *A Night to Remember*. New York: Henry Holt.

LYOTARD, JEAN-FRANÇOIS 1984: *The Postmodern Condition: A Report on Knowledge*. Geoff Bennington and Brian Massumi (trs). Minneapolis: University of Minnesota Press.

MCGANN, JEROME J. 1985: *The Beauty of Inflections: Literary Investigations in Historical Method and Theory*. Oxford: Clarendon Press.

—— 1988: *Social Values and Poetic Acts: The Historical Judgment of Literary Work*. London and Cambridge, Mass.: Harvard University Press.

—— 1989: 'The Third World of Criticism'. In Marjorie Levinson, Marilyn Butler, Jerome J. McGann and Paul Hamilton, *Rethinking Historicism: Critical Readings in Romantic History*. Oxford: Blackwell, pp85–107.

—— 1993: *Black Riders: The Visible Language of Modernism*. Princeton, N. J.: Princeton University Press.

MCGUINNESS, FRANK 1986: *Observe the Sons of Ulster Marching Towards the Somme*. London: Faber and Faber.

MCKENDRY, EUGENE 1991: Review of Loreto Todd, *Words Apart: A Dictionary of Northern Ireland English* (1990). *Linen Hall Review* (April), pp27–8.

MACLEAN, SORLEY 1971: *Poems to Eimhir*. Iain Crichton Smith (tr.). Newcastle upon Tyne: Northern House. (First published in Gaelic 1943.)

MCLELLAN, DAVID (ed.) 1971: *Marx's Grundrisse*. London: Macmillan.

MAIKA, PATRICIA 1984: *Virginia Woolf's* Between the Acts *and Jane Harrison's* Con/spiracy. Ann Arbor: UMI Research Press.

MANNING, D. J. 1976: *Liberalism*. London: Dent.

MARCUS, GEOFFREY 1969: *The Maiden Voyage*. New York: Viking Press

MARX, KARL 1970: *Economic and Philosophical Manuscripts of 1844*. Dirk J. Struik (ed.), Martin Milligan (tr.). London: Lawrence and Wishart.

—— 1971: *A Contribution to the Critique of Political Economy*. S. W. Ryazanskaya (tr.). London: Lawrence and Wishart.

MARX, KARL and ENGELS, FREDERICK 1974: *Marx and Engels on Literature and Art*. Lee Baxandall and Stefan Morawski (eds). New York: International General.

MENDELSON, EDWARD (ed.) 1977: *The English Auden: Poems, Essays, and Dramatic Writings, 1927–1939*. New York: Random House.

— (ed.) 1989: *W. H. Auden: Selected Poems*. New edition. New York: Vintage. (Selection first published 1979.)

MILLER, J. HILLIS 1991: *Hawthorne and History: Defacing it*. Oxford: Blackwell.

MITCHELL, W. J. T. (ed.) 1981: *On Narrative*. Chicago and London: University of Chicago Press.

MONTROSE, LOUIS A. 1989: 'Professing the Renaissance: The Poetics and Politics of Culture'. In Veeser (1989), pp15–36.

MULHERN, FRANCIS (ed.) 1992: *Contemporary Marxist Literary Criticism*. Harlow: Longman.

NICOLSON, NIGEL and TRAUTMANN, JOANNE (eds) 1975: *The Flight of the Mind: The Letters of Virginia Woolf. Volume 1: 1888–1912*. New York: Harcourt, Brace, Jovanovich.

— (eds) 1980: *The Letters of Virginia Woolf. Volume VI: 1936–1941*. New York: Harcourt, Brace, Jovanovich.

NORRIS, CHRISTOPHER 1992: *Uncritical Theory: Postmodernism, Intellectuals and the Gulf War*. London: Lawrence and Wishart.

NORRMAN, RALF 1982: *The Insecure World of Henry James's Fiction: Intensity and Ambiguity*. New York: St Martin's Press.

O'CONNOR, RICHARD 1956: *Down to Eternity. How the Proper Edwardian and His World Died with the Titanic*. New York: Fawcett Publications.

OLSEN, TILLIE 1978: *Silences*. New York: Delacorte Press/S. Lawrence.

ORMSBY, FRANK (ed.) 1990: *Poets from the North of Ireland*. Second edn. Belfast: Blackstaff Press.

ORWELL, SONJA and ANGUS, IAON (eds) 1968: *The Collected Essays, Journalism and Letters of George Orwell. Volume 1: An Age Like This 1920–40*. London: Secker and Warburg.

OUSBY, IAN 1982: 'The Convergence of the Twain: Hardy's Alteration of Plato's Parable'. *The Modern Language Review* 77(4), pp780–96.

PATTERSON, LEE 1993: 'Making Identities in Fifteenth-century England: Henry V and John Lydgate'. In Cox and Reynolds (1993), pp69–107.

PEARSON, HESKETH 1977: *Conan Doyle: His Life and Art*. New York: Taplinger Publishing. (First published 1943.)

PRECHTL, ROBERT (pseud. Robert Friedländer) 1938: *Titanic: A Novel*. Erna McArthur (tr.). London: Martin Secker. (First published 1937 as *Titanensturz*, Vienna and Leipzig: Saturn Verlag.)

PURDY, RICHARD LITTLE and MILLGATE, MICHAEL (eds) 1978: *The Collected Letters of Thomas Hardy. Volume four, 1909–1913*. Oxford: Clarendon Press.

RIMMON, SHLOMITH 1977: *The Concept of Ambiguity – the Example of James*. Chicago: University of Chicago Press.

ROBBINS, BRUCE 1984: 'Shooting off James's Blanks: Theory, Politics, and *The Turn of the Screw*'. *The Henry James Review* V(3), pp192–9.

RODWAY, ALLAN 1970: 'Generic Criticism: The Approach Through Type, Mode and Kind'. In Malcolm Bradbury and David Palmer (eds), *Contemporary Criticism*. Stratford-Upon-Avon Studies 12. London: Edward Arnold, pp82–105.

ROGERS, BYRON 1994: 'In Another Country'. *Times Literary Supplement*, no. 4742, 18 February, p8.

—— 1995: 'A Job's Worth'. *The Guardian Weekend*, 29 July, p53.

RONFARD, JEAN-PIERRE 1986: *Le Titanic*. Ottawa: Théâtre Leméac.

RORTY, RICHARD 1982: *Consequences of Pragmatism: Essays 1972–1980*. Brighton: Harvester.

RUBEN, DAVID-HILLEL 1977: *Marxism and Materialism*. Hassocks: Harvester Press.

RYLE, GILBERT 1971: *Collected Papers*. Vol. II, *Collected Essays 1929–68*. London: Hutchinson.

SAID, EDWARD W. 1993: 'Figures, Configurations, Transfigurations'. In Cox and Reynolds (1993), pp316–30.

SCHRERO, ELLIOT M. 1981: 'Exposure in *The Turn of the Screw*'. *Modern Philology* 78, pp261–74.

SERLING, ROBERT 1993: *Something's Alive on the Titanic*. New York: St Martin's Press. (First published 1990)

SHERRY, VINCENT 1987: *The Uncommon Tongue: The Poetry and Criticism of Geoffrey Hill*. Ann Arbor: University of Michigan Press.

SINFIELD, ALAN 1992: *Faultlines: Cultural Materialism and the Politics of Dissident Reading*. Oxford: Clarendon Press.

SKELTON, ROBIN (ed.) 1964: *Poetry of the Thirties*. Harmondsworth: Penguin.

SLAUGHTER, MARTINA 1966: 'Edmund Wilson and *The Turn of the Screw*'. In James (1966), pp211–44.

SMITH, MARY D. 1966: 'Downstairs from the Upstairs: A Study of the Servants' Hall in the Victorian Novel'. Dissertation: Harvard University.

SPEDDEN, DAISY CORNING STONE 1994: *Polar the Titanic Bear*. Boston, Mass.: Little Brown.

SPENDER, STEPHEN 1975: *W. H. Auden: A Tribute*. New York: Macmillan.

THOMPSON, JOHN B. 1984: *Studies in the Theory of Ideology*. Berkeley: University of California Press.

THOMSON, A. W. 1965: '*The Turn of the Screw*: Some Points on the Hallucination Theory'. *Review of English Studies* VI(4), pp26–36.

TICHI, CECELIA 1987: *Shifting Gears: Technology, Literature, Culture in Modernist America*. Chapel Hill and London: University of North Carolina Press.

TILLYARD, E. M. W. 1972: *The Elizabethan World Picture*. Harmondsworth: Penguin. (First published London 1943.)

TOKER, LEONA 1993: *Eloquent Reticence: Withholding Information in Fictional Narrative*. Lexington, Ken.: The University Press of Kentucky.

TRAVERSI, D. A. 1957: *Shakespeare From 'Richard II' to 'Henry V'*. London: Hollis and Carter.

TSCHACHLER, HEINZ 1989: 'The Cost of Story: Ideology and Ambivalence in the Verse Narratives of E. J. Pratt'. *Canadian Literature* 122–3, pp93–106.

VARIOUS AUTHORS 1912: Programme: *Dramatic and Operatic Matinée in Aid of the Titanic Disaster Fund. Tuesday May 14th, 1912, at 2. o'clock*. London.

VEESER, H. ARAM (ed.) 1989: *The New Historicism*. New York and London: Routledge.

VIDAL-NAQUET, PIERRE 1992: *Assassins of Memory: Essays on the Denial of the Holocaust*. Jeffrey Mehlman (tr.). New York: Columbia University Press. (First published in French 1987.)

WADE, WYN CRAIG 1979: *The Titanic: End of a Dream*. New York: Rawson, Wade Publishers.

WALSH, MICHAEL 1995: 'Raising the Titanic'. *Time* 145(10) (March 13), p110.

WALTON, PETER 1993: 'Details'. *Agenda* 31(3) (Autumn), p51.

WAUGH, PATRICIA 1992: *Practising Postmodernism Reading Modernism*. London: Edward Arnold.

WEST, MURIEL 1964: 'The Death of Miles in *The Turn of the Screw*'. *PMLA* 79, pp283–8.

WEST, PAUL 1981: 'Drowning as One of the Fine Arts'. *Parnassus* 9(1), pp91–109.

WHITE, HAYDEN 1973: *Metahistory: The Historical Imagination in Nineteenth-Century Europe*. Baltimore, Md. and London: Johns Hopkins University Press.

—— 1981a: 'The Value of Narrativity in the Representation of Reality'. In Mitchell (1981), pp1–23.

—— 1981b: 'The Narrativization of Real Events'. In Mitchell (1981), pp249–54.

—— 1992: 'Historical Emplotment and the Problem of Truth'. In Friedlander (1992), pp37–53.

WILLEY, BASIL 1934: *The Seventeenth Century Background: Studies in the Thought of the Age in Relation to Poetry and Religion*. London: Chatto and Windus.

—— 1940: *The Eighteenth Century Background: Studies in the Idea of Nature in the Thought of the Period*. London: Chatto and Windus.

WILLIAMS, LINDA RUTH 1995: *Critical Desire: Psychoanalysis and the Literary Subject*. London: Edward Arnold.

WILLIAMS, RAYMOND 1977: *Marxism and Literature*. Oxford: Oxford University Press.

—— 1980: *Problems in Materialism and Culture: Selected Essays*. London: Verso.

WILSON, RICHARD and DUTTON, RICHARD (eds) 1992: *New Historicism and Renaissance Drama*. Harlow: Longman.

WIMSATT, W. K. and BEARDSLEY, MONROE 1949: 'The Affective Fallacy'. Repr. in W. K. Wimsatt 1954: *The Verbal Icon: Studies in the Meaning of Poetry*. London: Methuen, pp21–39.

WIRTH-NECHER, HANA 1994: 'Final Curtain on the War: Figure and Ground in Virginia Woolf's *Between the Acts*'. *Style* 28(2), pp183–200.

WOOLF, LEONARD 1964: *Beginning Again: An Autobiography of the Years 1911 to 1918*. New York: Harcourt, Brace and World.

WOOLF, VIRGINIA 1970: *Between the Acts*. New York: Harcourt Brace. (First published 1941.)

WOOLFSON, CHARLES 1982: *The Labour Theory of Culture*. London: Routledge.
WRIGHT, IAIN 1994: 'Historicising Textuality or Textualizing History?: The Turn to History in Literary Studies'. *Proceedings of the 1993 Conference of the Australasian Association for Phenomenology and Social Philosophy.* Canberra (Australia).

INDEX